2⁄2

TWO IF BY SEA

TWO IF BY SEA

THE DEVELOPMENT OF AMERICAN COASTAL DEFENSE POLICY

Robert S. Browning III

Contributions in Military History, Number 33

Greenwood Press
Westport, Connecticut • London, England

Library of Congress Cataloging in Publication Data

Browning, Robert S.
  Two if by sea.

  (Contributions in military history, ISSN 0084-9251;
no. 33)
  Bibliography: p.
  Includes index.
  1. United States—Coast defenses—History.
2. United States—Military policy. I. Title.
II. Series.
UG410.B76 1983   355.4'5'0973   83-1638
ISBN: 0-313-23688-7 (lib. bdg.)

Library of Congress Catalog Card Number: 83-1638
ISBN: 0-313-23688-7
ISSN: 0084-9251

First published in 1983

Greenwood Press
A division of Congressional Information Service, Inc.
88 Post Road West
Westport, Connecticut 06881

Printed in the United States of America

10 9 8 7 6 5 4 3 2 1

To My Mother and Father

Contents

Illustrations

Preface

This book began as a study of American fortification programs in the nineteenth century. However, as I progressed I became increasingly aware that the story of American fortifications was really a part of the larger and more important story of American coastal defense policy. So I altered my course, setting out to investigate this larger story and discovering that American coastal defense policy was one of the most pervasive and consistent policies followed by American military and civilian leaders.

Indeed, from the time the first colonists came ashore, Americans recognized that the ocean would be the avenue of approach for any hostile power. Lurking out-of-sight offshore, enemy raiders or fleets could swoop down on the exposed settlements along the seaboard with little or no prior warning. However, since the colonists had no centralized military establishment, seacoast defense was a problem handled locally, with the construction of defenses usually undertaken only in response to an immediate crisis or threat. Not until after the War of 1812 did national leaders move away from this tradition by attempting to centralize control over the planning of seacoast defenses and, more important, committing the government to a large-scale program of peacetime construction. An important part of this shift was the creation of a Board of Engineers in 1816. This board soon established itself as the preeminent planning body in regard to coastal defenses. The views and principles it developed would remain fundamental to the doctrines of coastal defense planners well into the twentieth century.

The basic goals of the coastal defense system were purely military. Although occasionally fears of invasion surfaced in arguments over the need to defend the coast, the primary concern was the possibility of a maritime enemy attacking a coastal city for loot or in order to establish a base for additional operations. A secondary consideration was that coastal defenses at the most important cities and anchorages would force an enemy to land at a considerable distance from his objective, giving time for American forces to mobilize, concentrate, and counterattack.

Both of these were defensive goals, the coastal defenses merely providing the means of defense if the nation was actually attacked. But a larger theme also pervaded the arguments in favor of an extensive coastal defense system, a theme which emerged very early and assumed greater and greater importance as the nineteenth century wore on. This was the belief that by their sheer existence, coastal defenses might cause an enemy to forgo attacking the United States at all. It was in this sense that engineer officer Quincy A. Gillmore argued in 1881 that their true function was "to avert war." Moreover, coastal defenses stood as an ever-present symbol of a determination to protect the nation's citizens and their property.

The belief that preparedness acts to prevent war, rather than lead to it, remains a part of American military policy, and thus American coastal defense policy seems to reflect a consistent theme in American military thought. For this reason it is surprising that so little has been done on the subject in the past. The intention of this book therefore, is to fill a void in the literature of American military policy. While I cannot claim that it represents the last word on the subject, I do hope that it suggests not only some of the ways in which American military thought has remained remarkably consistent, but also some areas which deserve fuller investigation.

Acknowledgments

No book, and least of all this one, is possible without the encouragement and support of a large number of people. First of all, I would like to thank Professor Edward M. Coffman who guided this work through its first metamorphosis and whose patient criticism improved its style immensely. Professors Richard Sewell and Norman K. Risjord also provided helpful and much needed advice.

Dale Floyd, then at the National Archives, was not only helpful in finding sources but his enthusiasm for the project was appreciated. I must also admit a debt to the staff of the library of the Wisconsin State Historical Society, particularly John Peters, Sharon Mulak, and Ellen Burke, who were of great help in dealing with the government documents I needed.

It is also necessary to thank the many friends and colleagues who read chapters and offered both their experience and counsel. Jim Schneider, Randy Roberts, and Terry Bilhartz all have my deepest gratitude.

I would also like to express my thanks to Judy Taft, who typed the manuscript, and Bill Pierce, who did the artwork.

Closer to home, I will never be able to repay the debt I owe to my wife, Joan, who was as determined to finish this book as I was and whose steady encouragement meant so much. Lastly, I need to thank Tristan and Dulcinea for simply being themselves.

All of these people contributed much to this book, and they must share the credit for what value it has. Any errors of omission or commission are mine alone.

TWO IF BY SEA

INTRODUCTION
The Colonial and Early National Tradition

When the United States went to war in June of 1812 it had a coastal defense network of twenty-four forts and thirty-two lesser enclosed works which mounted a total of 750 guns of various calibers and extended from Maine to New Orleans.[1] This network of fortifications stood in mute testimony to one facet of the young country's evolving military policy, one stage in a defensive tradition that, going back to the colonial period, would continue to grow until it became a fixed, integral part of American military policy throughout the nineteenth century. To understand this persistent national policy of coastal defense, and gain a fuller understanding of American military policy, it is first necessary to examine the ways policymakers altered or continued the traditional approach to the problem of coastal defense in the early national period. Just as this period witnessed the creation of durable and continuing political institutions, the early national period saw the beginnings of the military establishment that exists today and the initiation of the policies that would give that establishment life and vitality.[2] And, as in developing other aspects of military policy, national leaders naturally relied on an already existing tradition when they began to grapple with the issue of defending the coastline.

Both of these were defensive goals, the coastal defenses merely providing the means of defense if the nation was actually attacked. But a larger theme also pervaded the arguments in favor of an extensive coastal defense system, a theme which emerged very early and assumed greater and greater importance as the nineteenth century wore on. This was the belief that by their sheer existence, coastal defenses might cause an enemy to forgo attacking the United States at all. It was in this sense that engineer officer Quincy A. Gillmore argued in 1881 that their true function was "to avert war." Moreover, coastal defenses stood as an even-present symbol of a determination to protect the nation's citizens and their property.

The belief that preparedness acts to prevent war, rather than lead to it, remains a part of American military policy, and thus American coastal defense policy seems to reflect a consistent theme in American military thought. For this reason it is surprising that so little has been done on the subject in the past. The intention of this book therefore, is to fill a void in the literature of American military policy. While I cannot claim that it represents the last word on the subject, I do hope that it suggests not only some of the ways in which American military thought has remained remarkably consistent, but also some areas which deserve fuller investigation.

This tradition went back to the beginning of English colonization in the New World. "Discontented natives" were one source of danger, but the small and widely scattered settlements were also threatened by England's European enemies. Both dangers were acknowledged in the London Company's instructions to its Jamestown colonists, and when the Pilgrims fortified their Plymouth colony, they chose a position which covered the harbor as well as the land approaches.[3] But whereas the French and Spanish sent trained military engineers to build the defenses of their settlements, the English left it up to each local community to provide not only the labor but the design for coastal defenses. In Massachusetts this took the form of a cooperative effort. Plymouth colony, for example, expected all the men to share in the labor, or forfeit ten shillings per day and pay for the work they were supposed to have done. Even with this inducement, however, work on local fortifications was often delayed and funds difficult to raise.[4] Untrained in the intricacies of military architecture, the English colonists built the simplest of protective works, the designs of which were often the result of "gross trial and error." With some notable exceptions, such as Castle William in Boston Harbor, the construction of a palisaded blockhouse or a basic earthwork (perhaps backed by stone or timber) was typical.[5]

Maintenance of these defenses was also a local concern, and tended to be erratic at best. While Castle William in Boston Harbor may have been the "strongest fort in the British colonies," it was in great need of repair by 1652 and needed work again in 1663.[6] Fort Frederica, in Georgia, parried a Spanish attack in 1742 but was found "decayed" in 1754 with over twenty cannon dismounted and ruined by lack of attention.[7] At Fort Johnston, in North Carolina, the tapia concrete used in construction was so poor that "large pieces fell out of the parapet" when the guns were fired.[8] Colonial governors constantly decried the poor state of fortifications. But the constancy of these complaints indicates that little change occurred. Colonial fortifications were in a constant state of disrepair.

The deterioration of coastal fortifications was partly due to the scarcity and expense of labor. Virginia attempted to overcome the short supply of money by imposing a "fort duty" on incoming ships. While the tax tended to increase over the years, shipowners complained bitterly, and ultimately the tax failed to provide a stimulus to better maintenance of the fortifications in the colony.[9] But the shortage of labor and money was not the only reason colonial fortifications fell into disrepair. More important was the fact that the British colonists perceived their fortifications solely in defensive terms. Large permanent works were not necessary against Indians, and the colonists implicitly relied on the British navy to protect them from European enemies.[10] Further, the symbolic nature of fortifications, their existence as ever-present reminders of the power and authority of the state, was not lost on the colonists. It was a common view in Europe that a permanent citadel represented a "refuge of tyranny" and a threat to community freedom.[11] In a colonial system that imposed the burden of defense on the local community, colonists were not likely to impose a greater burden on themselves than absolutely necessary. They relied on a temporary system of coastal defense, one under immediate and local control, in much the same way they relied on a militia to meet manpower needs. Small, cheap, and simple fortifications could be hurriedly built at times of crisis. When the crisis was past, just as the militia was disbanded and went home, the various fortifications were ignored and allowed to deteriorate. Such an approach did not provide a long-lasting system of defenses, but was in perfect harmony with the emerging colonial political theories. This approach kept costs to a minimum, as did the use of local construction materials and the small size of colonial defensive works, thus placing as small a burden as possible on the community. Above all, the entire process of decision making remained, as with other military matters, on the local community level.[12]

The American Revolution did little to change this tradition. The need to build defenses quickly actually reinforced the now traditional use of easily available local materials and the simplest of construction techniques. Fort Moultrie, on Sullivan's Island in Charleston Harbor, was built of palmetto logs laid in parallel rows sixteen feet apart with sand filling the spaces in between. Seemingly weak, the fort proved surprisingly resistant to cannon fire when, still incomplete, it beat off a British attack in 1776.[13]

Although such crudely constructed fortifications proved surprisingly effective, the Continental Congress recognized the need for trained engineers who could design and build stronger ones. Since no Americans possessed the necessary skills, Congress relied on the services of foreign engineers, largely French or French trained. One French engineer, Louis Lebeque Duportail, eventually rose to the command of all Continental engineers, reaching the rank of Major General by the end of the war. Another foreigner in American service, the French-trained Pole, Thadeusz Kosciuszko, served as Chief Engineer of the Southern Army and was largely responsible for fortifying the American post at West Point and the American position at Saratoga. However, despite the efforts of such men most of the numerous defensive works built during the Revolution continued to be constructed from impermanent materials. After the war these works rapidly deteriorated until by the early 1790s only a handful remained serviceable.[14]

Separated from possible European enemies by three thousand miles of ocean, the newly independent United States concerned themselves initially with internal questions, frontier expansion, and the creation of a new form of government. Such military questions as arose centered on the issue of a standing army for frontier service rather than on any remote and largely theoretical threat from overseas. The outbreak of European war in 1793, however, placed the United States in a difficult international situation. Despite American desire to remain neutral, the commercial relationships between the United States and the belligerent powers threatened to drag the country into the conflict. "Our disposition for peace," Washington noted in December of 1793, could ". . . be drawn into question by the suspicions too often entertained by belligerent nations."[15] The French had relaxed trading restrictions in the West Indies, opening opportunities to American merchants. British response was to invoke the "Rule of 1756" (which stated that trade closed in peacetime may not be opened to neutrals during war) and authorize the seizure of neutral vessels trading to or from the French West Indies. Hundreds of American ships were seized and some 150 vessels condemned in British Admiralty Courts, arousing the Atlantic coast, and making war a real possibility.[16]

Sincerely interested in avoiding war, Washington sent Chief Justice John Jay to England to negotiate a settlement. In the interim the administration faced the prospect of conflict. "There is a rank due to the United States among nations," Washington stated, "which will be withheld, if not absolutely lost, by the reputation of weakness. If we desire to avoid insult, we must be able to repel it; if we desire to secure peace . . . it must be known we are at all times ready for war."[17] Congress agreed and in January 1794 appointed a committee to investigate the need for coastal fortifications. This committee quickly reported back in February with the nomination of sixteen ports and harbors in need of defensive works. Because of the need for speed, the committee recommended the construction of earth parapets and redoubts. The estimated cost of the proposed fortifications was just over $76,000, with the cost of providing ordnance estimated at $96,645.[18]

Debate on this proposal was brief. Congress added four additional ports and harbors and the bill cleared on March 20, 1794. The following day Congress appropriated the necessary money for construction and ordnance. The act established no priority among the sites to be fortified and left execution of the plan to the President. After brief debate in April, Congress added one further site to the list, Annapolis (which gave a final total of twenty-one sites to be fortified), and granted a further $30,000.[19]

The program of fortification this legislation authorized was the first such program undertaken by the national government. For this reason it is known historically as the "First System." Such a designation is useful to distinguish between this 1794 program and later ones, and insofar as it represents the first time the national government spent money on coastal fortifications the label is appropriate. This program was, however, something less than a "system" if that term is meant to imply a coordinated and centralized effort with design consistency of the resulting forts and batteries. In this 1794 program the War Department exercised only a minimal coordinating function. In most respects this program really represented a continuation of the colonial tradition.

Lacking trained American engineers, Secretary of War Henry Knox appointed seven former Continental engineers, all French or French trained, to supervise the construction. This group included Stephen Rochefontaine, Swiss-born J. J. Ulrich Rivardi, and Pierre L'Enfant (the future designer of Washington, D.C.). Knox assigned each to a particular region and ordered them to cooperate closely with state officials.[20] Knox made this last point particularly clear in his instructions to the engineers. Each engineer was to notify the state governor of his appointment, submit necessary surveys to the governor, and proceed with construction only with the governor's approval. Such a procedure naturally left a great deal of authority in local hands. But if such a procedure reduced the ability of the central government to control the construction of coastal defenses, it was eminently sound politics. Localism was still a strong part of the American political philosophy. While the Constitution provided the framework of a strong central authority, the Founding Fathers consciously avoided making the relationship between the federal and state governments one of superior to inferior. For the federal government to assume a function, coastal protection, previously handled entirely as a state matter, might reawaken dormant fears about central authority. The struggle over the Constitution was only six years in the past in 1794; the Federalists already had a growing opposition within Congress, and in the midst of a severe international crisis, Knox clearly did not wish to create a new point of contention.[21]

Perhaps reflecting this emphasis on local control, Knox also delegated the actual scope and design of each work to the engineer on the spot. Knox supplied fairly detailed guidelines which specified the construction of redoubts, barracks, blockhouses, and a furnace for heating cannon shot at each site. He also instructed the engineers that the works were to be of earth, perhaps backed by timber or stone (works which in this regard differed little from colonial or Revolutionary War fortifications). Yet Knox made it clear that what he was supplying were only guidelines. "It has not been intended," Knox told Rochefontaine, " . . . to point out the particular manner in which the works are to be executed. Outlines only have been given. . . ." To Charles Vincent, supervising construction at New York City, Knox wrote, "The choice of the ground . . . with all the combinations and effects depending thereon, will rest upon your judgment."[22]

The need for speed in construction plus the limited funds available meant that the works would be small. Knox thought that redoubts and enclosed batteries should be large enough for 500 men, but permanent garrison houses or blockhouses would only need to hold fifty men. If the garrison went beyond this latter number, Knox told the engineers, "tents must be used." Naturally, with the emphasis on local control, the works constructed varied somewhat within the limits Knox set forth.[23]

As in the past, the construction program begun in 1794 was in response to an immediate crisis. Although the federal government provided the money, control over design and location of particular fortification was kept at the local level. The fortifications were small, relatively cheap, and built largely of earth. Also traditional was the fact that as the crisis of 1794 faded so did interest in coastal defense. When Knox resigned as Secretary of War at the end of the year, he urged the continuation of the fortification program. A time of peace and prosperity, he argued, was the proper time for a nation to "perfect its system of defence." Washington also attempted to keep Congressional interest in coastal fortifications alive by hopefully proposing that Congress would "not omit to inquire whether the fortifications . . . be commensurate with our exigencies." Congress was not persuaded. The War Department requested an additional $500,000 in December 1794. Congress grudgingly appropriated a tenth of that amount the following March.[24]

In January 1796 the new Secretary of War, Timothy Pickering, reported on the state of the fortifications begun in 1794. Works at sixteen of the twenty sites he discussed (Pickering did not report on Boston since the state of Massachusetts retained title) were incomplete, although Pickering presented many of these as essentially finished. On the other hand construction at five sites (Wilmington, Annapolis, Alexandria, Ocracoke Inlet, and Georgetown, South

Carolina) had ceased altogether. Pickering conceded that only "actual or impending" war would cause a resumption of building at Ocracoke Inlet and Georgetown, but argued that it was simply prudent to fortify "the few ports of the highest importance" with "fortifications of such kinds and extent as cannot be suddenly erected."[25]

In May a Congressional committee responded to this by noting that a considerable part of former appropriations remained unspent. Hence, the committee felt "no further legislative provision, relative [to fortifications] is necessary at this time." The sole exception was New York City, for which very extensive fortifications were planned. But although the committee recommended a sum for New York be appropriated, the majority of the House of Representatives disagreed and made no such appropriation.[26]

Without the funds for maintenance, the fortifications of the 1794 program soon began to deteriorate. Secretary of War James McHenry noted in February 1797 that "nature was altering" ungarrisoned posts while the garrisons at other positions had to make repairs and additions.[27] In debate that same month Representative William Smith of South Carolina reported that the only fort in Charleston Harbor would soon be swept away by the sea, while Samuel Smith of Maryland pointed out that at the best site for protecting Baltimore, "cattle had also free intercourse with the barracks, nor was there defense against them." Both men urged a suitable sum be given for maintaining the existing fortifications. In March Congress granted $24,000 in the annual military appropriation for fortifications.[28]

By June, however, the rising possibility of war with France revived interest in coastal defense. The high passions of the XYZ Affair and the resultant Quasi-War were both a year away, but in response to French snubbing of United States Minister Charles Cotesworth Pinckney and French seizures of American ships, some Federalists were already talking war. Guided by an estimate from McHenry, a House committee under Robert Livingston of New York proposed that $200,000 be appropriated for fortifications. This proposal sparked a hot week-long debate. Some die-hard Republicans argued against fortifications on principle. William B. Giles of Virginia, for example, bluntly stated that he did not believe fortifications "a proper kind of defense for the country." Giles was not alone, but the major stumbling block was that New York had not yet ceded the land for fortifications to the federal government as the law required. Finally, Congress reached a compromise: states could subtract any amount spent on fortifications from any debt owed the federal government. That issue resolved, Congress went on to appropriate $115,000 for fortifications.[29]

Although some Congressmen, like Giles of Virginia, opposed the creation of a system of coastal defenses in any form, most clearly believed that it was necessary to provide at least some way of protecting the coastal region, especially the valuable and vulnerable ports. The more commercially minded Federalists were even more adamant about this last point, for as Uri Tracy of Connecticut argued in 1794, if the country could not protect its commerce that commerce would soon disappear.[30] President John Adams returned to this same theme in a message to Congress in May of 1797:

> The commerce of the United States has become an interesting object of attention, whether we consider it in relation to the wealth and finances or the strength and resources of the nation. With a seacoast of near 2,000 miles in extent, opening a wide field for fisheries, navigation, and commerce, a great portion of our citizens naturally apply their industry and enterprise to these objects. Any serious and permanent injury to commerce would not fail to produce the most embarrassing disorders. To prevent it from being undermined and destroyed it is essential that it receive an adequate protection.

Adams suggested that a strong navy was the best defense for American commerce, but it was still necessary to "protect it here at home, where it is collected in our most important ports." The purpose of coastal defenses was not, in Adams's view, to repel an invasion attempt (since it was extremely unlikely that any such attempt would be made), but instead to deter "sudden and predatory incursions" made in the hopes of plunder or destruction by enemy privateers or warships.[31]

Many Republicans shared the Federalists' concern over protecting the coastal cities and their associated commerce. As the Federalists continued to press for a comprehensive military program, which included monies for increased coastal protection, that portion of their program enjoyed substantial Jeffersonian support. In May of 1798 Congress appropriated $250,000 for coastal fortifications. Debate was brief, but despite the crisis atmosphere not all Congressmen agreed with the need for fortifications. Particularly the Jeffersonians refused to be prodded by the belief, now being voiced by some Federalists, that French invasion was now imminent.[32] Albert Gallatin of Pennsylvania acknowledged the possibility of raids for plunder along the coast, but was firmly convinced "there was . . . no real danger of invasion."[33] That being so, argued Gallatin, the additional troops desired by the Federalists, and by implication the other aspects of their preparedness program, were intended to preserve order rather than for defense. Gallatin was personally willing to support those measures which were clearly defensive in character, such as fortifications, but particularly after the passage of the Alien and Sedition Acts in June and July of 1798, his warning began to strike a responsive chord in his fellow Jeffersonians. As the threat of outright war with France faded during 1799 so did Jeffersonian support for the military preparations, including fortifications, urged by the Federalists. At the same time the Federalist party itself split, at least partly over the issues raised by their preparedness program (in particular increases in army strength). In such circumstances the possibility that Congress would authorize large-scale military spending, even for defensive fortifications, simply vanished.[34]

The possibility remained slim following the defeat of the Federalists, and the rise to power of the Jeffersonians in 1801. As a party, the Jeffersonians were concerned about the need to protect the coast, but they were even more committed to retrenchment in military spending. With the end of the Quasi-War, there were no calls for a renewed program of fortification construction. Indeed, in his first annual message Jefferson suggested that the cost of coastal fortifications was large enough to make "it questionable what is best now to be done."[35] In the absence of any apparent threat, Congress naturally elected to do very little. During the period from 1794 to 1801 the United States spent nearly $830,000 on coastal fortifications, an amount representing just over 5 percent of all military spending during those years.[36] In contrast, from 1802 to 1805 Congress appropriated only $113,000 for such defenses, a total that represents only 3 percent of a substantially reduced military budget. Even this amount is undoubtedly somewhat high since Congress included fortification appropriations in the annual military appropriation as part of a sum for armories, magazines, and arsenals as well as fortifications.[37]

Although this parsimony reflected to some extent the traditional Jeffersonian antipathy towards the military, fiscal tightfistedness and an antimilitary philosophy were not the only reasons coastal defenses received less support after 1801. One reason, as already mentioned, was that the end of the Quasi-War removed any apparent threat to the nation's coast. In addition, though, there were those who questioned the effectiveness of permanent defenses. Among these was the administration's chief military expert, Secretary of War Henry Dearborn, who believed that permanent coastal batteries were not the best means of defending the coastline. He expressed his opinion most forcibly in regard to New York harbor. "That the harbor of New York is not susceptible of such defence as ought to be relied on by permanent or fixed batteries," wrote Dearborn, "must be evident to every one who will reflect upon the subject; and, consequently, . . . some other system ought to be adopted." Arguing from his experience in the Revolution, Dearborn believed that an enemy ship could easily bypass batteries firing across a channel. A better system, he suggested, would involve some fixed defenses, a number of "moving batteries," and a "sufficient number of well constructed gun boats."[38]

Other Jeffersonians distrusted fortifications as well. William B. Giles of Virginia reminded the House that he had opposed fortifications since 1797. It was, Giles asserted, "not to be expected that an enemy would choose to come to precisely the place where a fortification stands." A raiding enemy, intent on plunder, would simply avoid the sites of fortifications, since an extensive seacoast like that of the United States could not be protected everywhere, and thus much of the effort to construct permanent defenses would be wasted.[39]

Recognizing the need to protect the nation's ports and harbors, yet unsure of the effectiveness of permanent fortifications, Jefferson enthusiastically promoted a system of gunboats for coastal defense. These relatively small shallow-draft vessels could, he argued, be quickly and easily manned in an emergency and would be less expensive than either larger naval craft or fortifications. And, unlike larger warships, gunboats were completely defensive in character, a feature that made them particularly attractive to Jefferson. Several prominent military and naval officers, including General James Wilkinson and Commodore Samuel Barron, endorsed the gunboat idea, and Congress quickly authorized construction. Ultimately some 177 gunboats may have entered service. However, the belief that they were a more economical form of coastal defense than permanent fortifications proved mistaken. As Secretary of the Navy Robert Smith pointed out in December 1807 even when laid up they decayed to some extent and thus needed increasingly expensive repairs. Furthermore, said Smith, the cost of providing the required number of gunboats would exceed $1,000,000 while the cost of keeping them in service would be over $2,800,000 annually. These were sums even larger than those seen as too much for permanent fortifications. Partly for this reason, and partly because there were increasing doubts about the effectiveness of gunboats (which, after all, were a completely unproven form of defense), enthusiasm for them began to wane fairly quickly. Yet, this short-lived experiment with an alternative to fortifications for coastal defense would leave an important legacy—a continuing fascination with various forms of floating defenses which would appear and reappear throughout the rest of the century.[40]

Nevertheless, although Jefferson and his supporters sought some alternative to fortifications as the primary means of coastal defense, his administration took a step which would have profound impact on future fortification planning as well as on the American military in general. With administration approval Congress separated the Corps of Engineers from the Artillery (a single organization since 1794) in March 1802 and legislated that this newly created corps would be based at West Point, and there "constitute a military academy."[41] In some respects this step constituted simply a formal recognition and approval of an already existing arrangement. There already existed a Corps of Artillerists and Engineers, created by Congress in 1794. Furthermore, technical instruction had been going on at West Point, the unit's principle station and the largest post in the United States, since 1796. However, despite a conscientious effort, this initial attempt at formal military instruction did not fare well. Undiscouraged, the Federalists, particularly Alexander Hamilton and Secretary of War James McHenry, continued to press for a military academy. Congress did not go quite so far, authorizing only the appointment of instructors along with a nominal increase in the number of cadets.

The Jeffersonians continued this somewhat informal arrangement, and in May of 1801 a suitable American was finally found to head the post at West Point. This man was Jonathan Williams. A relative of Ben Franklin, Williams was educated in Europe (where he had spent most of his life) and was a vice-president of the American Philosophical Society (through which he came to Jefferson's notice). Eminently suited to the position, Williams became Inspector of the Fortifications and senior officer of the engineers. The legislation of March 1802 made him, effectively, the first superintendent of the Military Academy.[42]

In terms of American coastal defenses the creation of the school had both immediate and far-reaching effects. Even though it developed slowly, the existence of the academy signaled the beginning of the end of what Dearborn called "the unpleasant necessity" of American dependence on foreign engineers. In the long run the dual identity of the school as both a Military Academy and part of the Corps of Engineers would create a situation in which the American engineers would have a vested interest in fortification building. Academy graduates, developing a conscious identity as professional officers trained in a military art, could (in peacetime) fully demonstrate their skill only in military construction.

The first graduates of the academy soon got a chance to demonstrate their newly acquired skills. In 1807 the Jeffersonians re-evaluated some of their views on coastal defense in response to the *Chesapeake-Leopard* affair, an event which suddenly and dramatically made war with England a real possibility. The United States met the potential threat to the coast in the time-honored manner. In January 1808 Congress appropriated $1,000,000 for coastal fortifications, the largest sum to date and a greater amount than the total appropriated up to that time.[43] Not surprisingly, Federalist Josiah Quincy argued forcefully in support of such a large appropriation. "The ocean," he declared in December 1807, was no longer " . . .

an insurmountable obstacle, an impossible barrier.'' Now it was ''a smooth and beaten path . . . a military road.''[44]

The overwhelmingly Jeffersonian Congress did not, however, abandon all restraint in coastal defense spending. Successive proposals in the House of Representatives to substitute $2,500,000, $1,500,000, and $1,250,000 all met defeat before the $1,000,000 appropriation carried. In these votes the Jeffersonian majority maintained its opposition to large increasing expenditures on coastal defenses. Along with fourteen Federalists, only nine known Jeffersonians and eleven Congressmen with no recorded party affiliation voted in favor of substituting $1,500,000 for the $1,000,000 finally approved. Ten of these twenty Congressmen were New Yorkers. Indeed, only one New York Congressman voted against increasing the appropriation.[45]

The conclusions which can be drawn from this and other votes are straightforward. In general, Federalists tended to support increased spending for coastal defenses while the opposition was consistently Jeffersonian, while New York's representatives in both the House and Senate were supportive of increased spending regardless of party affiliation. Neither of these conclusions is startling. The Jeffersonians are traditionally viewed as cautious in terms of military spending, and New York City was already the nation's most important port and financial center. The New York representatives naturally sought to add to the city's defenses. Despite the tendency of Jeffersonians to oppose increased military spending, however, it must be noted that since they firmly controlled both House and Senate, any appropriation had to enjoy substantial Jeffersonian support in order to pass. By and large, Congressmen and Senators seem to have voted on how they judged the issue rather than on a party or regional basis. The same Congress which voted down an additional sum of $1,000,000 in February and March of 1809 would approve a further $750,000 in June.[46] That there was some justice to their hesitation in appropriating large additional amounts of money for coastal defenses is demonstrated by the fact that in December 1809 Secretary of War William Eustis reported as complete nearly all the works at a total of thirty-one sites, and in February 1810 further reported an unspent balance of $560,000.[47] Given such information Congress naturally reduced the appropriations in 1811 and early 1812. Even then, however, the sums appropriated matched War Department estimates.[48]

This building program, begun in 1807, is historically termed the "Second System." As with the program of 1794, the term "system" is only partially accurate. There continued to be considerable variation in the design of coastal fortifications. The 1807-1808 program included mere open batteries, low earth forts similar to those of 1794, and an increased use of masonry both as a backing for earth walls and as a substitute for the earth. This increased use of masonry was coupled with a new and somewhat novel design approach advocated by Chief Engineer Jonathan Williams.[49]

The theory of fortification Williams urged was based on the theories of the French engineer and writer the Marquis de Montalembert. Earlier works were based largely on the bastion system, a system which placed great emphasis on flanking fire brought to bear along the main walls of any permanent fortification. However, while the bastion system took its name from the projecting, angled "bastions" which allowed fire down the main walls, the system (when fully developed) involved much more. A complex array of advanced positions could be built, each of which would be placed so as to interact with all the others in a mutually supporting whole, and with all exposed masonry protected by sloping banks of earth.[50]

While modest in size compared with European models, American seacoast fortifications tended to be simplified versions of the complex bastion system. Even a crude fortification, built entirely of earth (more closely resembling a "fieldwork" than a fortification) would attempt to carry out the ideal of interlocking and flanking fire.[51] Montalembert's ideas challenged much of the prevailing theory, but the most important aspects of his thought for Americans were those that dealt with a "perpendicular" approach to fortification instead of the more traditional "horizontal" style. Montalembert argued that towers could be used to gain height and then, taking advantage of this height, guns could be mounted in tiers in internal chambers called casemates. These guns would then fire through embrasures, or shuttered openings in the wall. The available number of guns would then be determined by the height of the wall and not the length.[52] The idea of firing through openings in a fort's wall was not new, but the system now advocated by

Williams represented a major break with the bastion tradition. Williams, in fact, believed he was the first to translate Montalembert into English.[53]

Williams was in a good position to advocate a new design for American coastal defenses. His position as Chief of the Corps of Engineers and Superintendent of the Military Academy gave his views authority and importance. Further, as the single head of the engineers he had the opportunity to actively direct subordinates. In fact, Williams assumed the responsibility of assigning and directing subordinate engineers in 1808, when he established a system of engineering districts (although that term was not yet used to describe the arrangement). So, while a French engineer like Louis de Tousard might grumble about the use of masonry and casemates, Williams was able to make his views prevail, and thus while the majority of "Second System" defensive works continued to echo the familiar forms, that system also included a small number of casemated "castles" as urged by Williams.[54] It was a significant development, for the casemated design would become the single most important American seacoast fortification design during the years before the Civil War.

By 1812 the "Second System," including the new Montalembert castles, was essentially complete. And by 1812 the traditional approach to coastal protection was different in several respects. The quick, inexpensive, and small earthen works typical of the colonial period, the Revolution, and the early 1790s were now increasingly giving way to more extensive masonry works which required a substantial investment of time and money to complete. The traditional reliance on foreign engineers was also gone, ended with the creation of the Military Academy. Graduates of that institution were eager participants in the design and construction of many "Second System" works. And finally, the establishment of a Corps of Engineers, with a single head, provided the foundation for a centralized controlling organization capable of actually imposing design uniformity on American coastal fortifications.

One issue left unresolved, though, was the fundamental purpose of such coastal defenses. Were they simply to deter raids for plunder or tribute, or were they intended to prevent full-scale invasion? In general, the former view on the purpose of fortifications predominated. Nonetheless, some supporters of coastal defenses raised the spectre of invasion, for whatever motives, in both 1798 and 1806-1808.[55] The issue was not one which could be dismissed lightly, for the acceptance of one view or the other would determine the scope of any fortification effort. A system designed to prevent or repel invasion would have to be more extensive and consist of stronger works than a system in which only the major port cities had to be protected from raids by marauding enemy vessels.

Lastly, in one way the traditional approach, from the colonial period, to the problem of coastal defense continued. American efforts to protect the coast continued to be undertaken only in response to an immediate crisis. (The period from 1806 to 1812 can easily be considered as a protracted, but nevertheless immediate, crisis.) The more complex Montalembert-type masonry casemated fortifications could not, however, be produced in a hurry. If such fortifications were to become the backbone of an American coastal defense system, they would have to be built during periods of peace. When, following the War of 1812, the engineers urged exactly this, it signaled the final break with the colonial and early national tradition and raised anew the issues of whether fortifications were the best means of coastal defense and, if so, how extensive such a system of fortifications needed to be.

NOTES

1. *American State Papers, Military Affairs,* vol. 1, pp. 307-311 (hereafter cited as *ASP, MA*).

2. For a summary discussion of the establishment of national military policy in the early national period see Richard H. Kohn, *Eagle and Sword: The Beginning of the Military Establishment in America* (New York: Free Press, 1975), ch. 14.

3. "Instructions given by way of advice . . . ," cited in Robert Arthur, *History of Fort Monroe* (Fort Monroe, Va.: Coast Artillery School Press, 1930), p. 6; John R. Mullin, "Fortifications in America: Application in the New World," *Periodical: The Journal of the Council on Abandoned Military Posts,* vol. 6, no. 1 (Spring 1974), p. 13; Robert Arthur, "Coast Forts of Colonial Massachusetts," *Coast Artillery Journal,* vol. 58, no. 2 (February 1923), p. 105.

4. Mullin, "Fortifications in America: Application in the New World," p. 13; Mullin, "Fortifications in America: Intention and Reality."

Periodical: The Journal of the Council on Abandoned Military Posts, vol. 6, no. 3 (Fall 1974), pp. 23-36. On the French and Spanish also see Willard B. Robinson, *American Forts: Architectural Form and Function* (Urbana: University of Illinois Press, 1977), ch. 1; Arthur, "Coast Forts of Colonial Massachusetts," pp. 106-107.

5. Emanuel R. Lewis, *Seacoast Fortifications of the United States* (Washington, D.C.: Smithsonian Institution Press, 1970), p. 15; Robinson, *American Forts,* p. 35; Lewis, *Seacoast Fortifications,* p. 15; D.P. Kirchner, "American Harbor Defense Forts," *U.S. Naval Institute Proceedings,* vol. 84, no. 8 (August 1958), pp. 93-94; Arthur, "Colonial Coast Forts on the South Atlantic," *Coast Artillery Journal,* vol. 70, no. 1 (January 1929), p. 49.

6. Arthur, "Coast Forts of Colonial Massachusetts," pp. 110-111.

7. Arthur, "Colonial Coast Forts on the South Atlantic," p. 54.

8. Ibid.

9. Arthur, *History of Fort Monroe,* p. 27.

10. Mullin, "Fortifications in America: Application in the New World," p. 14.

11. Duffy, *Fire and Stone: The Science of Fortress Warfare, 1660-1860* (London: David and Charles, 1975), pp. 22-23. Duffy quotes Carnot of the French Revolution: "A citadel is a monstrosity in a free country, a refuge of tyranny which should be the target of the indignation of every free people and every good citizen" (p. 23). See also Jacqueline Thibaut, "Deciphering Fort Mifflin," *Military Collector and Historian,* vol. 27, no. 3 (Fall 1975), pp. 101-112.

12. Lewis, *Seacoast Fortifications,* p. 4. On the local nature of the colonial military see John Shy, *Toward Lexington* (Princeton: Princeton University Press, 1965), ch. 1. Also see Boorstin, "A Nation of Minutemen," *The Americans: The Colonial Experience,* pt. 13.

13. Edward M. Riley, "Historic Fort Moultrie in Charleston Harbor," *South Carolina Historical and Genealogical Magazine,* vol. 51, no. 2 (April 1950), pp. 63-64.

14. *Webster's American Military Biographies* (Springfield, Mass.: G. and C. Merriam Co., 1978), pp. 109-110, 221-222; Lewis, *Seacoast Fortifications* lists only three: Castle Island (Boston), Goat Island (Newport, R.I.), and Mud Island (Fort Mifflin), p. 17.

15. James D. Richardson, ed., *Messages and Papers of the Presidents,* vol. 1 (Washington, D.C.: Government Printing Office, 1896), p. 139.

16. Robert G. Albion and Jennie B. Pope, *Sea Lanes in Wartime,* 2nd ed., enlarged (New York: Archon Books, 1968), p. 73.

17. Richardson, *Messages and Papers,* vol. 1, p. 140.

18. *ASP, MA,* vol. 1, pp. 61-62.

19. *Statutes At Large,* vol. 1, pp. 346-347; *Annals of Congress,* 3rd

Congress (vol. 4), pp. 1423-1424 (hereafter *Annals*); Portland, Maine; Portsmouth, New Hampshire; Gloucester, Salem, Marblehead, and Boston, Massachusetts; Newport, Rhode Island; New London, Connecticut; New York; Philadelphia; Wilmington, Delaware; Baltimore and Annapolis, Maryland; Norfolk and Alexandria, Virginia; Cape Fear River and Ocracoke Inlet, North Carolina; Charleston and Georgetown, South Carolina; and Savannah and St. Mary's, Georgia.

20. *ASP, MA,* vol. 1, pp. 72, 77-78, 82, 87, 93, 101.

21. On the issue of localism and the framing of the Constitution see John P. Roche, "The Founding Fathers: A Reform Caucus in Action," *American Political Science Review,* vol. 55 (1961), pp. 799-816; Jackson T. Main, *The Antifederalists* (Chapel Hill: University of North Carolina Press, 1961), pp. 255-259, 261-281.

22. *ASP, MA,* pp. 73, 78.

23. Ibid., pp. 77-106, passim; Timothy Pickering, "Report from the Department of War Relative to the Fortifications . . . ," *Annals,* 4th Congress, 2nd session, pp. 2571-2574. Also see Lewis, *Seacoast Fortifications,* pp. 21-22; Robinson, *American Forts,* p. 63.

24. Knox to Speaker of the House, Nov. 28, 1794, Record Group 107, National Archives, Copies of War Department Correspondence and Reports, 1791-1794. Microcopy T982, Roll 1. Cited in Arthur P. Wade, "Artillerists and Engineers," Ph.D. dissertation, Kansas State University, 1977, p. 30; Richardson, *Messages and Papers,* vol. 1, p. 167; *ASP, MA,* vol. 1, pp. 107-108; *Statutes At Large,* vol. 1, pp. 438-439.

25. Pickering, "Report Relative to the Fortifications," *Annals,* 4th Congress, 2nd session, pp. 2571-2574.

26. *ASP, MA,* vol. 1, p. 115; *Annals,* 4th Congress, 1st session (vol. 5), pp. 1359-1374.

27. *ASP, MA,* vol. 1, p. 116.

28. *Annals,* 4th Congress, 2nd session (vol. 6), pp. 2211 and 2219; *Statutes At Large,* vol. 1, pp. 508-509.

29. *Annals,* 5th Congress, 1st session (vol. 7), pp. 299-324; *ASP, MA,* vol. 1, pp. 117-118.

30. *Annals,* 3rd Congress (vol. 4), p. 448.

31. Richardson, *Messages and Papers,* vol. 1, pp. 236-238.

32. *Statutes At Large,* vol. 1, p. 554. For a discussion of the Federalists' expressed fears of French invasion, see Kohn, *Eagle and Sword,* pp. 206, 213-214, 225.

33. *Annals,* 5th Congress, 2nd session (vol. 8), p. 1407. In fact, President Adams shared this view. See Kohn, *Eagle and Sword,* p. 230.

34. *Annals,* 5th Congress, 2nd session (vol. 8), p. 1482. For a detailed analysis of the way Congressional factions emerged and behaved on defense issues in the late 1790s see Rudolph M. Bell, *Party And Faction In*

American Politics: The House of Representatives, 1789-1799 (Westport, Conn.: Greenwood Press, 1973), pp. 150-192. Bell suggests that neither party affiliation nor state origin was a sure guide to voting behavior in these years. His data indicate, however, that while neither of these factors was a consistent predictor of voting behavior, Federalists tended to support military preparedness measures and the most consistent opposition came from Jeffersonians. Another good discussion of the way military issues of the late 1790s were affected by politics (focusing on the intra-Federalist split) may be found in Kohn, *Eagle and Sword,* ch. 13, passim.

35. Richardson, *Messages and Papers,* vol. 1, p. 330.

36. *ASP, MA,* vol. 1 (Serial 016), pp. 152-153, 192-197. Getting an accurate figure for the amounts spent on fortifications in the 1790s is extremely difficult since few sets of figures agree. A War Department report of 1800 indicates that $512,381.90 had been spent by October 1799. Another War Department report in 1801 gives a different total for the same period, and still a third amount is provided in a Treasury Department report of 1820. The figures used here are those reported by the War Department in 1801 since these were also used by Secretary of War Henry Dearborn in 1806. Figures for annual War Department or federal expenditures, here and throughout, are from United States Bureau of the Census, *Historical Statistics of the United States: Colonial Times to 1957* (Washington, D.C.: Government Printing Office, 1960), pp. 718-719.

37. *Statutes At Large,* vol. 2, pp. 183, 227-228, 249-250, 315.

38. *ASP, MA,* vol. 1 (Serial 016), pp. 193-194.

39. *Annals,* 5th Congress, 1st session (vol. 7), p. 240.

40. Richardson, *Messages and Papers,* vol. 1, p. 372; *American State Papers, Naval Affairs,* vol. 1 (Serial 023), Document 60, pp. 163-164 (hereafter *ASP, NA*); Howard I. Chapelle, *The History of the American Sailing Navy* (New York: W. W. Norton and Company, 1949), pp. 217-218, 226; *ASP, NA,* vol. 1 (Serial 023), Document 65, pp. 168-169; *ASP, NA,* vol. 1 (Serial 023), Document 76, pp. 198-199. Even among Jeffersonians there was not a complete consensus on the value of gunboats. John Randolph, leader of the Quids, was a persistent critic of the scheme. However, he and the other opponents of gunboats were in a clear minority. For a brief discussion of this issue see Norman K. Risjord, *The Old Republicans: Southern Conservatism in the Age of Jefferson* (New York: Columbia University Press, 1965), pp. 81-82.

41. *The Debates and Proceedings of the Congress of the United States,* 7th Congress, 1st session, p. 1312. Cited in Sidney Forman, "Why the United States Military Academy Was Established in 1802," *Military Affairs,* vol. 29, no. 1 (Spring 1965), p. 26.

42. Wade, "Artillerists and Engineers," pp. 48, 50-59, 68, 74-84, 109-110, 115-118, 139; *Webster's American Military Biographies,* p. 482.

43. *Statutes At Large,* vol. 2, p. 453.

44. *Annals,* 10th Congress, 1st session (vol. 17), pp. 1198-1199.

45. *Annals,* 10th Congress, 1st session (vol. 14), pp. 1204, 1227; *Statutes At Large,* vol. 2, pp. 516-517.

46. *Statutes At Large,* vol. 2, pp. 547-548. The February and March votes are in *Annals,* 10th Congress, 2nd session (vol. 16), pp. 452, 1521.

47. *ASP, MA,* vol. 1 (Serial 016), pp. 245-247.

48. *ASP, MA,* vol. 1 (Serial 016), p. 296.

49. *ASP, MA,* vol. 1 (Serial 016), pp. 245-247.

50. There are numerous excellent descriptions of the fortification systems of this period. In particular see Ian V. Hogg, *Fortress* (London: Macdonald and Jane's, 1975), pp. 54-69; Duffy, *Fire and Stone,* pp. 47-80; James R. Hinds and Edmund Fitzgerald, "Permanent Fortification in the United States," *Periodical,* vol. 9, no. 3 (Fall 1977), pp. 40-53. Also see Thibaut, "Deciphering Fort Mifflin."

51. James R. Hinds and Edmund Fitzgerald, "Fortifications in the Field and on the Frontier," *Periodical,* vol. 9, no. 1 (Spring 1977), pp. 41-49.

52. Descriptions of Montalembert's system can be found in Hogg, *Fortress,* pp. 78-79; Robinson, *American Forts,* pp. 70-77; Wade, "Artillerists and Engineers," pp. 186-191.

53. *Annals,* 9th Congress, 2nd session (vol. 16), p. 444.

54. Williams to Dearborn, February 29, 1808. Buell Collection (National Archives Microfilm). Cited in Wade, "Artillerists and Engineers," p. 212; Tousard's view is in his *American Artillerist's Companion, or Elements of Artillery,* reprint ed. (New York: Greenwood Press, 1969). Cited in James R. Hinds and Edmund Fitzgerald, "Permanent Fortifications in the United States," p. 43.

55. James Elliott of Vermont claimed that since the French had so soundly beaten the Prussians, " . . . upon every sober and solid principle of human calculation, it is our turn next." He went further and raised the far-fetched image of "our militia" fighting "three millions" of French veterans. He offered several resolutions regarding national defense which were quietly tabled. *Annals,* 9th Congress, 2d session (vol. 16), pp. 161-164, 199-200.

ONE
The Creation of a System

In the past the conclusion of a crisis meant an end to concern for seacoast defense. But the War of 1812 was scarcely ended when President James Madison called for a continued effort to put the seacoast in a defensible state. At the time he submitted the draft of the Treaty of Ghent to Congress (in 1815), Madison told the assembled legislators, "a certain degree of preparation for war . . . affords also the best security for the continuance of peace." He urged just such preparation in the form of continued support of the regular army and navy as well as the necessary appropriations to "improve all the means of harbor defence."[1]

Madison's Secretary of War, James Monroe, supported these sentiments, pointing out to the Senate Military Affairs Committee, "The late war has shewn [sic] our vulnerable ports . . . our defenceless situation. It is our duty to put these ports in a proper state of defence now that we have a fair opportunity for it."[2] Thus, Monroe joined his President in attempting to persuade Congress to support a program of coastal defense construction during peacetime and in the absence of any clear threat from an overseas enemy. In doing so, Madison and Monroe took the necessary first step towards the inauguration of a program of coastal defense which would, in altered form, continue for the rest of the century.

With the experiences of the War of 1812 still fresh in their minds, most Congressmen were not inclined to question the view of the executive branch. Although the regular army was cut sharply in size, Congress continued to fund the navy and supplied appropriations totaling $600,000 for coastal fortifications for the remainder of 1815. Such continued support for defensive measures, coming after the removal of a threat rather than in response to one, marks a watershed in the development of American coastal defense policy.[3]

Certainly the War of 1812 provided supporters of a national program of defenses with ample evidence to buttress their arguments. British raids in the Chesapeake Bay during 1813 and 1814 were not only destructive but led to the humiliating loss and burning of the capital in August 1814. Returning Congressmen in 1815 had visible evidence of the threat a superior naval power posed to an extensive and exposed seacoast. Yet, in perfect counterpoint, the stirring and well-publicized defense of Fort McHenry outside Baltimore, just weeks after the destruction of Washington, demonstrated that a tenacious defense, supported by sound, carefully constructed, and well-defended shore fortifications, could effectively resist an enemy fleet. Thus, for a time arguments in favor of continued spending on coastal defenses were made in an especially favorable environment.[4]

On the other hand, while Congress was willing to appropriate money for fixed shore defenses, there also existed an apparent belief that more expert advice and guidance on the utilization of those funds was necessary. As early as mid-1815 Monroe suggested the hiring of up to four advisers, in addition to the officers in the existing Corps of Engineers.[5] Congress did not authorize this large a contingent, but in April 1816 Senator James Barbour of Virginia easily secured passage of a resolution which authorized the President to employ a "skillful" assistant to the Chief of Engineers.[6]

The man chosen to fill this unusual position was Simon Bernard, a highly regarded French engineer. Bernard, a former aide to the Emperor Napoleon, came highly recommended by the American Ambassador, Albert Gallatin, and the Marquis de Lafayette. His appointment, of course, harked back to the old dependence on foreign engineers, a dependence supposedly eliminated by the creation of West Point. Born in 1779 Bernard received his training at the famous French school L'Ecole Polytechnique. During the Napoleonic Wars he rose to the rank of General, and served as an aide-de-camp to the Emperor. Accepted into royal service following the Restoration of 1814, Bernard rejoined Napoleon during the

Hundred Days. Surprisingly, he was allowed to reenter royal service after Waterloo, an indication of the regard held for his talents as a military engineer. Despite being accepted into royal service, however, Bernard soon came under a cloud and, forced to leave France, offered his services to the United States. Monroe found him a "modest, unassuming man," and both he and Madison considered him a valuable addition to the American military establishment.[7] Not everyone agreed with this assessment.

The Chief of Engineers, Joseph G. Swift, in particular, considered the appointment of Bernard both an insult and a dangerous precedent. It conveyed, said Swift, "the humiliating idea that the government [does] not repose sufficient confidence in the talents of the Corps of Engineers." Swift declared himself "mortified" by the situation, and argued that Bernard's appointment was not only a slap at the Corps of Engineers but an indication that his "talents as Chief Engineer [are] seen as inferior to those of General Bernard." Swift further protested that it was poor policy to hire foreign engineers to construct American defenses. Such a procedure, he contended, would give those officers a "knowledge of all our assailable points." If the government truly needed Bernard's knowledge and expertise, Swift believed he should be employed as an instructor at the Military Academy.[8] Swift's arguments were sound in several respects, but he was apparently correct in his assumption that the government viewed his and the other engineers' talents as inferior to those of Bernard. In any event, his protests at Bernard's appointment fell on deaf ears.[9]

Despite a claim that he would cooperate with Bernard, Swift was persistently critical of the Frenchman's skills. Swift believed Congress was in awe of the man's supposed brilliance as a military engineer, a situation that galled him for Swift believed Bernard's expertise to be overestimated. In contrast to the positive perception of Madison and Monroe, Swift disparagingly described Bernard as an "excellent bureau officer, a cold-hearted man; not in any sense a man of genius." While willing initially to submit to the situation, however grudgingly, Swift soon found his position intolerable. In November 1818 he resigned.[10]

Madison and Monroe were well aware that the hiring of a foreign engineer might wound the feelings of American engineers, many of whom deserved a good deal of praise for their work during and after the War of 1812. Nevertheless, both men earnestly desired Bernard's expertise. In an effort to get it, and simultaneously mollify American egos, Madison or Monroe (the authorship is unclear) devised a scheme which would have far-reaching effects but would fail in its immediate purpose. They created a board of officers to "examine the whole coast and report such works as are necessary for its defense to the Chief Engineer, who shall report the same to the Secretary of War . . . to be laid before the President." This arrangement, wrote Monroe, would ensure that "the feelings of no one can be hurt." The board would consist of three permanent members, Bernard and two Americans, and two additional members depending on the area being investigated: the engineer officer assigned to that district and a naval officer. In this situation, for Bernard's views to carry the day, four Americans would have to agree with him. Or, as Monroe phrased it, "We shall have four of our officers in every consultation against one foreigner, so that if the opinion of the latter becomes of an essential use, it must be by convincing his colleagues when they differ that he has reason on his side."[11]

If Bernard's appointment was a retrograde step in the sense that the United States was again turning to a foreign engineer, the creation of the board was a step forward for it systematized the selection of fortification sites and laid the foundation for the numerous later Boards of Engineers which would plan the nation's system of seacoast defenses. Certainly, it provided an opportunity to devise a true system of defenses, in which all the components were part of a larger whole, as well as allowing the assigning of priorities to certain sites. In the past the Chief of Engineers made the key decisions. He assigned engineers to various districts, reviewed the plans they submitted, and, summarizing those he approved, requested funds for construction via the Secretary of War. He could be guided by the obvious wishes of Congress or the Secretary, but by and large, the selection of sites and the approval of plans depended upon his judgment. The Chief of Engineers alone was in a position to see the whole system; one or two engineers, working in isolation at a limited number of sites, might see the interrelationships between positions at a particular locale, but would not necessarily have a connection to engineers at other sites and hence might not have an idea of how their work fit into some overall scheme.[12] Obviously, the creation of the Board of Engineers changed this arrangement. For one thing, the board would submit unedited recommendations to the Secretary of War, after, presumably, the members had thrashed out all the problems among themselves. More important, however, was the fact that the newly created board was responsible for developing plans for the entire coast. The engineer at a single locale might recognize the primacy of one site over another within his jurisdiction, but he worked alone. Each engineer had to rely on his own judgment, not only with regard to the design of fortifications, but also, given limitations of time and money, in determining the function of those fortifications and which ones were the most immediately necessary. Now, instead of relying on individual judgment, differing from place to place and engineer to engineer, the board could establish priorities even within a single locale, applying the same collective judgment to every site. Simultaneously, as a part of the grappling with priorities, the board would be forced to deal with the question of what the system of coastal defenses was to achieve—to decide, in other words, the function and purpose of the coastal defense system. The almost accidental creation of the first Board of Engineers fundamentally altered the past practice of American coastal defense planning, and for the first time made the development of a true system of coastal defenses possible.

But while Madison and Monroe expected the creation of the board to mollify the feelings of American engineers, who were bruised by the appointment of Bernard, it did not. Indeed, the new board had a rocky start. Swift's resignation in November 1818 was followed four months later by that of William McRee, perhaps the preeminent American military engineer of that time. McRee was one of the two American officers expected to serve as permanent board members. His resignation left as the sole remaining American permanent member his slightly junior colleague Joseph G. Totten.[13]

Totten was a consistent presence in American seacoast defense planning during the years before the Civil War. Born in 1788 he graduated from the Military Academy in 1805. Although he resigned his commission in 1806, he soon returned to the army as a lieutenant of engineers in 1808. For a time Totten worked directly under Swift, helping supervise the construction of fortifications in New England. During the War of 1812 he earned two brevet promotions for gallantry in service on the northern frontier. By 1816 Totten was a highly regarded member of the Corps of Engineers and a natural choice to serve with McRee and Bernard on the newly created Board of Engineers. His extant letters give little insight into the personal aspects of Totten's life. Instead they show a man dedicated to his work, reinforcing the image of a man described as "disciplined to obedience" and always aware of his duty.[14]

Like McRee and Swift, Totten expressed dismay at the appointment of Bernard. Unlike his colleagues, however, Totten did not resign. While it is clear that he never formed a close friendship with Bernard, he nevertheless preserved at least a nominal working relationship with the Frenchman until Bernard returned to France in 1831. With Bernard gone, Totten then became the nation's premier expert on matters of national defense and fortifications. In 1838 he advanced to the post of Chief Engineer, a position he held until his death in 1864.[15]

For almost fifty years then Totten was a major figure in the planning and development of the country's system of seacoast defenses. Partly as a result of such long service his reputation grew steadily, and his impact was enormous. Totten's name appeared on every major report dealing with the issue of coastal defense in the period before the Civil War. Indeed, he wrote most of them. Admired and respected by his fellow engineers, he was unchallenged within his field while remaining remarkably consistent in his views. Totten revised his, and thus the Engineer Department's position very little; often he repeated phrases and on occasion whole reports verbatim. As Presidents and Secretaries of War came and went, as views in Congress altered and shifted, the views expressed by Totten and the engineers remained unaltered, faithful to the principles and goals that Totten helped originate.[16]

Of course, these principles did not come into existence immediately. With the internal turmoil caused by Bernard's appointment, the new board was not ready with an overall plan for coastal defense for some time. The board began to submit reports and recommendations in 1818, but these first reports were concerned with particular regions, such as the Gulf coast or the Canadian border. Not until 1820 did it begin to develop a basic definition of the extent and function of the various defensive works being proposed.[17]

Finally, in February of 1821 the Board of Engineers submitted to

Congress the country's first comprehensive plan for coastal defense. Since Bernard was generally recognized as head of the Board of Engineers, this report is often referred to as the "Bernard Board Report."[18] Now seen as a particularly significant development in the history of American coastal defense, it is worth noting that the importance of the report was seen at the time as well. It was disseminated widely, being reprinted *in toto,* for example, in *Niles Register.*[19] Then, of course, the report attracted attention essentially because it was the first overall plan yet developed. It would remain historically prominent even if that was all it represented. But, in fact, from a historical perspective, this 1821 report means much more. It may be said to have established the foundation of a "Third System" of coastal defenses, separated both organizationally (since it came much closer to being a true system), and to some extent architecturally, from the earlier "First" and "Second Systems." Totten certainly thought so, for he originated the term "Third System" to describe the works proposed by the 1821 report and those proposed in subsequent reports until the Civil War. The format of the 1821 report was subsequently followed by all the major reports issued by the Board of Engineers. Most important, however, the 1821 report enumerated the fundamental goals of a coastal defense system from the point of view of the Board of Engineers. Those goals remained basically unaltered throughout the antebellum period. For this reason, especially, the 1821 report is worth examining in some detail.

The board argued that a coastal defense system should meet six criteria. First, it must close important harbors to the enemy. Second, it should deprive an enemy of so-called strong positions where he could fix a permanent, or even temporary, lodgment as a base for operations along the seaboard. Third, the system must cover the country's major cities. (In most cases these were also the important harbors, but a few, notably Washington, were not.) Fourth, the system should prevent the blockade of the routes of interior navigation. Closely related to this was criterion five: the system should cover coastal and internal trade by providing naval bases or havens for merchant vessels. Finally, the coastal defenses should protect naval yards and rendezvous anchorages. Few, if any, of the defensive works proposed by the Board of Engineers could fulfill all these criteria, but the board emphasized that all the proposed works met at least one of them.[20]

Almost at the very start, the board noted that the existing fortifications had not been planned as part of a single system. These existing forts, stated the Board, "only defend single points, and satisfy only a few essential conditions . . . they have not been planned . . . as one great and combined system, whose several parts should be connected, and should mutually support each other." Thus, the board contended, a "defensive system for the frontiers of the United States is . . . yet to be created." The board argued that such a system had four essential parts of which fortifications were only one. A true system included a navy, good interior communications by land and water, and a regular army backed by a "well organized militia." Diplomatically, the board accorded the navy primacy as the foremost element in a soundly designed coastal defense system. After making this gesture, however, the board's report went on to argue that "a navy can neither be augmented nor secured without fortifications." Only after the coast was secure from invasion, said the board, could all attention be devoted to the expansion of the navy, a force which, admittedly, could settle national quarrels on the ocean and away from the coast. Nevertheless, until that time came, fortifications were a necessary and vital first step.[21]

Of course, creating the kind of system envisioned by the board was an involved process, one that could not be done in a single step. The board carefully pointed out that not all the recommended fortifications were of "pressing necessity." Some could wait while others, more vital, were built. In keeping with this assessment, the board devised a system of priorities, arranging the proposed fortifications in three classes. First-class works were those believed immediately necessary to keep an enemy away from major ports and harbors. Placed in the second class were works intended to protect naval stations and commercial cities of "secondary importance." In some cases cities already had defensive fortifications and there was less need to add new works, or rebuild old ones right away. Deferred to the third class were works which would complete the system by covering open anchorages and small coastal towns and prevent landings at suitable points between the major port cities.[22]

The board contended that any system of coastal defense had to be built in harmony with the principles of "modern" war, and their scheme of classification demonstrates clearly the degree to which they drew upon the best available thought dealing with fortifications. Due to the continuing international reputation of Vauban and later French engineers, as well as the current fascination with the French armies under Napoleon, the most generally relied-on texts and treatises dealing with fortification were French. Bernard was naturally completely familiar with this literature and the American engineers were not strangers to it. They were undoubtedly particularly aware of Gay de Vernon's 1805 work, *A Treatise on the Science of War and Fortification,* originally written for the use of cadets at L'Ecole Polytechnique, and on its way to becoming the standard text at West Point. In regard to the development of a system of coastal defenses, de Vernon stated that such a system ought to consist of two elements: one being a chain of fortresses to enclose and protect harbors and prevent disembarkations, the second a series of smaller forts and batteries built between harbors to deny access to favorable landing sites and as points from which to observe the movements of the offshore enemy. De Vernon briefly reminded readers that maritime fortresses served to ''enclose depots, magazines and arsenals, whose preservation is an object of the greatest importance; . . . they should be sheltered and secured from the bombardments and conflagrations that the enemy may attempt by water or temporary debarkations.''[23]

The Board of Engineers' classification scheme followed the same line of argument emphasizing those works intended to cover major ports and harbors, and placing less emphasis on those works expected to protect smaller ports and intermediate landing areas. The board echoed de Vernon in its repeated insistence that the proposed fortifications were to cover ''the great commercial cities against attack by land or sea.''[24] On the other hand the Board of Engineers also stressed the importance of protecting coastal navigation, a concern not given much attention in the European literature. In a country which lacked an extensive road network, however, water transportation was vital. Particularly important was the ability to move goods along the coast and in large coastal waterways like the Chesapeake Bay. American experience in both the Revolution and the War of 1812 indicated that a superior navy, able to roam freely in coastal waters, could wreak havoc with this trade. More than most European countries the United States depended upon coastal trade, and the Board of Engineers was well aware of this dependency. The forts projected for the harbor of New York were not only to protect the city from attack, but were also expected

> to protect its numerous shipping; to prevent, as much as possible, the blockade of that immense river [the Hudson], which will soon have added to the wealth of its own shores the productions of the boundless regions on the northern and western lakes; and to cover the interior navigation which is projected to connect the waters of the Delaware with those of the bay of New York, by a canal from the Raritan.

Similarly, the works projected for the southern coast from Savannah to Georgetown, South Carolina had "for object to secure the communication between the sea and the interior; to prevent the blockade of the rivers and harbors of these States . . . necessary in guarding the coasting trade."[25]

The board projected a total of fifty works, in all three classes, to cover the major ports, anchorages, and coastal trade routes. In several cases there were multiple works to protect the same city or location. Five forts, for example, were proposed to cover the city and approaches to New Orleans, while two protected the lower Chesapeake Bay. Work on some of these positions was already underway, and in some cases the defensive works already existed (such as Fort St. Philip, on the Mississippi below New Orleans). Nevertheless, the completion of the system would be expensive. The board estimated the total cost at nearly $18,000,000 with the forts in the first class alone expected to cost over $8,000,000.

The financial investment in construction was, furthermore, not the only cost to be considered. Fortifications required garrisons, and the board estimated that peacetime garrisons would total over 4,600 men for the entire system. Twenty-five hundred men would be needed for the first-class works alone.[26] Such figures were obviously going to cause difficulty, and the board sought to forestall critics by insisting that the cost of constructing the necessary fortifications and providing them with garrisons would be cheaper in the event of war than doing without. In one six-month campaign, contended the board, the cost of raising enough troops to defend the coast would come to more than $16,500,000. With fortifications, only one-third the number of troops would be required, and the cost would be only $5,500,000. This savings of nearly $11,000,000, according to the board's calculations, essentially equaled the cost of construction. The forts would pay for themselves in a single six-month campaign. Furthermore, the ability of an enemy with superior naval power to strike at points of his own choosing without any foreknowledge of his intentions made defending the coast a difficult task. The existence of fortifications altered this situation. With "the points of attack . . . reduced to a few," argued the board, "we shall force an enemy to direct his efforts against these few points with which we shall be well acquainted beforehand, and which we shall have disposed to withstand all his attempts." With the enemy forced to attack where the defense expected him to, there was every reason to believe that he would be defeated at the very start of hostilities. The existence of a fortification system would make this possibility apparent to any potential enemy, and knowing in advance the likelihood of defeat, such an enemy might hesitate to attack at all. The board, however, was more certain, leaving out any intimation that an enemy would ignore the obvious. "There is no doubt," contended the board, " . . . that such circumstances will render an enemy more backward in risking his expeditions, and that we shall not only be better able to resist attack, but that we shall also be less frequently menaced by invasion."[27]

Here, then, in clear language, the board expressed the goal of the seacoast defense system. Not only would it serve to protect the major ports, the coastal navigation, and the points of naval rendezvous, but it would also act as a deterrent, lessening the chances of a crisis erupting into war. In every sense, from the board's point of view, the system of fortifications was "a real and positive economy."

President Monroe was pleased with this report and largely accepted the board's reasoning. In an extensive reference to the problem of coastal defense in his second inaugural address a few weeks later, the President used many of the same arguments, contending that fortifications would assist the United States in maintaining its neutrality during European wars by forcing belligerent naval vessels to keep their distance from the coast and protecting the government from insult. Monroe even went the Board of

Engineers one better by making their defensive and deterrent character explicit. "They have been dictated," he said, "by a love of peace, of economy, and an ernest [sic] desire to save the lives of our fellow citizens." Fortifications were, argued Monroe, "the best expedient that can be resorted to to prevent war."[28]

Carefully developed though it was, and despite the eager approval of it by the Chief Executive, the report did include several points of possible contention. One involved a subtle bit of numerical legerdemain in the board's calculation that the cost of building the proposed fortifications would be no more than defending the coast with those works that already existed. The board calculated the cost of defending six ports and harbors (New Orleans, Norfolk, Baltimore, Philadelphia, New York, and Narragansett Bay) with the fortifications already existing to be $16,750,000. Some 67,000 troops under pay and a further 53,000 within call were viewed as necessary and were included as part of the estimate. On the other hand, contended the board, only 23,720 men would be needed under pay and 36,280 within call for the coast to be defended with the proposed works. The cost of defending the coast under these circumstances totaled only $5,653,000. The board found the difference between defending the coast with the existing fortifications and defending it with the proposed works to be just over $11,000,000. This was, by the board's reckoning, nearly the cost of erecting the proposed defenses at the six ports and harbors listed.[29] But, of course, the board developed its figures for those six locations alone, and not all the projected works for those places were in the first class. Indeed, projected first-class works at Boston and Portsmouth (New Hampshire), supposedly among those works "indispensable," were not a part of the board's calculations, which, in fact, included completed works on both sides of the equation.[30] By presenting the numbers the way it did, however, the board avoided drawing attention to the fact that the complete system would cost nearly $18,000,000 rather than $11,000,000. Obviously, to be fully effective the system would have to be complete. Furthermore, the board was unrealistic in presenting a proposal which ultimately required 4,600 men for garrison duty at a time when Congress was reducing the maximum strength of the army to 6,000 men. Finally, and most significantly, the board's statements contained a subtle but significant shift in the perceived purpose of the fortification system. The board's language stressed the point that the system was meant to prevent, or at least make supremely difficult, an enemy invasion; the use of the term invasion implied that it no longer existed solely to deter enemy plundering of hit-and-run attacks on American port cities.

Congress did not welcome the board's 1821 report with any obvious enthusiasm. A clear majority favored continued funding for coastal defenses, but the impulse toward fiscal retrenchment meant that money would be forthcoming only for works considered clearly necessary. Less than three weeks after the board submitted its report, an effort to increase the fortification appropriation from $172,000 to $300,000 failed by a wide margin in the House of Representatives. Initially, no appropriation at all was provided for defensive works at Mobile Bay, a fact that led to a spirited defense of the fortification system by Kentucky Congressman Francis Johnson, who argued that the projected works for Mobile Point and Dauphin Island (in Mobile Bay, Alabama) were vital for the defense of New Orleans. After a good deal of debate, an additional $30,000 appropriation for Mobile Point cleared the House, but an equal amount for Dauphin Island failed to get through by a vote of thirty-one to eighty-five.[31]

Congressional disagreement with the Board of Engineers over the necessity for a fort on Dauphin Island was made even more explicit the following year. Even though Monroe supported the project, the House Military Affairs Committee contended that the proposed work, expected to mount 108 guns, would not prevent blockade of Mobile Bay, protect the coasting trade from New Orleans, or even serve as a depot for naval stores, since for nearly a mile out from shore the water was too shallow for even the smallest national vessels. Two reports by Bernard himself were cited in support of the project, but Congress remained unconvinced. As in 1821 it appropriated money for Mobile Point but not for Dauphin Island.[32] Clearly, Congress was not willing to accept the board's proposals without question. Significantly, Congress in 1821 appropriated money by fortification rather than as one lump sum. This practice would continue throughout the antebellum period.

The decade of the 1820s was a tempestuous one in American politics. In many ways it marked the beginning of a period often referred to as the "Age of Jackson," an era of rhetoric exalting the common man and an era of often intense antimilitary expression. The presentation of the annual military appropriation bill, which generally contained the provision for fortifications, often sparked long and hard debate in Congress. Congressman William van Wyck of New York set forth one aspect of these debates in 1822 contending that when war threatened, the country had always relied "on ourselves, or rather on the militia of our country." Van Wyck believed that "the same confidence may be restored."[33] John Rhea of Tennessee also questioned the need for military preparedness. "We are told," he argued, "that, to preserve peace, we must be prepared for war. If so, then, when will war be, and with whom? . . . With any of the nations of Europe there is no probability that the United States will soon be at war."[34] Rhea and van Wyck were not unique. Many Congressmen contended that fortifications were unnecessary. The nation should rely instead on the militia, "who are the strong bulwark and impregnable defence of this nation." There was no real danger of invasion, and fortifications required an expensive standing army to garrison and maintain them. As one Congressman expressed it, "our fortifications must be locked up in the breast of every freeman of America."[35] Sometimes, of course, this opposition ran afoul of local interests. When in 1824, John Cooke of Tennessee attempted to get an appropriation for a fort in New York harbor eliminated, he was immediately opposed by Representatives Silas Wood and Peter Sharpe of New York.[36] This illustrates that support for fortifications was sometimes rooted less in principle than in the perennial wish to have government money spent in one's home state or district. Representative Durfee of Rhode Island staunchly defended continued fortifications appropriations, especially in Narragansett Bay.[37] In a speech questioning the size of the 1826 appropriation, Representative Forsyth candidly complained that "not a dollar is allotted to the state from whence I come."[38] When Ambrose Spencer of New York argued his opposition to fortifications in March 1830, he remarked that the apparent purpose of these works was less the need for defenses than the benefits of the government expending money in the part of the country where these works would be built. In any case, he asserted, fortifications were a "lavish and useless expenditure."[39]

Since the decade of the 1820s was at least nominally a part of a one-party period in American politics, support of or opposition to the fortification effort was not a party issue. It is not surprising, however, that to some extent the state or region from which a Congressman came apparently influenced his vote. New York's representatives tended to support fortifications just as they had in the past. So did those from the New England states. Opposition tended to come mainly from southern and western states, although this was not consistently the case. For example, in 1824 Ohio's delegation voted overwhelmingly (thirteen of fourteen) in favor of reducing the appropriation for fortifications, while Kentucky's Representatives and those of North Carolina did so with similar unanimity. Yet, South Carolina's Representatives voted against lowering the appropriation, as did the delegations from Tennessee and Virginia. Indeed, opponents of the fortification appropriation could muster only a third of the votes in 1824, losing 62 to 120. So, despite their rhetoric, the opponents remained by and large a vocal minority in Congress. Appropriations for coastal fortifications continued, aggregating by 1820 a total of over $8,500,000. While far less than the engineers desired, this total represented some 11 percent of all military spending and it equaled nearly half of the original estimate for the complete system. Since the Board of Engineers had admitted that the building of the system would take a long time, the figures indicate that steady progress was being made.[40]

Nevertheless, the engineers continued to urge even greater spending on coastal defenses. There was little doubt in Totten's mind that the country needed the defensive system recommended by him and his fellows. Both he and his colleagues sought and found support for their views in history. Although the Board of Engineers paid lip service to the idea that the navy was the foremost element in their system of defenses, they consistently argued that actual defense of the coast by the navy was both financially and strategically unfeasible. Totten pointed out that if the coast was defended by the navy alone, then the defending force at every potentially threatened point had to at least equal the attacking force. Since no one could predict in advance the place of attack, the ultimate size of the necessary defending forces was huge.[41] The cost of providing a navy of this magnitude would be unbearable. The only sure way was to defend the coast by the use of a fortification system. History amply demonstrated the superiority, as well as the economy, of this approach. In his 1846 book, *Military Art and*

Science, Henry W. Halleck devoted an entire chapter to an analysis of American seacoast defense. Going back to the 1790s he paraded a series of ship-to-shore duels, each of which was a further example of the superiority of shore batteries over attacking naval vessels. From the American point of view, the most relevant examples were those drawn from the War of 1812. In that conflict, Halleck noted, British fleets proved unable to shake the defenders at Fort McHenry, Fort Bowyer (guarding Mobile Bay), and Fort St. Philip (below New Orleans). In each case the British had to withdraw. The only successful reduction of a seacoast fort was the capture of Fort Washington, on the Potomac River, abandoned by its garrison despite the strength of its position. However, Fort Washington was not a good example, contended Halleck, since he dismissed it as small, inefficient, and badly designed by an incompetent French engineer. Furthermore, in 1814 the fort was still unfinished. Even examples from European history of naval victories over shore batteries were, in Halleck's view, used as counterevidence only by those who misunderstood the actual facts of each case. In the instances he cited, fleets either stayed out of range of small-caliber shore guns, managed to slip by inattentive garrisons, or (as at the attack on St. Jean d'Acre in 1841) the shore guns were badly sited and unable to fire effectively on the attacking ships. Naval success in such a case was at best only a "doubtful victory." Halleck insisted that "there are no exceptions to the general rule of the superiority of guns ashore over guns afloat."[42] Further, Halleck countered what he thought misconceptions that recent improvements in naval weaponry would allow a ship to compete on equal terms with a fort. Halleck argued that history proved such ideas "groundless" and "absurd." Halleck was basically reiterating the traditional views. Thus, it is not surprising that Totten used similar, sometimes identical historical examples to make exactly the same points. American seaport towns lay exposed to the attacks of an enemy fleet. Seizure of any single major port would be a grievous blow to the American economy and richly rewarding to the successful fleet. Such ports were coveted prizes. It was, furthermore, folly to rely on the navy to protect them. According to Totten, the only sure way was through the use of coastal fortifications:

> There has been but one practice among nations, as to the defence of ports and harbors; and that has been a resort to

fortifications. All the experience that history exhibits is on one side only: it is the opposition of forts, or other works comprehended by the term *fortification,* to attacks by vessels; and, although history affords some instances wherein this defence has not availed, we see that the resort is still the same. No nation omits covering the exposed points on her seaboard with fortifications, nor hesitates in confiding in them.[43]

As Totten said, the construction of a large-scale system of coastal fortifications was the accepted means of providing coastal protection. Totten and his fellow engineers were firmly and unalterably convinced that the United States must do the same.

The engineering course work at West Point reinforced this point of view, emphasizing that a sound fortification scheme was the surest way to protect the coast. Like de Vernon, and doubtless relying upon him, the influential academy professor Dennis Hart Mahan argued that the ideal coastal defense was a twin chain of fortifications protecting each major port. The first of these chains protected the avenues of approach by water, preventing an enemy from coming close enough to bombard a port and simultaneously forcing him to land his troops (assuming an attempt to seize the port by land) some distance from the defenses. This ensured that any surprise assault would be out of the question. A further benefit was that the distance between the enemy's land and naval forces made cooperation between them difficult. Yet, Mahan saw the forts protecting the water approaches as only the exterior line of the defenses. All land approaches needed protection as well by permanent forts placed to keep the enemy from approaching close enough so that siege batteries could bombard the city or harbor. These landward forts also served as an "entrenched field of battle" for the defending troops. This, argued Mahan, was an important factor since those troops would, in all likelihood, be poorly trained militia. The "walled front" protecting the land approaches would "require a regular siege for its reduction," and "the enemy, in any attempt to carry [it] by open assault will be made to suffer heavily even if he is not repulsed."[44]

Such at any rate was the ideal. Mahan realistically noted that this system could not be fully implemented in the United States. The natural centers of wealth, almost invariably the same seacoast cities which needed such protection, were constantly expanding in size and population. This constant expansion, and the inevitable changes in local features which followed, made reliance on permanent works to guard the land approaches impractical. In these circumstances Mahan suggested the construction of temporary fortifications which he believed could be relied upon "with confidence."[45] These temporary works could be altered from time to time to meet the changed needs of an expanding city. By no means, however, could permanent fortifications be dispensed with altogether. "Without permanent defences," argued Mahan, "both our land and sea-board frontier would be left open." On the other hand, "with permanent works of a proper character at suitable points . . . our harbors would be secured and our large roadsteads . . . could be effectively closed against an enemy's squadrons." Furthermore, permanent fortifications

> "would serve as places of resort for our own vessels of war . . . where they could lie in security, and watch for a favorable moment of action. They would serve as covering points for our fleets, in event of any disaster. . . . They would form the natural rallying points for floating batteries, moved by steam."[46]

Mahan consciously and deliberately echoed European thinking on all these points. The theories he derived his arguments from were European, and the system he described was similar in scope and purpose to European fortification systems. The image he created of walled coastal cities evokes images of European coastal cities rather than the expanding, open American cities of the nineteenth century. Mahan, and Totten and Halleck, did, in fact, visualize American defenses on European terms. They visualized an extensive and intricate system of fortifications rivaling the most impressive of European approaches to the problem of seacoast fortification, which is why the system proposed by the engineers grew steadily in size and scope throughout the years preceding the Civil War.

The first revision of the Bernard Board Report of 1821 appeared in 1826. In it the board increased the number of proposed sites from fifty to over ninety. This increase was hidden to some extent by reduction in overall cost estimates. However, many of the sites listed in 1826 carried the notation "not yet projected" (meaning no plans had yet been drawn up for them) and for those sites the board did not include any estimated costs. If estimates had been provided, the overall costs would undoubtedly have risen accordingly and the savings thus less real than apparent.[47]

By 1836 the number of proposed defensive works in the entire system reached 124, and these works were now divided into four classes rather than three. The board described many of the newly proposed works as "batteries and redoubts," obviously something less than full-scale fortifications. Yet the designation for many sites was the plural term "works at," which implies the projection of more than one structure at that locale. This was clearly a more ambitious system than the one originally proposed in 1821 and it had an equally ambitious price tag of $31,500,000. Also larger was the garrison requirement for this system. In contrast to the total of 4,600 men in 1821, the board now estimated that nearly 6,000 men would be needed to garrison the proposed works. This was unrealistically large since the total strength of the army (much of which was fighting the Seminoles in Florida) was less than 10,000 officers and men.[48]

This kind of expansion in the proposed system of seacoast defenses continued. In 1851 Totten presented a plan for national defenses which included 186 works arranged in six classes. Although the acquisition of Texas, the Oregon Territory, and California meant a huge increase in the shoreline to be protected, this was still a vast increase over the number of works projected in previous proposals. Indeed, only twenty-eight of the works were for the West coast. The rest remained concentrated on the East and Gulf coasts, the same areas emphasized in previous reports. The entire system had a steep cost. In addition to some $20,000,000 already spent, Totten estimated a further $24,000,000 would be necessary to construct the eastern and Gulf defenses and $15,000,000 for the construction of those on the Pacific. Armament would cost a further $8,500,000 while the entire system called for peacetime garrisons of forty-seven and one-half companies.[49]

A survey of the various proposals concerning the defenses of Boston Harbor allows the expansion of the system to be seen from a different perspective. At the beginning of the War of 1812 Boston Harbor had works on Castle Island and Governor's Island (Forts Independence and Warren, both old forts repaired during the construction after 1808). Three small circular batteries completed the defenses, which mounted (or were expected to mount) a total of ninety-four guns. The Bernard Board Report of 1821 proposed an additional fort on George's Island to cover the main ship channel into the harbor. The revised report of 1826 included this new fort, which would mount 389 guns. The 1826 report further proposed a twenty-gun battery for Hog Island, a position that covered the harbor proper and supported the older, pre-1812 forts. By 1840 Totten listed the two oldest forts as having an armament of 139 guns, while the work on George's Island would now have 336 guns. (This work on George's Island was now named Fort Warren, the previous Fort Warren being renamed Fort Winthrop.) By 1851 the oldest of the forts, on Castle and Governor's Islands, carried 189 guns. Supporting batteries on Governor's Island added sixteen guns. Fort Warren, on George's Island, was listed as having an armament of 334 guns. The projected battery on Hog Island, together with a new work proposed for Nantasket Head, would mount a further 334 guns. Thus, from a total of 500 guns in 1826, the projected defenses of Boston were planned for over 850 guns in 1851. To be sure, many of the works projected in 1851 were low on the priority scale, but the comparison nonetheless indicates the expansion of the system proposed by the Board of Engineers during these years.[50]

Although the engineers' projected system grew steadily larger on paper, by and large it remained there as well. Of the 186 proposed in Totten's 1851 report, forty-two were in the first category as "Old Works of the First and Second Systems to be Retained." These fortifications included such forts as Castle Williams in New York harbor, Fort McHenry at Baltimore, Fort Mifflin south of Philadelphia, and Fort St. Philip on the Mississippi River below New Orleans. In a second category were an additional seventeen works of the third system, "completed or so nearly completed as to be able to use all, or nearly all their batteries." These works included Fort Warren on George's Island in Boston Harbor, Fort Monroe on Old Point Comfort, Virginia, and Fort Pulaski on Cockspur Island outside Savannah, Georgia. A final ten works were in a third category of those "under construction, and more or less advanced." Thus, by 1851 the original system proposed in 1821 was complete. The United States had a defensive network of some fifty-nine fortifications completed and a further ten abuilding, or about one-third the number being proposed. None of these were on the Pacific coast.[51]

Compared to the system of coastal fortifications which existed in 1812, or indeed during the 1820s, this array of defensive works represented an apparent increase in the amount of protection for the coast. However, not only were many of the coastal works now aging and in various stages of dilapidation, but both these and many of the newer fortifications were at best only partially armed. Of some 4,572 guns of all calibers seen as necessary to arm the forts of the first two classes in 1851 (just those works actually completed or nearly so), only 1,864 guns were actually in place.[52] To those involved with the planning of the coastal defenses, this situation was exasperating but not surprising. Armament was a problem between the years 1816 and 1860. As early as 1822 the Chief of Ordnance, George Bomford, pointed out that of some 1,500 cannon, mortars, and howitzers required for the fortifications then either built or planned, only 300 were available in existing stocks.[53] In 1829 Bomford noted that the fortifications expected to be completed in 1832 would require a total of 2,587 guns of all calibers. Yet at the then current rate of appropriation for the purchase of ordnance ($100,000 per year), it would take until 1850 to arm those forts. Bomford proposed to increase the annual appropriation to $250,000, which would allow the forts to be fully armed in 1837— still five years after the anticipated completion date.[54] Bomford's proposal fell on deaf ears. While occasionally the annual appropriation was increased, the disparity between the number of cannon necessary and the number available grew as the planned system of the engineers evolved. In 1836 Bomford claimed that the number of guns needed was over 10,000. Without any apparent sarcasm he added, "It is to be remarked here that partial armaments are now in a rapid state of completion for many of the forts . . . and that in the course of a short time there will have been mounted in various forts along the whole maritime frontier from seven to eight hundred heavy cannon complete."[55] Bomford listed only ten fortifications "in which cannon are actually mounted." By 1845 ordnance officer George Talcott stated that the forts already built and those under construction would need some 4,800 guns. Available were 2,900 guns of suitable quality, leaving a deficiency of just under 2,000. Talcott based his calculations only on the forts either built or those actually under construction, a procedure which reduced the total number of guns required from Bomford's earlier claim of 10,000. Talcott did note, however, that the proposed fortifications, not yet under construction, would need an additional 3,500 guns.[56]

Talcott went on to provide a detailed statement of the numbers of guns provided for each fort on the coast, a listing which gives more than a glimpse of the actual state of readiness of the coastal defenses. Fort Warren, planned for 334 guns, had no armament at all. Nor did Fort Trumbull at New London, Connecticut, Fort Calhoun at Hampton Roads, Virginia, or many of the other forts. Most had only a part of their planned armament. Fort Adams in Newport Harbor, Rhode Island, was short 303 heavy guns of its projected complete armament of 452. Fort Monroe, yet ready for only 159 guns, was planned for 359 and had been supplied with ninety-eight. Fort Pulaski, Georgia, ready for 113 guns and planned for 150, had only twenty. In fact, of the fifty-nine coastal forts and batteries making up the nation's coastal defense system, twenty-seven, or nearly half, had no part of their armament and a further twenty-two were only partially armed. Of the ten works either fully armed or short only a few guns, four were at New York and only three south of Washington. Four of these fully armed works mounted twenty-one guns or less.[57]

A simple list of the number of guns supplied to the various fortifications is not a complete indicator of the actual state of the seacoast defenses. Ordnance Colonel Henry Knox Craig protested in 1856 that to supply cannon for fortifications, as requested by Totten, would not be advisable even though enough guns were on hand to meet the request. Most of the forts Totten mentioned as ready for their armament were actually unfinished and without garrisons, argued Craig. This situation would ensure that the guns placed in those works would not be cared for. Inevitably, said Craig, "the guns . . . will become rusted and scale off in the bore: the wood work of the carriages will spring and become warped and twisted and will decay at the joints, and the iron will rust." Craig argued sensibly that this situation would involve more than just the injury to the guns themselves. The forts so equipped would be reported as armed, although "when a necessity arises for their use it will be found they have become unserviceable from remaining neglected and uncared for." And, continued Craig, "we may thus be lulled into a feeling of security from a fallacious estimate of our state of efficient preparation."[58] Since most of the seacoast fortifications, once completed, were ungarrisoned (as Craig claimed) or provided with a token caretaker force (sometimes a single man), many of the guns at the fully or partially supplied positions were doubtless in various stages of decay.

In any case, most of the seacoast forts remained unarmed up to the eve of the Civil War. In 1858 Craig reported to Secretary of War John B. Floyd that 6,114 cannon of all calibers were required for the armament of fortifications; yet of the available stocks of 4,222 heavy iron seacoast guns, Craig reported only 3,791 fit for service.[59]

While the shortage of cannon certainly acted to prevent full realization of the Board of Engineers' system, other problems also slowed the completion of the coastal defenses. One of the most important of these was that there were never enough engineer officers available to supervise construction, let alone undertake new projects. Beginning with Joseph G. Swift, every Chief Engineer complained about the shortage of engineers and urged the Congress to increase the size of the corps. Swift indicated in 1816 that fifty-seven posts between Portland, Maine and St. Marys, Georgia required repair, a situation which would employ thirty officers for three years. Another ten officers were needed to supervise the works being built or those about to be started. Other duties, including teaching at the Military Academy, demanded more officers and ultimately Swift found a need for eighty-two engineers although the corps at that time was only twenty-two strong.[60] Little was done about this problem for the strength of the corps was only twenty-five in 1823, and only twenty-two in 1833.[61] The strength of the Corps of Engineers did increase slightly during the ensuing years, nearly doubling by the mid-1850s. This number was still insufficient, however, since not only had the system of fortifications grown larger but the acquisition of Texas and California had dramatically added to the nation's length of coastline, and hence to the areas of engineer responsibility. In 1853 Totten pointed out that of forty-three officers in the Corps of Engineers, fifteen were involved in the coastal survey, serving at the Military Academy or on the Board of Engineers, while a further six were young and had "not yet had the experience requisite for taking charge of operations." Six of the remaining twenty-two officers were on the West coast, leaving just sixteen officers to handle the responsibility for more than forty fortifications on the East and Gulf coasts.[62]

Although the shortage of engineers and the lack of enough cannon to arm all the coastal fortifications were among the reasons the engineers' projected system of coastal defenses was incomplete by the 1850s, the reason most often cited—by both the engineers at the time and later historians—was Congressional refusal to appropriate enough money. There is support for such an argument; financial considerations were an important factor, and antimilitary rhetoric often flourished in Congressional debates. Nevertheless, by 1860 Congress had granted some $30,000,000 for the coastal defense system.[63] And that system, as originally envisioned in 1821, was substantially complete. Moreover, few members of Congress or members of the executive branch argued that coastal defenses were completely unnecessary. Nor did Congress as a whole or any individual Congressman or Senator advance a fully developed alternative system or scheme of defense. Debate in Congress was consistently centered on how much money to provide for completing the system proposed by the engineers. As indicated, that proposed system continued to expand throughout the antebellum years, making the disparity between funds appropriated and funds requested correspondingly larger as well. Focusing on alleged Congressional tightfistedness (and by implication Congressional imprudence, if not negligence) tends to obscure the fact that a clear majority of Congressmen believed some system of defense was necessary and voted funds to support it. What was at issue was not the need for coastal defenses, but the extent and purpose of such a system.

Secretary of War Lewis Cass was among those who questioned the necessity for the kind of defense system projected by the engineers, while acknowledging that providing for some form of defense was a "paramount obligation" of the government. On the other hand, Cass rejected any notion that the function of the coastal defense system was to forestall a full-scale invasion. Was it reasonable, he asked, to expect "that any enemy will be able and disposed to debark upon our coast an army sufficiently powerful to lay siege to our fortifications . . . and to endeavor by this slow and uncertain process to obtain possession of them?" Cass answered his own rhetorical question with a clear "No," arguing that any force landing on American shores "would command little more than the position it actually occupied." Unlike European countries, the United States had no central, vital point. Even if Washington were again captured, he insisted, its fall would only be an emotional blow for an enemy would soon be forced to retreat "with as few laurels as he won by its possession." Any invasion would be a "quixotic enterprise" for no enemy could expect to seize and "retain permanent possession of any port in this country."[64]

Cass saw the system of coastal defenses proposed by the engineers as one modeled on those of Europe, and thus unsuited to American needs. What was important, he maintained, was protecting the major coastal cities from potentially destructive raids or plundering expeditions. Doing this would require some permanent works, he acknowledged, but he clearly regarded many of the engineers' proposed works as larger than necessary and their system, on the whole, as too extensive.[65]

Cass's critique, made in 1836, went to the heart of the issues surrounding the question of coastal defenses. Not surprisingly, the engineers, led by Totten, vigorously defended their proposals and a fair proportion of the Board of Engineers' 1840 report is aimed at refuting Cass's arguments. Still, other national leaders returned to the same ground to suggest similar conclusions. Joel Poinsett, for example, Secretary of War from 1837 to 1841, was a staunch defender of the Board of Engineers, clearly expressing his faith in their judgment. Yet, while urging Congressional support for coastal defenses, Poinsett specifically referred to those works "of the first class" positioned to protect the most important trading centers, harbors, and naval yards.[66]

In 1851 Secretary of War Charles Conrad reexamined this same issue when he responded to Totten's major report on national defenses. Conrad came to the same conclusions as Cass and Poinsett had over a decade earlier. He readily acknowledged that some defenses were necessary, but all of those proposed, he said, were not. Conrad was well aware that many of the existing defenses were only partially armed at best, and nearly all of them were ungarrisoned. Given the situation with regard to both cannon and manpower, it was likely that any additional defenses constructed would suffer the same problems. Weakly armed and essentially ungarrisoned works posed no real obstacle to an attacker; they could be easily captured and once in enemy hands become very difficult to retake. Based on the proposals presented by the engineers, Conrad calculated that garrisoning the East coast alone would require over 62,000 men, while garrisoning the posts along all coasts would require 100,000 men. Totten and his fellow engineers suggested that local militia should be used for this, but Conrad pointed out that since the enemy might appear at any moment, the militia would have to remain on constant duty. This was not the kind of intermittent, emergency defense the militia traditionally supplied. There was no advantage, Conrad concluded, to the use of militia instead of regulars.

In addition, Conrad pointed out that completing the entire proposed system would be very expensive. He estimated that building all the recommended defenses—as well as finishing those already under construction—would cost $25,000,000 on top of around $20,000,000 already expended. Conrad, closer to the public mood than the engineers, did not believe the country would be willing to pay the price. The result would be a string of unmanned and unarmed works along the coast, of "questionable utility" and as much a liability as an asset to the country's defense.[67]

Thus, as the proposals of the engineers grew more ambitious, American political leaders began to increasingly question the need for the extensive system of coastal defenses being projected. The issue was increasingly important as the defenses around the nation's major ports neared completion in the 1850s. By that time as well, criticisms of the projected system began to emerge from within the Corps of Engineers itself, largely the work of a young and gifted engineer officer, James St. Clair Morton. Beginning in 1857 Morton submitted a series of memoirs to Secretary of War John B. Floyd which argued that "each generation should build and pay for its own fortifications," and that "such defences of all sorts should be cheap, and allow of such money as may be in the treasury being spent on . . . maintaining a large army and navy, and amassing magazines of powder and shot and artillery and military stores, rather than building masonry forts.'' Morton accepted the notion that a European power could mount an invasion of the United States, but considered it likely that any invading force would land at an open beach and invest the defending fortifications rather than attack them directly with a fleet. Not only were American forts, as currently designed, unable to prevent such an occurrence, said Morton, but they were also too small. "So far from their being a necessity for our sea coast fortifications be defensible with a minimum ration of men," he contended, "it is probable that . . . thousands of volunteers . . . would . . . flock to the rescue of any important seaboard city menaced by a naval military expedition from [Europe]." Morton believed American forts should be designed to hold the greatest possible number of soldiers so the United States could "rest the defence of our soil and our harbors upon such numbers, and upon the marksmanship and personal bravery and strong arms of our militia, instead of relying on inaccessible stone walls, iron-bound, and iron-shuttered embrasures, and gloomy ranges of casemates piled in crowded symmetry upon each other."[68]

Morton had other complaints about the system as then proposed and designed by the Board of Engineers. It was, he claimed, "no longer compatible with the modern principles of the art of defense, either in this country or any other." Further, he asked: "When will [it] be finished? It would seem certain that, at the rate the construction of the forts has been progressing, the present generation will not derive the benefit of the works it pays for." Even though Morton accepted the premise that an invasion of the United States was possible, he found the system of defenses then extant wanting. "No one branch of such [a system of military preparation], as that of fortifications, should be allowed to present an anomaly to the rest, to be conceived on such extravagant as well as ineffectual and ill-suited theories, as those which generate the costly and slow growing castle-like structures which dot our shores."[69] Morton's critique of the system found a favorable reception with Secretary Floyd. Switching from support of the permanent fortifications, Floyd reported in 1859, "It does not appear necessary to request considerable appropriations for additional masonry works. Such as are not strong enough . . . may, when the situation arises, be reinforced at a small expense by earthen batteries."[70]

The points raised by Cass, Poinsett, Conrad, and Morton were among the most thoughtful criticisms of the engineers' system raised during the antebellum years. Yet, none of them suggested abandoning all use of permanent fortifications as an element of the national defense system. Instead, they questioned the need for the kind of extensive network of forts the engineers envisioned. In this regard Morton was unusual in suggesting the possibility of a full-scale invasion. The others shared the far more common opinion that invasion was highly unlikely. Such men had a good deal of justification for their point of view. Realistically, the only power which could have mounted a major threat to the coast of the United States was Great Britain. The Board of Engineers clearly saw Britain as the main enemy. Yet, after the 1820s, and until the Civil War, American relations with Britain verged on war only for a brief period in the 1840s. That dispute (over the Oregon Territory) ended with an amiable settlement, and the furor passed quickly. Other European naval powers, particularly France, could have managed only raids along the coast, and in any case war with France was (aside from a short flare-up over Quasi-War claims in the 1830s) even less likely than with Great Britain. The Atlantic was still a formidable barrier in the early nineteenth century and no European power would have been able to turn its back on its neighbors and invest the time and effort necessary to mount a serious threat against the United States. Granting that this assessment involves hindsight, and that no one in this period could predict how long such relatively favorable relations with Europe would last, it is still evident that more men saw the situation continuing than were excited by the fears raised by the Board of Engineers. As memories of the War of 1812 dimmed, and peace continued, it is not surprising that interest in a massive program of coastal defense was not overwhelming, or that the extent of the system proposed by the engineers was questioned.

Critics of the engineers' system were not only concerned with the question of whether invasion was possible or not. A large portion of their criticism was based on technological changes which foreshadowed changes in the means and methods of defense. Morton, for example, was only one of many critics who argued the usefulness of electrically fired torpedoes (mines) as a major auxiliary to fortifications. Other critics noted the development of steam-powered ships and developments in naval ordnance (especially the invention of the Paixhans shell) and questioned whether or not such technological advances altered the traditional means of defense supported by the Board of Engineers. Steam vessels were less at the mercy of wind and current than sailing vessels, argued some, and could thus pass channel fortifications much faster. Once such a fort was bypassed, such critics pointed out, it became use-less. Some additional or even radically different form of defense was necessary in such a case, and proposals to augment or supplant the coastal fortifications with floating batteries, powered in some cases by steam, appeared with increasing frequency. Concerns about the proper means of defense were not new, but the persistence of such proposals acted with equally persistent concerns about costs to put a brake on the rapid development of the coastal defense system advocated by the Board of Engineers.

The engineers reacted to all criticism of their system by pointing to both historical examples and the current practices of other nations. As Totten expressed in a letter to W.A.M. Lea in 1841:

> When we see the truly military powers, those with whom war is a resort rather than necessity, departing from their old reli-ances, and adopting new ones of a different nature, we may suppose that some great change in the Art has really occurred . . . but while we see them still cherishing their line-of-battle ships and their fortifications . . . our conclusion should be that Paixhans guns, the steam battery and other new inven-tions, may be improvements on, but not destroyers of, that system of war, which is the offspring of experience and has grown up out of [a] trial of fire.[71]

Totten remained convinced of the correctness of the engineers' approach. In 1851 he referred back to his report of 1840 and remarked that "its statements and opinions have been confirmed by all my subsequent meditation on the subject." Furthermore, critics of the Board of Engineers' system "misunderstood" or "misrepresented" the design and extent of it. "Our system of sea-coast fortification is a good and sufficient one," he declared.

Despite the fact that it was largely ungarrisoned and the fortifications already built suffered from a shortage of armament, Totten was adamant that the fortification system was a strong one, well suited to the needs of the United States. "I do not hesitate to insist," he said, "that there is no system superior to it on any coast, either in general adaption to its ends, in its details of design, or in its manner of execution."[72]

Convinced of the correctness of his position, Totten was taking pardonable pride in a system of coastal defenses he considered the best in the world. The work on this system had gone steadily forward, sometimes slowly and sometimes vigorously, but with enough consistent support that by the eve of the Civil War the coastal defense system was a fully institutionalized part of American military planning.

NOTES

1. Richardson, ed., *Messages and Papers of the Presidents, 1789-1897,* vol. 1 (Washington, D.C.: Government Printing Office, 1896), p. 553.

2. Stanislaus M. Hamilton, ed., *The Writings of James Monroe,* vol. 5 (New York: G. P. Putnam's Sons, 1901), p. 324 (hereafter *Monroe*).

3. *Statutes At Large,* vol. 3, pp. 223, 224.

4. British Operations in the Chesapeake are covered in John K. Mahon, *The War of 1812* (Gainesville: University of Florida Press, 1972), pp. 109-122, 289-316. Fort Bowyer, defending the entrance to Mobile Bay, La., also successfully resisted a British attack, made as a prelude to the New Orleans campaign of 1814-1815. In the attack the British flagship, *H.M.S. Hermes,* had to be destroyed by its crew. See Wilburt S. Brown, *The Amphibious Campaign for West Florida and Louisiana, 1814-1815* (University, Ala.: University of Alabama Press, 1969), pp. 44-46. Senator James Barbour of Virginia used the imagery of a burned Washington in a speech against an attempt to reduce further the peacetime army. Upon his return to Washington, Barbour said, "I found the capital of my country smouldering in its ruins. . . ." *Annals of Congress,* 14th Congress, 2d session (vol. 30), p. 157 (hereafter *Annals*).

5. Hamilton, *Monroe,* p. 326.

6. *Annals,* 14th Congress, 1st session (vol. 29), p. 344. Barbour introduced his resolution on April 26 and it cleared the House of Representatives the following day with no apparent debate in either chamber.

7. Hamilton, *Monroe,* Monroe to Jackson, December 14, 1816, pp. 348-349; William H. Carter, "Bernard," *Journal of the Military Service*

Institution of the United States, vol. 51, no. 179 (Sept.-Oct. 1912), pp. 149-155.

8. Swift to William H. Crawford, May 21, 1816 and Swift to Crawford, July 1, 1816, Miscellaneous letters sent, Office of the Chief Engineer, vol. 1, pp. 11-12, 12-13, Entry 4, RG 77, National Archives (NA); Joseph G. Swift, *The Memoirs of Joseph Gardner Swift* (Privately printed and edited by Harrison Ellery, 1890), pp. 142-146, 149.

9. Marcus Cunliffe contends that after the War of 1812, Monroe and Crawford were awed both by military professionalism and by the reputation of the French armies under Napoleon. In his view this fascination for the French led to Bernard's appointment and the replacement of Alden Partridge as Head of the Military Academy by Sylvanus Thayer, who had studied military engineering in France. Interestingly enough, plans were afoot to bring over some additional French professors for the academy. See Marcus Cunliffe, *Soldiers and Civilians* (New York: Free Press Paperback, 1973), pp. 258-259. Bernard's appointment supports this contention.

10. Swift, *Memoirs,* pp. 149, 177-180.

11. Hamilton, *Monroe,* Monroe to Andrew Jackson, pp. 348-349.

12. Swift described this procedure in a letter to William H. Crawford protesting Bernard's appointment. Swift to Crawford, May 21, 1816, Miscellaneous letters sent, Office of the Chief Engineer, vol. 1, pp. 11-12, Entry 4, RG 77, NA. The kinds of reports the Chief Engineer received may be found in reports on fortifications and topographical surveys (1812-1823), Entry 221, RG 77, NA. See especially pp. 30-36, 47-49, 57-66, 74, 91-95.

13. Bvt. Maj.-Gen. George W. Cullum, *Biographical Register of the Officers and Graduates of the U.S. Military Academy at West Point, N.Y., From Its Establishment in 1802, to 1890,* 3d ed. (Boston: Houghton, Mifflin and Co., 1901), pp. 60-63.

14. Ibid., pp. 64-67. Totten's letters are preserved in letters and reports of Col. Joseph G. Totten, Chief of Engineers, 1803-1864, 10 vols. Entry 146, RG 77, NA.

15. Totten to Swift, June 2, 1816, Letters and Reports . . . , vol. 1, Entry 146, RG 77, NA, p. 13. Totten's feelings about Bernard are further revealed in a letter to Charles Gratiot (at that time Chief Engineer) in 1828. About a disagreement with Bernard over the plans for fortifying Pensacola, Totten wrote that he and Bernard were at an impasse "so totally irreconcilable as to forbid all compromise." He demanded that his plans no longer be submitted to Bernard. "His views," said Totten, " . . . I consider radically different from mine. My plans would not therefore aid him—and I submit whether in justice to me even if assistance could be derived from consulting them, such assistance should be given." In my

judgment this is not a letter from a man who shared a close working relationship with Bernard. See Totten to Gratiot, vol. 2, Entry 146, RG 77,
NA, 159.

16. On Totten, see Cullum, *Biographical Register,* John G. Barnard,
"Eulogy on the Late Joseph G. Totten," Annual Report of the Smithsonian Institution, House Exec. Document 102, 39th Congress, 1st
session, 1866, Serial 1265. Varina Davis, the wife of Jefferson Davis
(Secretary of War in the 1850s) described Totten as "an exceedingly elegant
man . . . most kind-hearted, . . . besides being a soldier in the scientific
sense of the term." Quoted in a footnote in James T. McIntosh, ed., *The
Papers of Jefferson Davis,* vol. 2 (Baton Rouge: Louisiana State University
Press, 1974), p. 383. On the tendency to repeat material from report to
report see "Board of Engineers Report on Defences of the U.S. Frontiers
(1822)," Miscellaneous Reports of Engineer Boards, 1821-1834, Entry 223,
RG 77, NA. This is a verbatim copy of a report in 1820. (See reports on fortifications and topographical surveys, Entry 221, RG 77, NA, pp. 422-432.)
Phrases and sometimes whole sections appear and reappear in all the major
reports produced between 1820 and 1860. For these reports see the appropriate citations below.

17. Reports on Fortifications and Topographical Surveys, Entry 221,
RG 77, NA, pp. 422-432.

18. *American State Papers, Military Affairs,* vol. 2 (Serial 017), Document 206, pp. 304-313 (hereafter *ASP, MA*). The report is reprinted in
Walter Millis, ed., *American Military Thought* (New York: Bobbs-Merrill
Paperback, 1966), pp. 102-111, and may be found as Document 98, Serial
54, 16th Congress, 2d session.

19. *Niles Register,* vol. 20 (1821), pp. 263-269, 285.

20. *ASP, MA,* vol. 2, Document 206, p. 305. These criteria are also
described in Samuel R. Bright, "Coast Defense and the Southern Coasts
Before Fort Sumter," M.A. thesis, Duke University, 1958, pp. 11-14. For a
brief discussion of the importance of this report see Russell F. Weigley, *The
American Way of War* (New York: Macmillan, 1973), p. 60.

21. *ASP, MA,* vol. 2, Document 206, pp. 309-310.

22. Ibid., p. 308.

23. Ibid., p. 305. Gay de Vernon, *A Treatise on the Science of War and
Fortification,* 2 vols., trans. by Capt. John M. O'Connor (New York: J.
Seymour, 1817), vol. 2, p. 14.

24. *ASP, MA,* vol. 2, Document 206, p. 306.

25. Ibid.

26. Ibid., pp. 308, 310-12.

27. Ibid., p. 309.

28. Richardson, *Messages and Papers,* vol. 2, p. 88.

29. *ASP, MA,* vol. 2, Document 206, p. 309.

30. Ibid., pp. 310, 313.

31. *Annals,* 16th Congress, 2d session (vol. 37), pp. 1270, 1275, 1283.

32. *ASP, MA,* vol. 2, Document 214, pp. 345-349. Further support for the Dauphin Island project by Monroe and a rebuttal of the Committee's report by Bernard may be found in *ASP, MA,* vol. 2, Document 223, pp. 368-375. Despite this additional support, Congress refused to appropriate money for fortifications on Dauphin Island at this time.

33. *Annals,* 17th Congress, 1st session (vol. 38), p. 1191.

34. *Annals,* 17th Congress, 1st session (vol. 39), pp. 1610-1611.

35. *Congressional Debates,* 19th Congress, 1st session (vol. 2, pt. 1), p. 1164.

36. *Annals,* 18th Congress, 1st session (vol. 42), p. 2461.

37. Ibid., pp. 2460-2461.

38. *Congressional Debates,* 19th Congress, 1st session (vol. 2, pt. 1), p. 1154.

39. *Congressional Debates,* 21st Congress, 1st session (vol. 6, pt. 1), p. 636.

40. *Annals,* 18th Congress, 1st session (vol. 42), pp. 2460-2461; House Document 75, 21st Congress, 1st session, Serial 167. Here and throughout, figures for annual military or federal expenditures are from United States Bureau of the Census, *Historical Statistics of the United States: Colonial Times to 1957* (Washington, D.C.: Government Printing Office, 1960), pp. 718-719.

41. *ASP, MA,* vol. 6 (Serial 021), 24th Congress, 1st session, Document 671, p. 378. This is a report by Totten on the system of defenses submitted in March of 1836. It may also be found in Senate Document 293, 24th Congress, 1st session, Serial 282, and as part of a collection of documents on the subject of fortifications and seacoast defenses in House Report 86, 37th Congress, 2d session (April 23, 1862), Serial 1145, pp. 86-87.

42. Henry W. Halleck, *Military Art and Science* (New York: D. Appleton & Co., 1846), p. 173 and ch. 7, passim Halleck had earlier presented this information to Congress via the Engineer Department in 1845. See Senate Document 85, 28th Congress, 2d session, Serial 451. The relevant portions of Halleck's book are taken verbatim from this report.

43. Joseph G. Totten, *Report of General J. G. Totten, Chief Engineer on the Subject of National Defences* (Washington, D.C.: A. Boyd Hamilton, 1851), p. 22 (hereafter *Report on National Defence*). This passage is taken verbatim from "Report on the Defence of the Atlantic Frontier, From Passamaquoddy to the Sabine" (Report of the Board of Engineers, 1840), Senate Document 451, 26th Congress, 1st session, Serial 360. In 1851 Totten claimed to have written the 1840 report, attributed at the time to the Board of Engineers.

44. Dennis H. Mahan, *An Elementary Course of Military Engineering, Part II: Permanent Fortifications* (New York: John Wiley and Son, 1867), pp. 156-517. Mahan's texts were originally printed via lithograph at the Military Academy and were used in that form for many years before being publicly printed.

45. Ibid., p. 159.

46. Dennis H. Mahan, *A Treatise on Field Fortification* (New York: John Wiley, 1848), p. 159.

47. "Revised Report of the Board of Engineers on the Defence of the Seabors," *ASP, MA,* vol. 3 (Serial 018), Document 327, pp. 283-302.

48. *ASP, MA,* vol. 6 (Serial 021), Document 671, p. 378, 24th Congress, 1st session. See note 41 for additional locations.

49. Totten, *Report on National Defenses,* p. 108.

50. *ASP, MA,* vol. 2, Document 206, pp. 304-313; *ASP, MA,* vol. 3, Document 327, pp. 283-302; Senate Document 451, 26th Congress, 1st session, Serial 360; Totten, *Report on National Defences,* pp. 92-107.

51. Totten, *Report on National Defences,* pp. 51-55.

52. Ibid.

53. Gen S. V. Benet, ed., *A Collection of Annual Reports and Other Important Papers Relating to the Ordnance Department* (Washington, D.C.: Government Printing Office, 1878-1890), pp. 65-74.

54. Ibid., p. 192. This is a report from Bomford to Secretary of War John Eaton, Nov. 30, 1829.

55. Ibid., pp. 319-320. This is a letter in reply to interrogatories, Bomford to Secretary of War Lewis Cass, April 5, 1836.

56. Ibid., vol. 2, pp. 78-83. This is a report from Talcott to Secretary of War W. L. March, Dec. 27, 1845.

57. Ibid.

58. Ibid., pp. 575-576. This is a letter from Craig to Secretary of War Jefferson Davis, Feb. 2, 1856.

59. Ibid., pp. 656-658. This is a letter from Craig to Secretary of War John B. Floyd, Aug. 26, 1858. Because of the obvious shortage of cannon for the armament of fortifications, as well as on the grounds of efficiency and cost, every Chief of Ordnance after the War of 1812 urged the creation of a national foundry. Congress never acted on these proposals.

60. Swift to Secretary of War W. H. Crawford, June 8, 1816. Miscellaneous letters sent, Office of the Chief of Engineers, vol. 1, pp. 9-10, Entry 4, RG 77, NA.

61. *ASP, MA,* vol. 2 (Serial 017), "Register of the Engineering Department for 1823," p. 516; *ASP, MA,* vol. 5 (Serial 020), Document 533, p. 79.

62. "Annual Report of the Chief Engineer, 1853," Senate Document 1, Serial 691, 33d Congress, 1st session, p. 202. In 1834 the Senate Military

Affairs Committee, while supporting the idea of an increase in the size of the Corps of Engineers, remarked that "more injury than benefit might result from an immediate increase of the Corps to the strength proposed. . . ." Instead the committee recommended a gradual increase in the corps strength. *ASP, MA,* vol. 5 (Serial 020), 23d Congress, 2d session, Document 588, pp. 450-42.

63. Thirty million is the generally accepted figure. Bright, "Coast Defense and the Southern Coasts," p. 99; James St. Clair Morton, "Memoir of American Fortification Submitted to the Honorable John B. Floyd" (Oct. 31, 1859), Senate Exec. Document 2, 36th Congress, 1st session, Serial 1024, p. 452.

64. Lewis Cass, "Message From the Secretarys of War and Navy Relative to The Military and Naval Defences of the Country," *ASP, MA,* vol. 6 (Serial 021), 24th Congress, 1st session, pp. 368-369, 372.

65. Ibid.

66. J. R. Poinsett, "Report From the Secretary of War . . . Relative to a Plan for the Protection of the North and Eastern Frontiers of the United States," Executive Document 199, 25th Congress, 2d session.

67. Charles M. Conrad, "Letter From the Secretary of War in Reference to Fortifications" (Dec. 8, 1851), Exec. Document 5, 32d Congress, 1st session (Serial 637), pp. 11, 13.

68. Morton, "Memoir of American Fortification," pp. 457, 519-520.

69. Ibid., p. 520.

70. John B. Floyd, "Annual Report of the Secretary of War" (1859), Senate Exec. Document 2, 36th Congress, 1st session (Serial 1024), p. 12. For an assessment of Floyd's change in attitude from 1857 to 1859 see Bright, "Coast Defense and the Southern Coasts," pp. 84-86.

71. Totten to Lea, July 29, 1841. Letters and reports of Col. Joseph G. Totten, Chief of Engineers, 1803-1864, Entry 146, RG 77, NA.

72. J. G. Totten, *Report on National Defences,* p. 3; Annual Report of the Chief Engineer, 1854, Exec. Document 1, 33rd Congress, 2d session (Serial 747), pp. 92, 95-96.

TWO
Engineer Training and Fortification Design

Coastal fortifications were the key element in the system of defenses developed and promoted by the Board of Engineers. Any criticism of the system, or any modifications of suggested changes in it, had to first come to grips with this fact. For this reason it is not only useful but necessary to examine briefly the training received by American engineers, the sources of their ideas, and the design of the fortifications they built.

The demanding nature of his occupation set the military engineer apart from his fellow officers almost from the start. Unlike officers of infantry or cavalry, engineering officers required specialized training in mathematics and architecture in addition to knowledge of military science. Although initially civilians trained outside of the military filled the need for engineer officers, by the eighteenth century European governments increasingly sought to develop a pool of trained engineering officers by creating specialized schools run by the military. Students at those embryonic military academies received some instruction in the general military art, but from the start the emphasis at these schools was on the technical training needed by engineers and, for similar reasons, by artillerymen.[1]

The motive behind the founding of the American academy at West Point in 1802 was the same. Up to this time the country had no school for technical training, and national interest as well as military necessity demanded one. While the United States could rely on the militia for its soldiers, few if any of the pool of militia officers were competent in the intricate skills of military engineering. As Charles Pinckney of South Carolina pointed out, an engineer needed education not required in the other branches of the military. In addition, engineers were a necessity for a nation which expected to rely on fixed fortifications for defense rather than on a standing army.[2] The need to rely on the services of foreign engineers was both embarrassing and potentially hazardous, for the supply of such officers was completely out of the hands of the national government. For these reasons, the new Military Academy was placed explicitly under the direction and control of the Corps of Engineers. While West Point was to be a military academy in the fullest sense of the term, the emphasis from the start was on engineering and science.[3]

The military engineering training at West Point reflected the country's early dependence on foreign engineers as well as the generally acknowledged preeminence of the French in this field. The texts used at the academy were, for years, either French or translations of French texts. One of the earliest such books available in the United States was a translation of the Chevalier de Clairac's *L'Ingenieur de Campagne,* or *Field Engineer.* Translated by Major Lewis Nicola and published in 1794, this 256-page book covered the whole subject of fortifications, "showing their defects and how to remedy them." The first text used as such at West Point, however, was a slim translation by Jonathan Williams of Henri de Scheel's *The Elements of Fortification.* Arranged in the form of questions and answers, this forty-nine-page book included a glossary of fortification terms and a series of sketches illustrating types of fortification. Williams referred to the book as only an "introduction" to the study of fortification but it remained the standard text at the academy until after the War of 1812. Some supplementary use was also made of Louis de Tousard's two-volume *American Artillerist's Companion,* first published in 1809.[4] A French-born officer, Tousard served with the Americans during the Revolution and was associated with the first attempts to establish a school of engineering at West Point. His book contained a section on the principles of fortification, but was never intended to be a text on the subject.

Officers and cadets at West Point were able to supplement the information in the texts through the meetings and discussions of the United States Military Philosophical Society, a group which included many prominent political figures as well as military personnel. At the meetings of the society, members could argue the best means of harbor defense, sometimes presenting or describing plans for fortifications. It was at such meetings that Jonathan Williams first presented the fortification theories of the Marquis de Montalembert.[5] Montalembert's eleven-volume work *La Fortification Perpendiculaire* appeared between 1776 and 1778, but was not translated into English until Williams undertook the task after 1802. As already noted, Montalembert's approach to fortification broke to a great extent from the Vauban tradition. His theories were not, in fact, accepted to any great degree among the French military engineers, most of whom continued to advocate the bastion system as defined by the systems of Vauban. Montalembert's emphasis on the multistory gun tower, however, did receive attention, particularly outside France, since this type of fortification offered the prospect of increasing a fort's firepower without any corresponding increase in the acreage occupied by the work. Williams was among the first in the United States to advocate the use of this system for seacoast defense, and the meetings of the Military Philosophical Society provided him with a forum in which to express his views.

It can be argued that Williams's support for Montalembert, together with the modifications to his system developed by American engineers, represented the beginning of an American approach to fortification and a lessening of the reliance on European theories. If so, however, it was a very small beginning, for in many respects American dependence on European theories increased rather than waned after the War of 1812. In 1817 Sylvanus Thayer replaced Alden Partridge as Superintendent of West Point. Recently returned from a tour of various European military schools, Thayer was especially impressed by the military skill and professionalism of the French. Thayer proposed to model West Point explicitly on the French schools of engineering and fortification, an effort for which he had the support of the Monroe administration in Washington.[6] At the same time, the French-educated engineer Claude Crozet replaced Partridge as Professor of Engineering and the cadets received a new text.

The new engineering text was Captain M. O'Connor's translation of Gay de Vernon's *Treatise on the Science of War and Fortifi-*

cation, originally developed as a text for L'Ecole Polytechnique, the French school of military engineering. It represented a large advance over previous texts since it was devoted almost entirely to the subject of engineering, although O'Connor added sections which dealt with other aspects of the military art. This translation of de Vernon remained the standard academy engineering text until the mid-1830s, supplemented by J. M. Sganzin's *Programmes des Lecons du Cours de Construction* and Hachette's *Traite des Machines.*[7]

Under Thayer's superintendency the quality of the engineering program steadily improved. Previously, under Partridge, "Engineering was less attended to than French or drawing, the greater number of cadets on graduating never having gone beyond the definitions to be found in Colonel Williams' little primer of 50 pages on the subject. . . . Many cadets scarce knew the difference between the ditch and the glacis of a fort save by the conventional colors adopted in their delineation."[8]

This state of affairs did not continue under Thayer's administration. Fourth-year cadets at the academy were divided into two sections. The first group studied "the entire course of engineering, military science and grand tactics," while the second section studied, "in connection with military science and grand tactics, field engineering only."[9] By the mid-1830s engineering was far and away the predominant field of study of West Point. Some 71 percent of the total classroom hours during the four-year curriculum were spent on the study of either engineering or the related disciplines of mathematics and natural philosophy (in modern terms, chemistry and physics). Not only was the scholastic emphasis placed heavily on the engineering subjects, performance in these classes was the key determinant in final class rank. Cadets who placed at the top of the order of merit had the opportunity to choose their branch of service. Only the very top graduates obtained entry to the Corps of Engineers. This practice ensured that the engineers were seen, and accepted, as the elite branch of the army.[10]

Partiality for the French approach to fortification continued throughout the antebellum period, a bias maintained by the academy's most famous and perhaps most influential instructor, Dennis Hart Mahan. Mahan served as Professor of Engineering from 1832 to 1871, and his course was designed around the use of French and French-derived texts, many of which Mahan developed himself. Mahan attended the academy from 1820 to 1824. His scholastic abilities were so evident that he served as Acting-Assistant Professor of Mathematics while still a cadet. Upon graduation, Mahan was the only member of his class recommended for appointment to the Corps of Engineers, a clear mark of both his scholastic abilities and the high regard of his instructors at the academy. Instead of leaving West Point to serve in the field, Mahan stayed at the academy for two years as Assistant Professor of Engineering. His health in poor condition, Mahan then obtained permission to convalesce in Europe while studying the operations of European military schools. He stayed for four years, and like his mentor, Thayer, Mahan developed a strong favorable bias toward the French methods of instruction and their theories of fortification.[11]

As Professor of Engineering, Mahan soon overhauled the engineering curriculum, replacing O'Connor's version of de Vernon with texts translated and written by himself. The first of his efforts was his *Treatise on Field Fortification*, which included a substantial section on the attack and defense of permanent fortifications. It went through at least six editions totaling some 10,000 copies. Not content, Mahan went on to supply a lithographed text on permanent fortification, derived largely from notes obtained during his years in France. Although Mahan's texts on military engineering were not available in published form until 1865 (although versions of his original notes were published in the Confederacy during the Civil War), with revisions they served as the basic West Point texts until the mid-1880s, when they were replaced by J. B. Wheeler's *Textbook of Military Engineering*. The two-volume 1865 edition of Mahan's *Elementary Course of Military Engineering* simply made more widely available the notes long used as the text at the widely available the notes long used as the text at the academy.[12]

Although his notes replaced de Vernon as the text for the study of military engineering, Mahan did little to change the obvious bias toward the French. In many respects, while Mahan updated and improved on O'Connor's version of de Vernon, the course material remained essentially the same. In words very similar to those of de Vernon, Mahan defined permanent fortification as "defences which, constructed of materials of a durable nature, and designed for permanent occupancy by troops, receive such a degree of strength that the enemy will be forced to the operations of either a siege or a blockade to gain possession of them.'' Mahan added to this simple definition by postulating a series of five general conditions which any well-designed fortification had to meet:

> 1st. They should be of sufficient strength to resist with success all the ordinary means resorted to by an assailant in an open assault.
>
> 2nd. Be provided with suitable shelters to protect the troops, the armament, and the magazines of provisions and munitions of war required for their defence against the destructive measures of the assailant of every description.
>
> 3rd. Be so planned that every point exterior to the defences within cannon range shall be thoroughly swept by their fire.
>
> 4th. Have secure and easy means of communication for the movements of the troops, both within the defences and to the exterior.
>
> 5th. And, finally, be provided with all such accessory defensive means as the natural features of the position itself may afford, to enable the garrison to dispute with energy the occupancy by the assailant of every point both within and exterior to the defences.

The true art of the military engineer, said Mahan, consisted "in a knowledge of the means which are employed to fulfil [sic] the above conditions, and of their suitable adaption to the natural features of the positions he may be called upon to fortify."[13] As with any set of general prescriptions, there was no single answer for every case. American engineers were trained in, or at least exposed to, all the various systems of fortification. From this variety of possible solutions to particular circumstances, the engineer could choose that which offered the best hope of meeting Mahan's basic conditions.

By and large, European fortification theories centered on the means of defending land borders. Designing and constructing seacoast defenses involved numerous difficulties not always explicitly covered by those theories. With their primary purpose the defense of a waterway (a river, a channel, the approach to a harbor), the main focus of any seacoast work had to be directed toward the water. Yet, fortifications on the coast also had to be designed to repel attacks by land as well as by sea. A work open or poorly designed on the landward side simply invited an enemy to land outside cannon range, march overland, and seize the position by assault. Seacoast defenses thus had to be designed to make difficult, if not impossible, any such seizure (called an *escalade* or *coup de main*), and thus force an enemy intent on taking the position to resort to a siege.

Of all the known systems of fortification, the traditional bastion system, a term which included the various "systems" of Vauban, remained a highly regarded design for resisting such escalades. Of course, no fortification could be expected to resist forever. Although no military effort promised success more surely than a siege, the bastion system forced a besieger to begin his attack some distance from the main walls of the fortification. From the American point of view, any delay or lengthening of the siege gave militia time to muster. An enemy undertaking the time-consuming and complicated operations of a formal siege would soon find himself in an ever more difficult position as the American relief forces gathered. Only a very powerful force could cope with the demands of a siege and simultaneously the need to defend itself from the attacks of American troops. If confronted by a position which could not be taken quickly, a weaker force, or one unwilling to risk the hazards of conducting operations in an increasingly hostile environment, might well avoid attacking the position altogether.

Because the bastion form was so basic to the design of fortifications it is worth examining the details of this design in greater detail (see Fig. 1).[14] In profile, the main walls of a bastioned fortification had three features. The masonry wall itself was the *scarp* rising as much as thirty feet above the ditch in front of it. Behind the scarp, to the inside of the fortification, was an earthen mound called the *rampart*. The rampart rose from ground level to the top of the scarp wall and formed a large, level area inside the walls. The flat upper surface of the rampart, called the *terreplain*, formed the area where troops served within the fort. From the terreplain those troops had a commanding view of the surrounding countryside. At

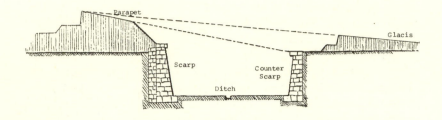

FIG. 1   Profile of a Bastioned Fortification.

the front edge of the rampart, atop the scarp, was the *parapet*. Up
to thirty-five feet thick at the base, the parapet protected the troops
and guns on the rampart and its massive bulk absorbed the shock
of enemy cannon fire. At intervals embrasures were cut in the parapet to allow the guns of the fortification to fire. A firing step, built
at the rear of the parapet, allowed troops to fire over the top as
well.

In front of the main wall (scarp, rampart, and parapet) and
immediately in front of the scarp was the *ditch*. Wet (as a moat) or
dry, the ditch was some twenty to thirty yards wide. On the side of
the ditch opposite the scarp there was a brick or masonry retaining
wall termed the *counterscarp*. This kept the edges of the ditch from
crumbling into and filling the ditch. Atop the counterscarp ran a
narrow walkway perhaps twelve feet wide (although in spots it was
much wider) called the *covered way*. Troops on the covered way
either returned fire or sallied to repulse attacks. A small bank of
earth thrown outwards protected the troops on the covered way.
This bank of earth, sometimes reinforced with a brick or wooden
retaining wall, was termed the *palisade,* and from it ran a gentle
slope away from the fort called the *glacis*. This last was a carefully
cleared area, devoid of any cover for an attacking enemy and completely exposed to the fire of the fortification. The height of the
palisade, that part of the glacis closest to the fortification, equaled
(or, in fact, slightly exceeded) the height of the masonry scarp wall.
Thus, the scarp was sheltered from direct enemy fire by the earth of
the glacis. No masonry was exposed to direct enemy shot.

Bastions were projecting constructions, built at the angles of the scarp and intended to provide flanking fire on any enemy who approached the main walls directly, Further structures could be built in the ditch to provide protection for the scarp. Termed *demi-lunes* because of their resemblance to a half-moon or crescent, these devices were similar, albeit smaller in scale, to the profile of the main wall. In addition, other works could be built inside the bastions, in front of the bastions, or in the spaces between the bastions and the demi-lunes. Each had its own name and various schools of fortification design emphasized some at the expense of others. The basic purpose, however, was the same for all of them. Each provided further protection for the main scarp wall and each added to the cross fire that could be brought to bear on the ground before the fort. At the same time they forced a prospective attacker to begin his operations at a greater distance from the main fortification, delaying if not preventing any direct attack on the scarp wall. This fact is important to remember, for the bastion system did not promise invulnerability; it only made the attacker's job more difficult. Using the siege methods first developed by Vauban in the sixteenth century, a besieger's only questions involved the time the siege would take. Given enough time, sieges succeeded no matter how well designed the fortification. Once a besieger worked his batteries into position on the covered way, the scarp wall was unprotected and a breach became inevitable.

Even granting that no engineer expected a bastion fortification to resist a siege indefinitely, there were problems with the bastion system, many of them technical in nature but nevertheless important. For one thing, the system was fully effective only when the proper relationships existed between the lengths and distances and angles of all the component parts.[15] On awkward or geographically difficult sites these relationships could not always be maintained. In such circumstances the fort was obviously less successful and in some cases incapable of fulfilling its purpose. Another problem, and a more important one, was inherent in the design. The bastions, while designed to flank the main scarp, were themselves vulnerable to enfilade fire from well-sited siege batteries. There were many ways to deal with this problem, none of which was completely satisfactory. Sometimes the attempt to overcome this problem threw the careful arrangement of the rest of the components out of sync, thus demanding further remedial measures until the whole system became unmanageable. Engineer Lieutenant Edward Holden condemned the flanking arrangement of the bastion system for just this reason: "In the last stages of the siege," he pointed out, "when its flanking arrangements are most required, they are either in ruins, or exposed to such a fire as prevents the serving of their batteries."[16]

As Holden also pointed out, Montalembert proposed to deal with this problem by utilizing a different design, that of the *tenaille trace* together with the use of multistory gun towers to provide firepower on the flanks. The tenaille consisted of a series of angles connected in a continuous series, presenting what one fortification analyst calls "a saw-edged front."[17] While the tenaille trace eliminated the need for bastions, and thus the problems those devices posed, Mahan found the arrangement a poor one. Each of the projecting angles was itself exposed to enfilade fire, and when compared to the bastion system, the design substantially reduced the available interior space.[18] Instead of the tenaille trace, American engineers were excited by Montalembert's suggestions regarding the use of casemated gun towers, a fortification design advocated by Williams before the War of 1812 and rapidly accepted in the United States as the proper design for coastal defense works.

American efforts at fortification were generally restricted to the seaboard where sites were often irregular and limited in acreage. The use of the multistory fortification, with the guns placed in tiers within reinforced interior chambers called casemates and firing through embrasures cut through the wall itself, offered a solution to the old dilemma of how to get large amounts of firepower from relatively small fortifications. Williams argued that "for every shot a traditional system could fire, these towers . . . would fire six, occupying only the same space of ground, and this without counting the cannon that might be mounted on the top of the whole."[19] A sixfold increase in firepower from the same ground area was exactly the prescription for a seacoast fort. Despite the fact that as a design it was never treated with unusual emphasis in the West Point texts, the multistory, casemated fortification became a key design after the War of 1812.

The idea of using casemates did not originate with Montalembert. They appeared in crude form as early as the fifteenth century. In land fortification, however, the advantages of the casemate were for some time outweighed by the disadvantages. One problem was that the dense smoke created by the firing of the guns could not escape from the interior of the fort, and soon drove the gun crews from their guns. Adequate ventilation was a technical problem that could be solved by the use of chimneys which drew the smoke out. A far more critical problem with the casemate idea was that the masonry wall of the scarp could not be masked with earth without effectively negating the whole effect. Exposed to the steady fire of a besieger's guns, the high, completely exposed masonry walls would soon be smashed down. The bastion system offered far better protection to the fortification, and by virtue of this attribute it remained the preferred system for land fortification.[20]

By the eighteenth century fortification theorists believed that the problem of exposure to an enemy's cannon fire was far less serious for a seacoast fort. As Muller's treatise of 1746 argued, a ship was in continuous motion which made accurate aiming of its guns nearly impossible. Muller calculated that a three-decked man-of-war, the largest type of ship a seacoast fort would have to face, would have an apparent superiority of as much as six guns to one over a land battery. Yet the ship had no better than a one-in-three chance of hitting the battery, at least according to Muller's calculations. American engineers accepted these conclusions. As long as the scarp was sufficiently thick, said Mahan, it could "withstand the fire of the heaviest guns within the range that ships can venture to attack."[21] Even if unable to resist the pounding of a well-sited and steady siege battery, the heavy masonry scarp of a fort was stronger than the thin wooden hull of a sailing ship. Furthermore, a brief comparison between the calculations of Williams and Muller indicates that the casemated fortification canceled the superiority of the ship in terms of number of guns. With the fort now able to produce six times the firepower from the same land area, and the ship presumably still faced with needing to fire three times for one hit, the overwhelming advantage in effective number of guns lay with the fort. In addition, the fort could mount heavier guns than the ship. During the War of 1812 ships' guns ranged up to thirty-two-pounders, meaning that they fired roundshot weighing thirty-two pounds each. At the same time Castle Williams in New York, among the first of the casemated designs finished, mounted fifty-

pounder guns on its upper tier. By 1818 guns firing 100-pound projectiles were in the American armory.[22] No contemporary warship
mounted guns remotely that heavy. Clearly, all the advantages lay
with the fort rather than the ship.

Once the idea of the casemated "castle" achieved acceptance,
American engineers rapidly set about improving on it. The problem
that particularly concerned them was the size of the opening—the
embrasure—in the scarp wall. Should shot pass through this opening it would certainly disable or destroy the gun behind it. Further,
a large opening invited the use of canister or grape shot as antiper-
sonnel devices by the attacking ships. And experiments soon
demonstrated that an even greater peril was the threat of splinters
of stone being flung through the opening as the cannon balls of
attacking ships chipped at the stone around the embrasure. The
smaller the opening, the less the possibility of any of these events
occurring, and the stronger the fort became.[23]

By the War of 1812, American embrasures had openings ranging
down from twenty-eight to eighteen and one-half square feet in
area. Dissatisfied with this, Totten designed an embrasure with an
exterior opening of only ten square feet. After 1815 these were the
embrasures built into American coastal forts. Incredibly, by the
1850s European embrasures still had exterior openings of fifty-four
square feet. Totten, during this same period, was in the process of
redesigning his embrasure, achieving an exterior opening of a bare
nine square feet. Yet, despite the far smaller exterior opening,
Totten's design allowed a traverse of sixty degrees, while European
designs allowed a traverse of only forty degrees.[24]

Totten supervised a number of experiments on embrasures during the 1850s. Aside from resulting in the redesign mentioned
above, these experiments shed a great deal of light on the mechanics
of the embrasure and its ability to withstand cannon fire. Totten
discovered that canister and grape shot broke up when it struck a
granite embrasure, and the small pieces continued through the
opening where they would be likely to injure or incapacitate a gun
crew. Totten proposed to protect the embrasure opening with
armor plate, in this case boiler plate, or lead concrete. "It may be
fairly assumed," he wrote, "that a plate, eight inches thick, of
wrought iron of good quality, kept in place by a backing of three
feet of solid masonry, will stop a solid ball from an eight-inch

Columbiad approximately sixty-five pounds in weight . . . from the distance of 200 yards.'' Damage, if the masonry was not firmly tied into the rest of the wall, would be severe. Provided, however, that the scarp above and below the embrasure was much thicker, the thickness of the scarp at the embrasure could be only five feet. After 1858 the throats of all embrasures had the reinforcement of just such eight-inch plates. For the further protection of the gun and crew, shutters of iron two inches thick covered the embrasure opening while the gun was being loaded.[25]

Totten also considered the possibility of protecting the entire scarp by armor. He remained convinced that naval gunfire was inadequate to breach well-constructed masonry, however, and concluded in 1857 that

> until there shall be much stronger reasons than now exist, or are now anticipated, for believing that well-constructed masonry batteries may be breached by naval broadsides, the cheaper construction can be safely followed—especially as, should such a necessity ever arise, they may be externally plated with iron.

As Brevet Brigadier-General Henry L. Abbot remarked in 1887, this was the first reluctant admission that a great change was about to occur in naval weaponry, a change that as Abbot said (referring to Totten) ''was destined even before his death to sweep away the system of forts he had elaborated by the labor of his whole life.''[26]

Although the first signs of this great change were perceptible by the late 1850s, the technical improvements and innovations made by American engineers in the design of casemated forts meant that, for their time, American seacoast fortifications were among the strongest in the world. In a series of lectures in 1887, General Abbot gave a useful description of these forts which, despite its brevity, indicates clearly their size and complexity. According to Abbot, most of the casemated works were

> masonry structures, usually placed but little above the water-level, rising into one, two or three tiers of casemates and surmounted by a tier in barbette. The scarps were built without any bonding of the masonry into the supporting piers (which

would cause unequal settling on such sites as most of these works occupy). In all later works the scarps of the waterfronts are 8 feet thick; where they are backed by the piers of casemates the reinforcement amounts to 2½ feet; the masonry of the casemate arch . . . extends a solid support to the whole structure over 30 feet thick.

Obviously, these were massive structures and it is not surprising that Totten and his fellow engineers long believed them impervious to the fire of ships' guns. In turn, these forts could bring an awesome amount of firepower to bear on any hostile naval force. "In plan," continued Abbot, "these works were usually hexagonal, often truncated on the land side . . . permitting the casemate guns on adjacent fronts to fire in parallel planes at their extreme traverse [thirty degrees]."[27] The wide traverse allowed by Totten's improved embrasure meant that even the guns on an unattacked front could be brought into action, creating a heavy cross fire on areas outside the fort.

Although the casemated fortifications were the most impressive of the antebellum fortifications on the coast, it must be pointed out that not all the coastal defense works followed the casemate ideal. Many coastal fortifications contained a combination of design forms, including elements of both the older bastion system and the newer casemated design. Fort Adams, for example, in Narragansett Bay, Rhode Island, had a landward front of earth ramparts and granite revetments very much in the bastion tradition. Designed by Simon Bernard, this portion of the fort naturally followed the form favored by the French military engineers. On the front towards the bay, though, the fort had two tiers of casemates, and provision for a third tier of guns in barbette. Fort Adams was thus a combination of architectural forms and, as built, had concentrated firepower for the seaward approaches while preserving the more traditional form to protect the fort from any potential land attack.[28]

Fort Pulaski, outside Savannah, Georgia, also exhibited a combination of design forms, although not to the degree of Fort Adams. Here the main fortification consisted of a pentagonal work of two casemate tiers surmounted by a tier of guns in barbette. When complete the fort was expected to mount 150 guns. Its brick walls were twenty-five feet high, and, according to Willard B.

Robinson, "The architectural form for Fort Pulaski is one of the clearest and handsomest expressions of structural function to be found in a North American fortification."[29] Because the fort was on a mile-long island, some provision for close defense was necessary. This took the form of a large V-shaped work (called a *ravelin*), which harked back to the bastion form. Although the design obviously combined architectural forms, the traditional bastion form for the land side was greatly simplified.

In cases where the fortification could not be directly attacked from land, the casemate design reigned supreme. This was particularly true in situations where the ground space was limited. Fort Sumter, in Charleston harbor, and Fort Jefferson, in the Dry Tortugas, are good examples of what might be termed the "pure" casemate design. Fort Sumter (see Fig. 2) was set atop a man-made island in the harbor, with work beginning in 1829. A pentagonal work with walls fifty feet high, the fort had two tiers of casemates on all sides except that facing the city of Charleston, and provision for a third tier in barbette. All the embrasures were granite, while the parapet for the barbette tier was brick. Although it never received its full complement of guns, Fort Sumter was designed to mount 136 guns.[30]

Also on an island, Fort Jefferson was a "tower bastion" design, meaning that small projecting towers were built at the angles. While called "bastions," these towers only barely resembled those of the older system, although their function of providing flank protection for the intervening walls remained the same. Aside from this distinctive feature, Fort Jefferson closely resembled Fort Sumter in form. It was, however, far larger and, without doubt, the most ambitious of the casemated fortifications designed during the antebellum period. Designed to mount the huge total of over 450 guns, Fort Jefferson was a hexagonal work with two tiers of casemates and provision for a tier of guns mounted in barbette. The scarp walls were forty-five feet high and the outer wall was six feet thick. Some 40,000,000 bricks were used in the construction of Fort Jefferson, which, begun in 1846, was never finished.[31]

Although by the middle of the nineteenth century European engineers were beginning to question the efficiency of the enclosed masonry fortification, American engineers continued to believe in the effectiveness of large casemated masonry works. Tradition and training were a part of the continued use of this particular design, but American engineers could and did cite evidence from contemporary European conflicts to support their views. Military missions sent to Europe during the Crimean War took pains to study the design of European coastal fortifications and pronounced American ones superior. Colonel Richard Delafield, a member of the military commission sent to observe the war, concluded that in the area of designing coastal defenses Americans "have less to learn . . . than of any other part of the art of war." After witnessing a British test conducted against a captured Russian fort at Bomarsund, Delafield reported that, despite firing 540 shot and shell, the ship was unable to inflict decisive damage on the fort or create a practicable breach. Delafield believed that this brief experiment confirmed American faith in the casemated masonry fort, for he thought European fortifications weaker than their American counterparts. "There are none of the granite scarps of our sea-coast defenses," he reported, "but what are very superior to either those of Bomarsund, the Malakoff, or [the] seaward batteries of Sebastopol; and we have some not surpassed by those of Cronstadt. This experience, then, should encourage us in every way to persevere in our sea-board defense."[32] In addition, Delafield suggested that the Crimean War also indicated that a European power could move an army 3,000 miles and maintain it on a hostile

FIG. 2   Cross Section of the Wall of Fort Sumter.

shore. Thus, the United States needed to be prepared. Even though "sea-coast defenses [can] be relied upon for security against the most powerful fleet that could attack them," it was critical that Congress appropriate enough money to continue construction and provide suitable armament for American fortifications.[33] American engineers, already secure in the belief that the masonry casemated coastal fortification was the key element in the nation's defense system, were undoubtedly encouraged by the evidence which seemed to vindicate all their claims.

NOTES

1. Such schools began in Russia in 1709, in England in 1741, and in France in 1748. See Andre Courvisier, *Armies and Societies in Europe, 1494-1789,* trans. by Abigail Siddall (Bloomington: University of Indiana Press, 1979), pp. 106-107. In *The Art of Warfare in the Age of Marlborough* (New York: Hippoorene, 1976), p. 282, David D. Chandler places the founding of the first Russian academies in 1728, and the English one in 1721. The general argument remains sound regardless of the actual dates.

2. Stephen E. Ambrose, *Duty, Honor, Country: A History of West Point* (Baltimore: Johns Hopkins University Press, 1966), p. 13.

3. For a time the academy was, in fact, the only technical school in the United States. Thus its graduates were in great demand and many went quickly on to work on the many canal and railroad projects under way in the country. See Daniel H. Calhoun, *The American Civil Engineer: Origins and Conflict* (Cambridge: MIT Press, 1960), pp. 43-46.

4. Sidney Forman, "Early American Engineering Books," *The Military Engineer,* vol. 46, no. 310 (March-April 1954), pp. 93-95. Gustave G. Fieberger, "Historical Sketch of the Department of Engineering," *The Centennial of the United States Military Academy at West Point, New York, 1802-1902* (Washington, D.C.: Government Printing Office, 1904), p. 275.

5. Arthur P. Wade, "Artillerists and Engineers," Ph.D. dissertation, Kansas State University, 1977, pp. 190-192.

6. Fieberger, "Historical Sketch," pp. 276-277; Russell F. Wiegley, *Towards An American Army: Military Thought from Washington to Marshall* (New York: Columbia University Press, 1962), p. 42; Archie P. McDonald, "West Point and the Engineers," *The U.S. Army Engineers: Fighting Elite,* Col. F. M. Davis and Lt. Col. T. M. Jones, eds. (New York: Franklin Watts, 1967), pp. 39-44; M. L. Welch, "Early West Point-French Teachers and Influence," *American Society Legion of Honor Magazine,* vol. 26, no. 1 (Spring 1955), pp. 27-43.

7. Fieberger, "Historical Sketch," p. 277.

8. George W. Cullum, *Biographical Register of the Officers and Graduates of the U.S. Military Academy at West Point,* 3rd ed. (Boston: Houghton Mifflin, 1891), vol. 3, p. 609.

9. Fieberger, "Historical Sketch," p. 277.

10. James L. Morrison, Jr., "Educating the Civil War Generals: West Point, 1833-1861," *Military Affairs,* vol. 38, no. 3 (October 1974), pp. 108-111.

11. Thomas E. Griess, "Dennis Hart Mahan: West Point Professor and Advocate of Military Professionalism, 1830-1871," Ph.D. dissertation, Duke University, 1968, pp. 101, 105, 115-118, 135, 141-142; Cullum, *Biographical Register,* vol. 1, pp. 319-320.

12. Sidney Forman, *The Military Engineer,* p. 95; McDonald, *The U.S. Army Engineers: Fighting Elite,* pp. 39-44; Fieberger, "National Sketch," pp. 278-279.

13. Dennis H. Mahan, *An Elementary Course of Military Engineering* (New York: John Wiley and Son, 1867), vol. 2, pp. 1-2.

14. For an analysis of the evolution of the bastion system see Quentin Hughes, *Military Architecture* (London: Hugh Evelyn, 1974), chs. 3, 4; William M. Black, Major General and Chief of Engineers, "The Evolution of the Art of Fortification," Occasional Paper no. 58, U.S. Army Engineer School (Washington, D.C.: Government Printing Office, 1919), pp. 47-77; and Ian V. Hogg, *Fortress: A History of Military Defense* (London: MacDonald and Jane's, 1975), chs. 3 and 4. Descriptions of works built to the systems of Vauban and other fortification designers may also be found in Mahan, *Elementary Course of Military Engineers,* pp. 2-14, and Major Hector Straith, *Treatise on Fortification and Artillery* (London: William H. Allen and Co., 1858), chs. 4, 5, 6, 9. A brief but very useful introduction to the subject of fortification design is James R. Hinds and Edmund Fitzgerald, "An Introduction to Fortification in the Musket Period," *Periodical: The Journal of the Council on Abandoned Military Posts,* vol. 8, no. 3 (Fall 1976), pp. 24-28.

15. Black, "Evolution of the Art of Fortification," p. 61; Edward S. Holden, *Notes on the Bastion System of Fortification: Its Defects and Their Remedies* (New York: D. Van Nostrand, 1872).

16. Holden, *Notes on the Bastion System.*

17. Hughes, *Military Architecture,* p. 140.

18. Mahan, *Elementary Course of Military Engineering,* p. 106.

19. *Annals,* 9th Congress, 2d Session (vol. 16), p. 445.

20. Straith, *Treatise on Fortification,* p. 262. In addition, some engineers feared injury to the gun crews from rock splinters flung back through the embrasure. Richard Delafield, to the Chief Engineer submitting . . . plans and estimates for rebuilding Fort Delaware (1836), in letters, reports, and other records relating to fortifications, 1810-1869. Fortifications and Defense, 1810-1920, Entry 219, RG 77, NA. Also see John Muller, *A*

Treatise Containing the Elementary Part of Fortification, Regular and Irregular (London: J. Nourse, 1745, reprinted by the Museum Restoration Service, Ottawa, Ontario, 1968), pp. 86, 205-207; Black, "Evolution of the Art of Fortification," p. 60; and Hinds and Fitzgerald, "Introduction to Fortification," p. 42.

21. Muller, *A Treatise of Fortification*, pp. 203-204; Mahan, *Elementary Course of Military Engineering*, pp. 25-26.

22. William E. Birkhimer, *Historical Sketch of the Organization, Administration, Material and Tactics of the Artillery, United States Army* (Washington, D.C.: James J. Chapman, 1884), p. 277.

23. Mahan, *Elementary Course of Military Engineering*, pp. 25-26.

24. Joseph G. Totten, *Report Addressed to the Hon. Jefferson Davis, Secretary of War, on the Effects of Firing with Heavy Ordnance From Casemate Embrasures*, Papers on Practical Engineering, no. 6 (Washington, D.C.: Taylor and Maury, 1857), p. 144.

25. Ibid., p. 142. In the North the scarps of seacoast forts were faced with granite, while in the South with brick. The latter material proved less durable. Z. H. Burns, *Confederate Forts* (Natchez: Southern Historical Pub., Inc., 1977), p. 58; Henry L. Abbot, *A Course of Lectures Upon the Defence of the Sea-Coast of the United States* (New York: D. Van Nostrand, 1888), pp. 139-140.

26. Totten, *Report on Effects of Firing From Casemate Embrasures*, p. 157; Abbot, *Lectures*, p. 140.

27. Abbot, *Lectures*, pp. 140-141.

28. Willard B. Robinson, "The Rock on Which the Storm Shall Beat!" *Periodical: The Journal of the Council of Abandoned Military Posts*, vol. 9, no. 1 (Spring 1977), pp. 3-16. While French engineers, particularly those trained in the late eighteenth and early nineteenth centuries, preferred the bastion form for land fortifications, they did accept the idea of casemates for seacoast forts as the nineteenth century wore on. The engineers of other European countries did so much faster.

29. Willard B. Robinson, *American Forts* (Urbana: University of Illinois Press, 1977), p. 111.

30. Robinson, *American Forts*, p. 107; Frank Barnes, *Fort Sumter National Monument, South Carolina*, National Park Service, Historical Handbook Series, no. 12 (Washington, D.C.: 1952, revised 1962).

31. Robinson, *American Forts*, pp. 111, 115; Sheldon H. Kinney, "Dry Tortugas," *United States Naval Institute Proceedings*, vol. 76 (April 1950), p. 425. For the numbers of guns these forts were expected to mount, see the tables attached to the report of Joseph G. Totten on the subject of national defenses, Exec. Document No. 5, 32nd Congress, 1st session, Serial 637.

32. Richard Delafield, *Report on the Art of War in Europe in 1854, 1855 and 1856* (Washington, D.C.: George W. Bowman, 1861), pp. 24, 25-26.

33. Ibid., p. 53.

THREE
Alternatives and Auxiliaries

Despite the historical evidence and apparently valid claims presented by Totten and his colleagues, the system of coastal defenses they designed and promoted did not go unquestioned. Not everyone was willing to accept completely the engineers' assumptions regarding either the cost-effectiveness or the military effectiveness of the fortification system. Periodically critics proposed the use of new devices, or older devices redesigned in keeping with technological advances, to supplement or even replace the fortifications. None of these critics argued that coastal defenses were unnecessary. Most, in fact, insisted that such defenses were vitally important, but the fortification system of the engineers was not the answer. Developments in warship design and improvements in naval ordnance led some critics to suggest that the shore battery was no longer superior to the ship. Another, and early, criticism was that even when the shore battery's superiority was assured, such batteries could not prevent enemy vessels from passing through the channels apparently swept by their fire. The increasing size and cost of the system proposed by the engineers was another issue. Like Lewis Cass, who declared in 1836 that the European-oriented fortification system proposed by the engineers was unsuited to American geographical and political needs, such critics sought either some alternative means of defense which could be substituted for fortifications or a means of defense which could act in support of, or as an auxiliary to, a less extensive system of fortifications.[1] In many cases the same means of defense might be viewed as either an alternative or an auxiliary to the engineers' fortification system. In any case, whether the motive was simply a belief in economic retrenchment or a sincere difference of opinion over the effectiveness of fortifications, these critics never argued that coastal defenses were unnecessary. Instead, they argued that a less expensive or more effective means of defense was needed.[2]

In general, the proposals for auxiliary or alternative means of coastal defense fell into two main categories: floating defenses (a category which included such disparate elements as floating batteries and the use of the navy in direct coastal defense) and submersible devices, essentially early forms of the electrically fired submersible mine. Proposals for the use of such alternative or auxiliary methods of central defense appeared periodically rather than consistently, but in nearly all cases the proponents of such measures began by questioning the effectiveness of fortifications and ended by arguing that only the use of some new and different method could really protect the coast.

Questions regarding the efficiency of fortifications went back to the first tentative construction programs begun in the 1790s and early 1800s. Jefferson's Secretary of War, Henry Dearborn, expressed a long existing belief in 1806 that fortifications could not prevent enemy ships from passing through a channel (specifically that of the Narrows at the entrance to New York Harbor). Dearborn was among the first to argue explicitly in favor of a combined coastal defense system, including fortifications, but supplemented by additional defensive devices, particularly gunboats, a favorite of the Jefferson administration. Dearborn's prescription of a defensive system which included auxiliaries to fortifications presaged the arguments of the post-War of 1812 period, in which proposals for floating defenses of many varied types consistently appeared.

The gunboats favored by Jefferson and Dearborn were only the first experiment in a floating defense system. Another quite different innovation put in an appearance before the end of the War of 1812. This was the *Demologos,* a massive, steam-powered ship designed to defend New York and break the British blockade of the port. One hundred and fifty-six feet long and fifty-six feet in the beam, the *Demologos* was the brainchild of inventor Robert Fulton and the first steam-powered war vessel ever constructed. Built in

1814, the project represented a gamble by the United States, desperately eager to break the British blockade. The hull design was innovative, the *Demologos* being double-hulled with the paddle wheel in a sixty-foot channel between them. The complete design of the ship—hull, boilers, and all other machinery—was Fulton's; but Captain David Porter demanded masts and sails, which Fulton provided. Armed with twenty guns, the vessel was not completed in time to see any service in the War of 1812. During a trial run in June 1815, the ship performed better than the government expected. During further trials in July and then in September, the *Demologos* proved capable of moving at five and one-half miles per hour, and two and one-half miles against the tide. Unhappily, Fulton died in February 1815, and did not see his vessel perform. With the war over and no apparent need for this vessel, the navy used the *Demologos* (renamed the *Fulton*) as a receiving ship in the Brooklyn Navy Yard, where it blew up in June 1829.[3]

The *Demologos* (or *Fulton*) did not immediately effect a revolution in American naval architecture. Nor, despite its excellent trial performance, did it lead to a reevaluation of coastal defense planning. The existence of this ship did, however, act as a spur to further proposals urging the adoption of a system of floating steam batteries for coastal defense.

John Stevens, an inventor and businessman from New Jersey, communicated a plan for a steam-powered vessel to Congress in 1821 which he believed would substantially strengthen the defenses of the coast. He proposed that the parts of the steam engines for these vessels be stored along with elongated shells (of his own design) in depots at each important port and harbor. Reviewing his proposal, however, the Board of Navy Commissioners argued that vessels such as this would not prove as useful as Stevens believed. Furthermore, the naval officers pointed out that Stevens had not provided any protection for the engines and other machinery on his vessel. The navy was, said the Commissioners, already experimenting with steam batteries of superior design and it suggested that any further investigation of Stevens's proposal was unnecessary.[4]

Stevens retorted angrily that the Navy Commissioners opposed his scheme because it was contrary to the current mode of naval construction and warfare. "If," complained Stevens, " . . . it would have a tendency to annihilate the present system of warfare, would it be expected that these gentlemen would feel kindly toward it?'' Stevens expressed his anger and his conviction that his designs were superior to the board's by offering to wager anywhere from $600 to $3,000 that his steamboat, the *Philadelphia,* could outrace the *Fulton,* which was the basis for the supposed designs of the board. Later, when he had calmed down, Stevens admitted that Commodore John Rogers and the board acted ''as the majority of mankind would have done.''[5] The steamers, or steam batteries, of the board, supposedly in the planning stages, were never built.

The concept of using floating defenses as an alternative to coastal fortifications, however, struck a responsive chord among at least some Congressmen. In 1822, when the House Military Affairs Committee recommended discontinuing the construction of a fortification on Dauphin Island outside Mobile, Alabama, it raised the possibility of using a floating defense force instead. The committee believed that such a force, in cooperation with a small fort on Mobile Point, would ''constitute a suitable defense for the Bay of Mobile.''[6] This argument echoed Henry Dearborn's pre-1812 contention that the best form of coastal defense was a combination of floating, permanent, and temporary defenses. Yet while Congress willingly ceased providing funds for the Dauphin Island fortifications, it did not supply money for any floating defenses either. The best that Louisiana Representative Josiah Johnston would persuade Congress to do in 1823 was to have a committee inquire into the expediency of constructing two steam batteries for the Mississippi.[7]

Interest in the possibilities of steam power and in the use of floating batteries for coastal defense, however, continued outside of Congress. During 1826 and 1827 Major General Edmund P. Gaines engaged in an inspection of the military posts under his command in the Western Department. As a part of his report on this tour of inspection, Gaines remarked on the defensive needs of the Mississippi Valley and particularly the city of New Orleans. The invention of steam-powered ships, argued Gaines, was a revolution which had already produced great changes in commerce and was destined to make even greater changes in military operations, ''particularly so in whatever regards the attack and defense of seaports, and of every description of military works upon and in the vicinity of rivers and bays.'' Gaines was already interested in the use of floating batteries moved by steamboats, and he approached the subject of the defense of New Orleans with those things in mind. Gaines began by contending that a "first-rate" steam engine could propel a seventy-four-gun warship (typical line-of-battle ship of the late eighteenth and early nineteenth centuries) more than a mile in six minutes (ten miles per hour) and that such a ship would not remain under fire from a coastal fort for more than twelve minutes. Gaines calculated that a heavy gun could not be fired more than once per minute, and thus would at best get off only about twelve shots at the ship. Because of the ship's speed, Gaines thought it unlikely that more than 30 percent of the shots would hit the hull or rigging of the ship, or that more than a tenth would be likely to hit a vital spot. For Gaines, the conclusion of this mathematical analysis was clear. It was impossible, he wrote "with all the fortifications designed and constructed for the protection of the large seaport towns of the United States, to secure any one of them from assault and capture by a respectable enemy, provided with a strong naval force aided by steam." To be effective, the coastal fortification needed the support of "several floating batteries . . . towed or propelled also by steam."[8]

Unlike Jefferson's gunboats, each of which mounted only one or two guns, the batteries envisioned by Gaines were massive in scale. Each, he thought, would carry from eighty to 160 heavy guns. Yet Gaines thought that the construction of such batteries would be simple and relatively inexpensive. Any desirable number of them, he suggested, could be obtained for not much more than double the value of the timber used in their construction. Aside from cost and efficiency, the system had other advantages. Gaines contended that the steamers used to propel the batteries would also serve as supply ships. In addition, the steamers would be protected by the sheer bulk of the battery in front of them and once the batteries were engaged, "the steamboats would take a position in the rear, where by suitable cables they would, without any risk, maneuver the batteries to the right and left and to the rear."[9]

Gaines believed so firmly in his proposal that he contended

that no experienced officer of the navy or army, after careful investigation of our means of defense, with those likely to be employed against us in the attack aided by steam, would venture to pronounce . . . important posts secure, or even in a very respectable state of defense, without at least two or more large steam frigates or other floating batteries.

Gaines was less than accurate in asserting this, for hardly any army or navy officers supported his claims. There was, in fact, at this time very little apparent interest in Gaines's proposals. Congress took no action, despite the fact that Gaines continued to expound his ideas to anyone who would listen.[10]

Despite a lack of official or Congressional interest, Gaines was not alone in contending that steam power would fundamentally alter the means of both attack and defense of the coast. An anonymous member of the United States Naval Lyceum complained in 1836 that, while steamers were neglected in the United States, England and France were "more alive to their importance." The writer went on to criticize the design of a steamer then under construction at the Brooklyn Navy Yard (the ship, in fact, was not actually completed), and concluded with the hope that it would not be long before "we shall be in condition to afford to our commerce . . . that protection, which can only be effectively rendered by a fleet of well-constructed, well-appointed and formidable steamers."[11] By the end of the 1830s, the navy was beginning to respond, and in 1839, laid down the keels for two side-wheel frigates, the *Mississippi* and the *Missouri*. At the same time interest was slowly growing in the applicability of steam power to coastal defense.[12]

As early as 1834, Secretary of the Navy Mahlon Dickerson requested authority to construct two or three steam batteries. "It can hardly be doubted," he argued, "that the power of steam is soon to produce as great a revolution in the defense of rivers, bays, coasts, and harbors as it has already done in commerce . . . in Europe as well as America." With regard to American defenses, Dickerson believed that if steam power had the effects anticipated, it would "diminish in some instances, the necessity of permanent fortifications on our coasts, by substituting those which may be moved from place to place." Dickerson welcomed steam power, for like observers of nearly every new military device or technological improvement, he foresaw "the application of steam" reducing "the frequency as well as the horrors of [maritime] war," for it would take from the attacker "his hope of success, and of course, his motive for action."[13] The House Committee on Naval Affairs echoed aspects of Dickerson's arguments in 1835 when it urged the building of an unusual "prow-ship" designed by Commodore James Barron. Powered by steam, the ship (really three ships joined together transversely) was equipped with an iron-bound pyramidal bow which would serve as a ram. Its cost was set at $75,000 and the committee went on to argue that the fortification system had multiplied at immense cost, and this ship represented a far cheaper means of coastal defense.[14] Congress never responded to the pleas to build the ship, however, although the same committee submitted an identical report a year later.[15] Nevertheless, the increasing cost of the engineers' fortification system was clearly spurring a search for alternative means of defense, and men concerned about the situation readily seized upon the old concept of floating batteries or similar devices.

Similar consideration motivated Lewis Cass's suggestion in 1836 that floating batteries, properly constructed, were floating forts, "almost equal to permanent fortifications in their power of annoyance and defence, and in other advantages far superior to them."[16] Cass made it clear that he believed such floating batteries should be employed as "accessories" to permanent fortifications. Like Gaines, however, he saw the mobility of these devices as a major asset. "Being transferable defences," he wrote, "they can be united upon any point." A hostile fleet in the Chesapeake would certainly have to take into account the existence of such powerful vessels. "During a calm," Cass argued, "they would take a distant position, insuring their own safety, while . . . their power of motion would enable them . . . to approach the fleet, and to retire, when necessary, where they could not be pursued."[17] Cass thought enough of floating batteries to assert that "our Atlantic frontier will not be properly secured till this means of efficient cooperation in its defense is introduced."[18] To ensure close and effective cooperation between the floating batteries and the permanent fortifications, Cass thought their care and management ought to be entrusted to the army; and he carefully separated them from steam warships for naval operations on the high seas.[19]

Even a few engineers shared Cass's enthusiasm for floating defenses and steam batteries. Major J. L. Smith thought it possible for the engineers to build in two months a "cannon-proof" steam battery, capable of ten to twelve miles per hour, for $15,000. His superior, Chief Engineer Charles Gratiot, passed this information on to Cass and agreed that such devices would be a powerful auxiliary to the existing defenses of the coast. Although Gratiot admitted that his department had no practical knowledge of the subject, he recommended the construction of a total of twenty-six such batteries, ten each for New York harbor and Chesapeake Bay and six for Delaware Bay. He estimated the cost of each, in contrast to Smith, at a level between $25,000 and $30,000.[20] Senator Thomas Hart Benton advanced the argument for the batteries, but his support was not enough to get a bill through.[21] Official support for the idea of floating batteries or steam batteries ended quickly when first Cass left the War Department and Van Buren then dismissed Gratiot from his post as Chief of Engineers.[22] Gratiot's enthusiasm for such devices was restrained, but the attitude of his successor, Joseph G. Totten, was clearly hostile.[23] Mahlon Dickerson (still Secretary of the Navy) was the only military authority who continued to press for their construction. He appealed to Senator Richard M. Johnson of the Senate Military Affairs Committee in 1838, with the argument that since European navies were developing "a system of defense as well as attack, by means of steam batteries," the United States needed to do so too.[24] On the other hand, Secretary of War Joel R. Poinsett contended that steam batteries

> ought only to be regarded in the light of auxiliaries to the permanent defence of the coast—important, it is true, but for reasons which it would be tedious to detail here, entirely inadequate, of themselves, to afford sufficient protection to . . . our Atlantic frontier, and . . . the Gulf of Mexico.[25]

These official pronouncements did not keep General Gaines from returning to the fray in 1840, when he submitted a long and detailed memorial to Congress on the necessity of providing floating batteries for the defense of the Mississippi. Gaines's views of fifteen years earlier remained unaltered. He proposed the immediate construction of from two to four floating batteries for New Orleans, "and from two to five others, for the defense of every other navigable inlet leading into any of the principle seaports of the United States.'' Each battery would be flat-bottomed, 200 to 300 feet long, ninety to 150 feet wide, and carry from 120 to 200 heavy guns. Gaines did not propose that these massive devices be self-propelled. Instead, each would have a suitable number of attending "tow-boats," some built by the government and others chartered when the need arose. Many of the latter, Gaines believed, would become available since they would be "thrown out of employment during a state of war."[26] As in the 1820s, Gaines believed such batteries might be built relatively cheaply. Perhaps in order to forestall questions of expense, however, he proposed a novel use for these batteries during peacetime. They could, he believed, be used to deepen channels of the river, "a work which may be accomplished with the most perfect ease, and to any desirable extent." To the bottom of each battery Gaines wanted to attach a framework of ploughs and iron scrapers which could be raised or lowered for dredging purposes. Gaines went on to propose both a new system of military education (aboard his batteries), which would unite theory and practice, as well as a system of seven national railroads connecting "the two central states of Tennessee and Kentucky to the seven grand divisions of the national frontier."[27]

As in the past, Gaines was convinced that no rational man could

> much longer shut his eyes against the obvious, self-evident truth, that steam power . . . must soon so change the nature of all military operations . . . as to render FIXED fortifications a butt, a mockery, a laughing stock, to the assailant, for any purposes of *national defence,* save and excepting only for the security of arsenals, or other deposits of munitions of war.[28]

His views did not, however, gain much support. The War Department refused to pay his expenses, incurred while collecting the information contained in his memorial, and bluntly told him there was no money available for the construction of the kinds of batteries he proposed. The Board of Navy Commissioners' response was wholly in accord with the views of the engineers on the efficiency of such a form of defense. "Although a few such or similar batteries might perhaps be useful in particular places," wrote Commodore Morris of the board, "it would not be expedient to adopt them generally as substitutes for fixed fortifications." Samuel Humphreys estimated the cost of such a battery at $700,000 to $1,400,000, an estimate which did not include any stores, armament, masts, or sails and which clearly countered Gaines's optimistic assertions regarding costs.[29]

In 1841 Secretary of War John C. Spencer did point out how useful railroads and canals were for the movement of troops and obliquely suggested that Congress might recompense states for the expenses of such improvements, but he merely alluded to Gaines's memorial and supported the views of both the navy and the engineers. The greatest military talent and experience of the country, said Spencer, had long been devoted to the development of the existing system of defense, "which has been so deliberately considered and so long matured, and . . . may now be regarded as the settled policy of the country."[30]

Ironically, in the face of this determined opposition from the War Department and the Corps of Engineers, the early 1840s witnessed the first attempts to construct floating batteries. One vessel, named *Union,* was the brainchild of Lieutenant W. W. Hunter of the navy. One-hundred and eighty-five feet long, with a beam of thirty-three feet and mounting four sixty-eight-pound guns, this vessel had a unique propulsion system known as the "Hunter wheel." Instead of the vertical arrangement of paddle wheels generally followed in steamer design, the "Hunter wheel" rested on its side. The whole assembly lay below the water line, and the wheel revolved at right angles to the keel of the ship. The *Union* had two of these wheels, each in a watertight compartment to keep the water flowing into the wheel from entering the ship itself. Altogether, this was an ingenious way of protecting the relatively fragile machinery of the paddle wheel, which on most steamers was a tempting target for an enemy's guns. Unhappily, the great flaw of the design was that since the entire wheel was below the water it had no "idle" side. Those paddles not actually working to propel the ship had to work to force water inside the watertight case. Despite this defect, readily apparent to most engineers, the Navy Department provided the money for the ship and it was completed by the end of 1842. Its performance was, however, disappointing. With the assistance of sails, the ship did reportedly attain a speed of twelve knots, but the average was closer to five knots with a daily consumption of eighteen tons of coal. Despite further experiments, as well as a larger engine, the performance of the ship failed to improve. Finally, the navy abandoned the effort in 1848 and like the *Demologos (Fulton)* the *Union* become a receiving ship.[31]

At the same time that Lieutenant Hunter's oddity was under construction, Congress authorized Robert L. Stevens to construct a shot and ball proof ironclad steamer costing no more than the average costs of the existing steamers *Missouri* and *Mississippi*. On April 14, 1842 Congress authorized $250,000 for the construction of the vessel, and in February of the following year Secretary of the Navy Upshur and Stevens formally agreed on a contract.[32]

Robert Stevens was the son of the inventor John Stevens, the proponent of the steam battery summarily rejected by the Board of Naval Commissioners in 1821. Robert Stevens's design was, however, entirely new. Based on a series of experiments conducted in the presence of a joint board of army and navy officers, Stevens argued that a series of wrought-iron boiler plates, riveted together to a thickness of four and one-half inches could resist sixty-four-pound shot at a distance of thirty yards. "It will be manifest," he contended, "that a steam vessel, or battery, fortified in the manner . . . described, and furnished with the means of rapid propulsion, would be able to approach an adversary's vessel so securely and so closely as to render it nearly impossible to miss her with shells fired horizontally."[33] No wooden warship, said Stevens, could stand against such a ship, and it was important that the United States be the first to build one. "The advantage of being first," he contended, " . . . must render us secure, for a long time, against the vessels of war of other nations, as these would require to be built anew." Basically, the House Committee on Naval Affairs agreed, stating that as an adjunct to fixed shore defenses, such a steam vessel or battery "must prove invaluable."[34]

Designed to be 250 feet long, 40 feet wide, carry an impressively heavy armament and an underwater ram, the Stevens steamer was a remarkably foresighted vessel. If built, it well might have transformed naval thinking long before the famous duel between the *Monitor* and the *Merrimac* during the Civil War. However, it never was built. Official enthusiasm waned quickly and in 1843 the Secretary of the Navy, David Henshaw, stopped payments. Stevens obtained another contract, but once more, in August 1849, payments stopped. At this point the Navy Department declared all the contracts void and declared its intention to sell the collected materials for scrap. Discouraged and deep in debt, Stevens appealed to Congress. By doing so he saved the materials and his contract, but continued delays meant that the floor timbers of the vessel were not laid until 1854.[35]

Robert Stevens died in 1856, leaving his brother Edwin to carry on the project. Edwin admitted that naval armament as well as warship design was no longer the same as in 1842, and he proposed completing the vessel with substantial modifications (which nearly doubled the length and increased the armor protection to nearly seven inches). By now, however, neither Congressional nor Navy Department interest could be aroused by the project. Ultimately the still-unfinished vessel was condemned by a joint board of army and navy officers in 1862. Abandoned by Congress to the Stevens family, Edwin willed it to New Jersey with funds to complete it. When the funds gave out in 1881, the vessel was broken up for scrap.[36]

Despite the persistent urgings of General Gaines and the dedicated labor of men like the Stevenses, the United States never actually built any of the floating batteries demanded by critics of the fortification system. Congressmen who did not accept the need for a fortification system were equally unwilling to support increased expenditures for other forms of defense. But while no batteries were built, the concept of floating or self-propelled defenses remained an important, if unheralded, part of American thinking on coastal defense.

Floating and steam batteries were not, however, the only alternative means of floating coastal defense proposed in the years before the Civil War. Uriah Brown, for example, submitted a memorial in the 1820s proposing the use of fireships as agents of coastal defense. Brown referred to his proposed vessel as a "Navis Conflagrator" and unlike the typical fireship, which was allowed to drift or sail into contact with an enemy ship before being set afire, his design called for the projection of an inflammable liquid onto the enemy ship. Brown's vessel was designed, in principle, to deflect enemy shot by the arrangement of "inclined planes," a design apparently similar in concept to the slope armor of modern tanks. Alden Partridge, for one, believed the idea worthy of notice. The *National Intelligencer* reported him as including Brown's fireships in his system of coastal defense. Simon Bernard thought the plan combined "strength of construction . . . with security to the propelling engine destined to reach within the proper range of the incendiary liquid." More restrained than Partridge, Bernard merely suggested that such a device "might become a very valuable auxiliary in the defence of our harbors and open bays." The House Committee on Naval Affairs, reviewing all the information available, urged a bill providing for experimentation under a board of engineers to determine if American coastal defenses would be strengthened by the inclusion of Brown's device.[37]

The use of the term "steam battery" by those critics who proposed using such devices as agents of coastal defense often leads to confusion, for the term was often used synonymously with "floating battery" or "war steamer." It is thus sometimes unclear whether proposals favoring the use of floating batteries and other such devices are making a distinction between floating defenses associated with a specific locale and naval vessels. In 1812, for example, the House Military Affairs Committee suggested the use of a "floating force" for the defense of Mobile Bay which included at least one "steam frigate," which by implication would be a seagoing vessel capable of fleet operations, as well as "gunboats," which in all likelihood would be designed to fight only in coastal waters.[38] In 1846 the House Committee of Naval Affairs recommended the construction of twelve war steamers, but while these ships would be able to be operated at sea, they were clearly expected to operate along the seaboard, making it "difficult for any fleet, however large, to remain long on our coast."[39] The steam batteries supported so vigorously by Secretary of the Navy Mahlon Dickerson were intended for the defense of "rivers, bays, coasts, and harbors." Yet, Dickerson added to the semantic confusion in 1838 when he discussed the advantages of "armed steamers" as a part of the coastal defense system, and then employed the term "steam battery" in a later paragraph without any distinction between the types of vessels involved. In all likelihood, the two terms meant the same thing to him just as they did to many military and civilian leaders.[40]

Most critics who proposed the use of floating or steam batteries did, however, make a distinction between the role of such devices and that of the navy proper. Lewis Cass believed floating batteries were, in fact, an army responsibility since, as he told Senator Thomas Hart Benton, they had no relation to vessels constructed for naval use.[41] Most navy men, too, carefully distinguished between the roles of coastal defense vessels and those for use at sea. Commodore Matthew C. Perry in 1851 made a particular point of regarding steam batteries "in contradistinction to steamers of war," although he did suggest that "much reliance could be placed on all vessels of war, particularly those moved by steam, whether intended for ocean or harbor service, as auxiliaries to the fortifications."[42]

All proposals to use floating defenses either implied or stated a criticism of the fortification system, and while engineer officers distinguished between the navy proper and auxiliaries, such as floating batteries, they used similar arguments to counter proposals to substitute either alternative for the existing fortification system. There were two main, although related, counterarguments to the use of floating defenses (and the use of the navy in direct coastal defense) advanced by the engineers. One was the cost of such defenses as opposed to the cost of permanent fortifications. The other was the efficiency of such defenses. Both lines of argument went back to at least 1822. At that time the Board of Engineers (headed by Simon Bernard) responded to the House Military Affairs Committee's proposal to employ a floating force in the defense of Mobile Bay, insisting that "the only species of force which can resist and repel the attacks to which a maritime frontier is exposed are heavy guns and mortars in vessels, or heavy guns and mortars covered by proof epaulments on shore." The first of these agents, a floating defense, was uncertain, however, and the board went on to enumerate the reasons why shore fortifications were superior. First of all, accidents "beyond the control of courage or skill" might take the floating force out of commission at a critical time. Furthermore,

> the enormous expense of this kind of defence . . . has amongst all nations caused, and must ever cause, its rejection as a means of local security; to be sufficient, it must be least

equal the threatening force at every point . . . because where
he is unknown and where he will attack is uncertain.

Beyond the initial expense, the board argued that floating defenses
were perishable and needed replacement frequently. The board
admitted that occasionally situations arose when floating defenses
might prove useful, but contended that the "only successful practice with this force has been to employ it where no other will avail,
or at most only as an auxiliary." The board came down firmly and
unequivocably in favor of fortifications as the soundest and most
economical form of defense. "All the nations experienced in war,"
said the board, "concur in one sentiment as regards their utility, at
least in relation to a maritime frontier; and all nations having such
a frontier rely upon them for their security."[43]

This 1822 position of the Board of Engineers continued to be the
basic argument of the engineers throughout the years before the
Civil War. The board report of 1840, written in large part by
Joseph G. Totten, repeated the contention that since the point of
an enemy's attack would be unknown beforehand, any naval
defense force had to be "at least equal in power to the attacking
force" at every point of attack. Thus the use of the navy as a
coastal defense force demanded a force as "many times greater
than in the attack as there are points to be covered."[44] The board
conceded that if the definition of the term "navy" included gunboats and floating or steam batteries as well as sea-going vessels,
there was some merit to proposals to use the navy in coastal
defense. However, the board argued that such auxiliaries to permanent fortifications were useful in only specific and isolated cases,
such as when secure anchorages were available to an enemy outside
gun range. "It is doubtful," maintained the board, "whether, as a
general rule, . . . floating batteries . . . would afford a better
defense, gun for gun, than gun-boats," and any probable number
of gunboats, said the board, would neither "impede or hinder for a
moment the advance of a hostile fleet." The same factors which
influenced the use of the navy as a coastal defense force, acted
upon other floating defenses as well:

It will be noticed [said the Board] that this kind of defence,
whether by gun-boats or floating batteries, has the same in-

trinsic fault that an inactive defence by the navy proper has; that is to say, the enemy has it in his power to bring to the attack a force of the same nature, . . . as that relied on for defence; hence the necessity not of mere equality, but of *superiority*, on the part of the defence, at every point liable to be attacked; and hence, also, the necessity of having an aggregate force many times larger than that disposable by the enemy as we have places to guard.[45]

Even steam power, according to the board, did not give an advantage to the defense, for steam-powered batteries were, it believed, no different from any other type of floating defense. "Although much has been said, of late, of the great advantage that defense is to derive from this description of force [steam batteries]," the board claimed, "we have not been able to discover the advantages; nor do we see that seacoast defence has been benefited, in any particular, by the recent improvement in steam vessels." Indeed, improvements in such vessels only made it likely than any steam-powered defense vessel would be attacked by similar sea-going ships; thus steam conferred no advantage to the defense. "Steam batteries," the board maintained, "cannot be substituted for shore defence." Only "a well digested system of fortifications will save a country from the danger attending every form of defence by naval means," and only such a system was "worthy of all reliance."[46]

If from a strategic or tactical point of view it was improvident to rely on a naval or floating force for defense of the coast, it was, said the engineers, also far more expensive to do so. Henry W. Halleck calculated in the mid-1840s that the average cost of constructing a vessel of war was $6,000 per gun, while the expense of maintaining such vessels amounted to more than 7 percent a year. War steamers, such as the *Missouri* and *Mississippi*, cost over $60,000 per gun by Halleck's calculations, making such ships even more expensive agents of defense. Furthermore, steam vessels cost more to operate and maintain. Fortifications, however, cost only about $3,000 per gun and Halleck argued that the cost of maintenance was negligible, only one-third of 1 percent annually of the original cost of the fortification. While Halleck contended ships could not be substituted for forts, no matter what the relative cost was, his calculations touched a sensitive issue for a fiscally conscious Congress.[47]

Both the army engineers and naval officers agreed that it was not the proper role for the navy to operate in coastal defense. In 1851 Secretary of War Charles Conrad queried both groups on a number of issues, including the possibility of relying on vessels of war or other floating defenses as substitutes for permanent fortifications. Almost unanimously, they suggested that little or no reliance could be placed on such defensive measures. Several naval officers did state that steam batteries or war steamers might prove useful auxiliaries but even these agreed with Commander R. B. Cunningham who said, "The indispensable and in fact imperative necessity of having *strong* permanent fortifications . . . is a settled and decided conviction of my mind; they will admit of no substitute."[48] Even Commodore Matthew C. Perry, who believed that the country could rely on all the navy's ships as a part of coastal defenses, repeatedly indicated that warships or specially designed floating batteries were auxiliary to fortifications. The engineers queried agreed with this. Typical of their responses was that of William H. Chase who stated, "any kind of floating defences is inferior, on every score, to land batteries."[49]

Ten years later nothing had changed. In 1861 Major John G. Barnard recalled Cass's statements of 1836:

> Barely twenty years have elapsed [said Barnard] since the, then, highest military authority of the government argued that reliance should be on the navy as the chief agent of coast defense, that the United States was not in danger of invasion, that in preference to fortification floating batteries might be used, and finally, that the system proposed by the Board of Engineers was unnecessarily large for its purpose.

Now, Barnard contended, "such opinions, though they are not *entirely* abandoned, have so few supporters that it would be wasting ink and paper to quote them for confutation." Great Britain, he pointed out, had only recently awakened to the need for coastal fortifications, an example that "furnishes now the most striking example that could be offered to us of the truth of *our* fundamental principle. That the essential and true basis of coast defense is fortification." Critics of the British commissioners' report might scoff, said Barnard, "but they cannot allege . . . that it was devised before the days of steam—of rifle-cannon—of ironclad floating batteries." The British were thoroughly familiar with all of these things and had as well recent experience in the Crimean War to draw upon. Barnard found it flattering to American military pride that Britain, a country "whose immunity from coast defense has been so long boasted," was now adopting in principle the same means of coastal defense as the Board of Engineers had proposed forty years earlier for the American coast.[50] To American engineers, floating defenses were costly and inefficient agents of coastal defense, which the British would ultimately find a failure. In the years before the Civil War, the engineers scorned such defenses and, as always, found the proof for their view in European arguments and European practice. However, floating defenses (including floating or steam batteries) were not the only form of auxiliary defenses discussed during the years before the Civil War. Another defensive weapon proposed was the electrically fired underwater mine—called a torpedo during this period. Like floating batteries, torpedoes appeared before the War of 1812. The ever-inventive Robert Fulton began trying to interest the British and French navies in both a submarine and in explosive torpedoes (or, in modern terms, submersible mines) during the early 1800s. Failing in this effort, he returned to the United States where, in August of 1807, on the third attempt, he successfully blew up an anchored brig in New York Harbor.[51] In 1810 Fulton wrote a brief pamphlet extolling the virtues of his devices which he submitted to President Madison and both houses of Congress. Fulton's device consisted of 100 pounds of gunpowder in a copper case, made buoyant by the attachment of a cork cushion. Linked to the copper case was a brass box containing a gunlock and a two-inch gun barrel. When triggered by a clockwork timer, this small flintlock fired a charge into the gunpowder causing it to explode. The mechanism could be set so that the torpedoes would explode at any predetermined time up to one hour after activation. Torpedoes anchored in place could be triggered by a ship making contact with a lever connected to the gunlock. Normally, these torpedoes hung suspended from a cork buoy at depths up to fifteen feet below the surface.

To this torpedo Fulton added a proposed refinement. He suggested the use of a harpoon gun in which the harpoon was attached to the torpedo by an attached line. These harpoon guns would then be mounted in twenty-seven-foot boats mounting two swivel-mounted blunderbusses for armament and with a twelve-man crew. When the harpoon gunner fired into the bow of a ship, the attached line would (said Fulton) pull the torpedo up against the keel where the resulting explosion would cause the most damage and, in Fulton's opinion, certainly destroy the ship.[52]

Fulton promoted his torpedoes as cheaper to build than ships. He believed that his invention, by destroying ships of war, would "produce that liberty so dear to every rational and reflecting man." Fulton recognized that some condemned torpedoes as a barbarous form of war. Fulton replied that "all wars are barbarous," adding, "It would be barbarous for ships of war to enter the harbor of New York, fire on the city, destroy property, and murder many of the peaceable inhabitants." Yet, this would happen, he said, unless means were devised to prevent it. Since he believed his torpedoes could prevent such an act, then perforce "the invention must be humane."[53]

Congress authorized further experimentation and appropriated $5,000, but trials made in New York harbor in September of 1810 proved a discouraging failure. No attempt was made to actually place a torpedo against the hull of a ship. Originally, the brig *Argus* was to have been the target of blank torpedoes, but the naval officers involved, especially Commodore John Rodgers, rigged the vessel with a net and spars to prevent boats from coming in contact with it. The officers contended that such means of defense were not only possessed by warships, but could be rigged in fifteen minutes. Confronted with this situation, Fulton admitted he was unprepared for an attack on the ship, and the experiment fizzled.[54]

The failure of Fulton's devices came as no surprise to the naval officers involved who had, in fact, set out to frustrate him from the start. Even before the experiments began, Rodgers referred to the torpedoes as "the most absurd visionary scheme that can be conceived to have originated in the brain of man not actually out of his senses," and he professed amazement that Congress had been "so far imposed on as to even notice it."[55] The committee appointed to report on the experiments, which included Chief Engineer

Jonathan Williams, reported that Fulton's system was "too imperfectly demonstrated to justify the Government in relying upon it as a means of public defence."[56] However, the committee suggested that future discoveries might make the system useful. Commodore Rodgers remained unimpressed. "Having attended all the experiments," he recorded in his journal his conviction that Fulton had not attempted to carry out the proposed experiments "owing . . . to an entire conviction, in his own mind, that such an attempt would only serve to prove more distinctly that the practice of every, or any part of his project would be found not only impossible, but that even its theory would be proved as conclusively absurd." As a means of national defense, said Rodgers, Fulton's torpedoes were "to say the least, comparatively of no importance at all."[57]

For a time Fulton continued to promote his theories and designs during the War of 1812. But he soon became more interested in the design and construction of his steam warship, the *Demologos,* and his interest in torpedoes waned. Fulton's abandonment of this line of research did not discourage a host of imitators from supplying plans and proposals for torpedoes during the war and in the years that followed. While no effort was made to actually employ such devices during the war, the continued publication of such proposals ensured that knowledge of the history of torpedo design as well as recent developments in the field become relatively widely available.[58]

Among those influenced by Fulton in the United States was Samuel Colt, more famous as the inventor of the Colt revolver. The exact genesis of Colt's ideas on torpedo design are unclear, but he undoubtedly drew many of his ideas from Fulton's earlier experiments.[59] Colt detonated his first underwater explosion on July 4, 1829, when he attempted to blow up a raft moored in a neighborhood pond and succeeded only in drenching a number of spectators. Undismayed, he continued to experiment and by the early 1840s was ready to submit his proposals to the national military authorities.[60] The major difference between the designs of Colt and Fulton was that Colt's torpedoes were fired electrically rather than by either contact or the clockwork mechanism used by Fulton. Fulton had been aware of this method but had not been able to overcome either the problem of determining when a ship was actually over the torpedo or how to protect the electrical wires while they were under water. Improvements in underwater cable design made the procedure technically feasible for Colt, and he also devised a method—which remains unknown—for determining when a vessel was over one of his torpedoes.[61]

Colt distrusted the professionals of both the army and the navy and appealed directly to political leaders with a series of public demonstrations. On July 4, 1842, Colt successfully blew up a drifting hulk in New York harbor. He destroyed a moored boat on the Potomac River on August 20, 1842, and returned to New York to sink a 260-ton brig on October 18, 1842. The climax of this series of demonstrations occurred on April 13, 1844, when he destroyed the ship *Styx* on the Potomac River before a large crowd which included President Tyler and numerous other government and military officials.[62]

Congress was impressed enough to appropriate $15,000 for continued demonstrations in late 1842. But the Congressional reaction to Colt's 1844 demonstration was a House resolution requiring the Secretaries of War and the Navy to report on whether his "combustible agent" was already known and if "the mode of its application to harbor defence be new; and if new, what objections there are against its adoption, if objections do exist."[65]

Although Colt asserted that the Navy Department had all the necessary information to assess his invention, Secretary of the Navy John Y. Mason claimed it did not. He confined himself to dealing with Colt only on financial matters and left any critique of Colt's device up to the War Department, to which Colt had steadfastly refused to divulge his secret. Lacking any specific information, Secretary of War William Wilkins referred the matter to Chief Engineer Totten, who had many objections.

Totten began by asserting that from a technological point of view, Colt's invention was not new. "The use under water," he wrote, "of gunpowder in blasting rocks, levelling foundations . . . and even blowing up vessels, is a matter of common notoriety amongst persons conversant in such operations." Even the use of electricity to fire the gunpowder charge was widely known.[64] Criticizing the originality of Colt's invention on a technological basis missed the point, of course, for whether or not the device was original had nothing to do with its potential as an agent for coastal or harbor defense. But Totten had objections on this score as well. Totten pointed out that Fulton's similar proposals were well known. Underwater explosive devices, said Totten, "are not new resorts as measures of defence, in the minds of ingenius men." Except "in certain positions and under particular circumstances," Totten believed that reliance on such devices as agents of defense would be "as utterly in vain as it would be unwise." Totten pointed out that it was impossible to determine accurately when a ship was actually over the explosive device. Lacking this ability, he asked, how could the device be effectively used? Even assuming an enemy hesitated, continued Totten, if the object of his attack was important enough, he would try to land and destroy the means of firing the devices. To prevent this landing, the defensive arrangements had to include either a force capable of defeating the landing party or a fortification with its garrison. Thus the defense would actually rest "either upon the fort or upon the army, and not upon the deposites [sic] of powder." As he did with regard to floating batteries or the use of steam, Totten insisted that the system of defenses then extant or under construction was far more reliable as well as being proven by experience. "Military experience has enacted," he argued, "as an inflexible law, that no device, however plausible, shall be admitted to confidence as a military resource, except as it shall make its way by success in actual war, or in a long and severe course of experience analogous thereto." Since the existing means of harbor and coastal defense were "the fruits of this kind of experience, they should give way only to means that have been proven superior, by trial not less thorough." As an auxiliary, Colt's device might have some utility, but "as a sole means of defence, it is wholly undeserving of consideration."[65]

Based on this condemnation of Colt's system, as well as Colt's continued refusal to divulge any information, Secretary of War Wilkins reported to Congress that Colt's invention was "liable to fatal objections" as a primary means of harbor defense and to "very strong objections" even as an auxiliary.[66] Colt responded to this by writing directly to Congress and pointing out that he had never claimed his device was original, only that his secret method for determining when a ship was actually over a torpedo was. Colt went on to submit a patent application (which the commissioner approved) and obtain a letter from scientist Thomas P. Jones which argued that Colt's device was not only novel but sure to succeed. The House Committee on Naval Affairs eventually reacted to this by producing a favorable report in early 1845 which recommended compensating Colt for the time spent on his experiments. Since Colt, however, continued to refuse to reveal his "secret," the committee did not recommend the adoption of his scheme.[67]

In analyzing the failure of Colt's attempt to gain acceptance of his device, one historian of the episode, Alex Roland, argues that the turnover in government officials and Colt's own secretiveness combined to prevent any favorable action by the government. While these factors are important, there are other factors which apply not only to Colt's invention but to all the other alternative means of coastal defense proposed and dismissed before the Civil War. The Navy Department had no organized body of experts to deal with the issue of coastal defense. While that encouragement for experimentation in alternative means of coastal defense came largely from the Navy Department (and it is significant that it did), the only group explicitly formed to deal with the problems of coastal defense was the army's Board of Engineers. This group reacted towards Colt's invention just as it had toward every other device proposed as an alternative or auxiliary means of coastal defense; it steadfastly maintained that the fortification scheme devised by the Board of Engineers was the only true means of defense.

Thus, while other means of defense might prove occasionally useful as auxiliaries, the fortification system was the only one which could be completely depended upon to protect the coast. The consistency of the engineers' views as well as the consistency of the board's leadership led both to a deference to them as the true experts on coastal defense and to a continued (if sometimes hesitant) reliance on their fortification system as the cornerstone of the coastal defense system. Only the coming of weapons which would demonstrate that the historical relationships on which that system was based had been fundamentally altered would shake the engineers' faith in it.

NOTES

1. Lewis Cass, "Message From The Secretarys of War and Navy Relative to the Military and Naval Defences of the Country," *ASP, MA,* vol. 6 (Serial 021), Document 671, p. 369.

2. Congressman Joshua Giddings of Ohio, a consistent foe of large military budgets, neatly summarized all these positions when he complained in 1850 that the engineers' fortification system was "unsuited to the age in which we live, expensive, and entirely useless." *Congressional Globe,* 31st Congress, 2nd session (vol. 20), p. 641.

3. Frank M. Bennett, *The Steam Navy of the United States,* 2nd ed. (Pittsburgh: Warren and Co., 1897), pp. 8-15.

4. *American State Papers, Naval Affairs,* vol. 1 (Serial 023), Document 193, p. 685.

5. Archibald D. Turnbull, *John Stevens: An American Record* (New York: The Century Co., 1928).

6. *ASP, MA,* vol. 11 (Serial 017), 17th Congress, 1st session, Document 214, p. 346.

7. *Annals,* 17th Congress, 2nd session (vol. 40), pp. 1041, 1076.

8. Edmund P. Gaines, "Report of a Tour of Inspection Commenced on the 11th December 1826, and Completed in April 1827 . . . ," *ASP, MA,* vol. 4 (Serial 019), Document 407, pp. 105-106.

9. Ibid., p. 106.

10. James Wesley Silver, *Edmund Pendleton Gaines: Frontier General* (Baton Rouge: Louisiana State University Press, 1949), p. 224.

11. "On Steamers of War, By a Member of the Naval Lyceum," *The Naval Magazine,* vol. 1, no. 4 (July 1836), p. 355.

12. Bennett, *Steam Navy,* pp. 34-35.

13. Mahlon P. Dickerson, "Annual Report of the Secretary of the Navy, (1834)," *Executive Document 2,* 23d Congress, 2d session, Serial 271.

14. *House Report No. 86,* 23d Congress, 2d session (February 4, 1835), Serial 276.

15. *House Report No. 674,* 24th Congress, 1st session (May 17, 1836), Serial 295. James P. Baxter III, *The Introduction of the Ironclad Warship* (New York: Archon Books, 1968, reprint of 1933 edition), p. 30.

16. Lewis Cass, "Message," p. 373.

17. Ibid.

18. Lewis Cass, "Annual Report of the Secretary of War (1835)," *ASP, MA,* vol. 5 (Serial 020), Document 613, p. 628.

19. Cass to Thomas Hart Benton, January 14, 1836, *Senate Document 76,* 24th Congress, 1st session, Serial 280.

20. Major J. L. Smith to Chief Engineer Charles Gratiot, *Senate Document 76,* 24th Congress, 1st session, Serial 280 (December 27, 1835), and Gratiot to Cass, January 11, 1836. See also, *ASP, MA,* vol. 4 (Serial 021), Document 624, pp. 11-12.

21. Bright, "Coast Defense and the Southern Coasts Before Fort Sumter," M.A. thesis, Duke University, 1958, p. 27. Bright's brief dis-

cussion of floating batteries and the system of coast defenses may be found on pages 25-28.

22. Gratiot believed that, as auxiliaries, the value of floating batteries was "undoubtedly great" and their value might, in addition, be found "sufficiently so to warrant the diminution, or even total omission, of some of the minor works." He argued, however, that to rely on them without extensive experimentation and proof of their efficiency "would be a dangerous experiment, that nothing but necessity could justify." Gratiot proposed the suitably diplomatic solution of having a Board of Officers (presumably the already established Board of Engineers) study the problem. Gratiot to Joel R. Poinsett, April 27, 1838, *Senate Document 412,* 25th Congress, 2d session, Serial 318, pp. 2-3.

An 1806 graduate of the Military Academy, Gratiot became Chief Engineer on May 24, 1838 and simultaneously obtained a brevet promotion to Brigadier General for "Meretorious service and general good conduct." President Van Buren dismissed him from the army on December 6, 1838 for "Having failed to pay . . . the balance of the moneys placed in his hands, in 1835, for public purposes . . . according to the President's order, communicated to him by the Secretary of War on the 28th Nov., 1838; and having neglected to render his accounts in obedience to the law of Jan. 31, 1823." Cullum, *Biographical Register,* vol. 1, pp. 70-71.

23. Totten often admitted that floating batteries might prove useful in certain situations, but he also insisted that such batteries "cannot be substituted for shore defences," an argument subtly but, I think, distinctly different from Gratiot's. See, for example, the Board of Engineer's Report in 1840, *Sentate Document 451,* 26th Congress, 1st session, Serial 360. Totten's views are discussed in more detail below.

24. Dickerson to R. M. Johnson, President of the U.S. Senate, June 26, 1838, *Senate Document 495,* 25th Congress, 2d session, Serial 319, p. 2.

25. Poinsett to Johnson, January 9, 1838, *House Executive Document 199,* 25th Congress, 2d session, Serial 327, p. 15.

26. Edmund P. Gaines, "Memorial of Major General Edmund P. Gaines," *Executive Document 206,* 26th Congress, 1st session, Serial 368, pp. 119-120.

27. Ibid., p. 120. Gaines took his case on this railroad system to the people. He and his wife went on a joint lecture tour. She spoke on "The Horrors of War" while he, in full uniform, lectured on the military needs of the United States and the virtues of his railroad scheme.

28. Letter, Gaines to New Orleans City Leaders, November 24, 1838, quoted in Silver, *Edmund P. Gaines,* p. 227. The arguments advanced by Gaines in his memorial to Congress are also expressed in this earlier letter.

29. Commodore Charles Morris (for the Board of Navy Commissioners)

to Secretary of the Navy James K. Paulding, April 25, 1840, *House Executive Document 206,* 26th Congress, 1st session, Serial 368, p. 148; Humphreys to Morris, April 22, 1840, *House Executive Document 206,* 26th Congress, lst session, Serial 368.

30. John C. Spencer, "Annual Report of the Secretary of War (1841)," *Executive Document 2,* 27th Congress, 2d session, Serial 1401.

31. Bennett, *Steam Navy,* pp. 47-50.

32. *Senate Report 120,* 32d Congress, 1st session, Serial 630; Bright, "Coast Defense and the Southern Coasts," p. 42.

33. *House Report 448,* 27th Congress, 2d Session, Serial 408, p. 11.

34. Ibid., pp. 12, 14.

35. *Senate Report 129,* 32nd Congress, 1st session, Serial 630; Turnbull, *John Stevens,* pp. 420-422; Bright, "Coast Defense and the Southern Coasts," pp. 57-58; Baxter, *Ironclad Warship,* pp. 48-52. *Senate Report 129* contains a useful summary of the history of the Stevens steamer up through early 1852.

36. Turnbull, *John Stevens,* pp. 425-428; Bright, "Coast Defense and the Southern Coasts," pp. 58-59.

37. *ASP, NA,* vol. 3 (Serial 025), Document 367; Baxter, *Ironclad Warship,* pp. 30, 53-54.

38. ASP, MA, vol. 11 (Serial 017), Document 214, p. 346.

39. *House Report 681,* May 20, 1846, 29th Congress, 1st session, serial 490.

40. Dickerson to R. M. Johnson, June 26, 1838, *Senate Document 495,* 25th Congress, 2nd session, Serial 319. In an attached letter Isaac Chauncey (writing for the Board of Navy Commissioners) also used the two terms interchangeably. The fact that during this period steam warships were often classified as "floating batteries" is pointed out by Harold and *Margaret Sprout in The Rise of American Naval Power, 1916-1918* (Princeton: Princeton University Press Paperback, 1939), p. 115. The Sprouts imply, however, that the blame for this semantic confusion lay with the army's Board of Engineers. The fact that naval officers also used the two terms synonymously indicates that in fact the confusion was far more widespread.

41. Cass to Benton, January 14, 1836, *Senate Document 76,* 24th Congress, 1st session, Serial 280.

42. Matthew C. Perry to Secretary of War Charles M. Conrad, July 25, 1852, *Executive Document 5,* 32nd Congress, 1st session, Serial 637, pp. 135-140.

43. *ASP, MA,* vol. 11 (Serial 017), Document 223, pp. 371-373.

44. *Senate Document 451,* 26th Congress, 1st session, Serial 360, p. 13.

45. Ibid., p. 77. (In *The Rise of American Naval Power,* Harold and

Margaret Sprout suggest that the Board of Engineers saw the only way a naval force could contribute directly to defense of the coast was "through a distribution of the vessels along the seaboard." (Paperback edition, p. 100.) The Sprouts do acknowledge that the engineers argued in favor of a "more efficient" fortification system, but they do not make clear (as the board's own reports do) that the engineers established the premises of using the navy in direct coastal defense only then to dispute them. The Board of Engineers was, in fact, insistent that a naval force of any size could not defend the coast alone (i.e., without fortifications) under any circumstances. The Sprouts further state that the engineers viewed the navy's role as they did because they had "no conception of fleet operations." (Paperback edition, p. 115.) This argument does not appear to reflect either that, one, the engineers established no role for the navy beyond suggesting that it should act offensively and not be tied to the coast, or, two, few (if any) naval authorities understood the fleet concept either. Both of the Sprouts' contentions appear to reflect their own Mahanian views of naval history more than the actual coastal defense theories of the Board of Engineers.

46. *Senate Document 451,* 26th Congress, 1st session, Serial 360, pp. 11-14.

47. Henry W. Halleck, *Military Art and Science* (New York: D. Appleton and Co., 1846), pp. 207-209.

48. R. B. Cunningham to Charles M. Conrad, September 29, 1851, Letter no. 3, *Executive Document 5,* 32d Congress, 1st session, Serial 637.

49. Major William H. Chase to Conrad, April 17, 1851, *Executive Document 5,* 32d Congress, 1st session, Serial 637.

50. Major John G. Barnard, *Notes on Sea-Coast Defence* (New York: Van Nostrand, 1861), pp. 12-13, 18, 27-30.

51. Alex Roland, *Underwater Warfare in the Age of Sail* (Bloomington: Indiana University Press, 1977), p. 114; Capt.-Lieut. F. Von Ehrenkrook, *History of Submarine Mining and Torpedoes,* trans. by Sgt.-Major Frederick Martin (U.S. Army, Engineer School of Application, Willets Point, N.Y., Paper no. 1. Originally published at Berlin, September 30, 1878), pp. 12-13.

52. *ASP, NA,* vol. 1 (Serial 023), Document 80, pp. 213-217. In a letter addressed to President Madison and both Houses of Congress, Fulton also described some of his earlier experiments with these devices.

53. Ibid., p. 223.

54. Roland, *Underwater Warfare,* pp. 115-116; *ASP, NA,* vol. 1 (Serial 023), Document 85, pp. 234-245. This document includes a number of letters from observers of the experiment and Fulton himself, as well as an extract from a journal kept by Commodore Rodgers.

55. Commodore John Rodgers to his wife, April 13, 1810, as cited in Roland, *Underwater Warfare,* p. 116.

56. *ASP, NA,* vol. 1 (Serial 023), Document 85, p. 235.

57. Ibid., pp. 242-243.

58. Roland, *Underwater Warfare,* pp. 120-126.

59. Philip K. Lundeberg, *Samuel Colt's Submarine Battery: The Secret and the Enigma* (Washington, D.C.: Smithsonian Institution Press, 1974), p. 7; Roland, *Underwater Warfare,* p. 134.

60. Lundeberg, *Colt's Submarine Battery,* p. 8.

61. Lundeberg, *Colt's Submarine Battery,* pp. 12-14; Roland, *Underwater Warfare,* pp. 135-136.

62. Lundeberg, *Colt's Submarine Battery,* pp. 25-26, 29-30, 33-34, 42-43; Von Ehrenkrook, *History of Submarine Mining,* pp. 16-17.

63. *Congressional Globe,* 28th Congress, 1st session (vol. 13), p. 538; Lundeberg, *Colt's Submarine Battery,* p. 47; Roland, *Underwater Warfare,* p. 142.

64. Joseph G. Totten to Secretary of War William Wilkins, May 1, 1844, *House Executive Document 127,* 28th Congress, 2d session, Serial 465, p. 7. Also attached to this document are letters by two scientists, Robert Hare and Joseph Henry, to Secretary Wilkins, which point out that in terms of materials Colt's device was not original.

65. Totten to Wilkins, ibid., p. 11.

66. William Wilkins to Speaker of the House J. W. Jones, May 8, 1844, ibid., p. 13. The letters and reports which make up Document 127 together with other relevant letters and documents, are reprinted in an appendix to Lundeberg, *Samuel Colt's Submarine Battery.*

67. Samuel Colt to Congressman Henry C. Murphy, June 3, 1844 and Patent Petition for Samuel Colt's Submarine Battery, June 8, 1844, both in Samuel Colt Papers, Box 6, Connecticut Historical Society, Hartford, Conn., contained in an appendix to Lundeberg, *Colt's Submarine Battery,* pp. 68-71; Letter, Thomas P. Jones to Samuel Colt, June 14, 1844, *House Document 127,* 28th Congress, 2d session, Serial 465, p. 24; Roland, *Underwater Warfare,* pp. 147-148.

FOUR
Technological Change and Coastal Defense

Joseph G. Totten and his colleagues received their training in engineering and military science during the last half-century of a long period of relative stagnation in the development of artillery. The cannon in use during the late 1830s were remarkably similar to those of the previous two centuries. Nineteenth-century guns were larger than their ancestors of the seventeenth and eighteenth centuries, but like the earlier models they were all smoothbore muzzle loaders which fired solid, cast spherical projectiles—termed either ball or shot. In this regard cannon had not changed from the time of their first invention. Accustomed as we are now to rapid and continuous change in weapons technology, it is difficult to realize fully how deeply this constancy of weaponry influenced thought. Totten, Halleck, and the other American engineers were on firm ground in looking to the past for examples of ship-to-shore engagements; the weapons these men knew and understood were the same weapons used in these earlier duels. Yet even as they formulated and expressed their views on the primacy of the masonry fortification, a technological revolution in weaponry was under way that would shatter both their carefully constructed notions and the fragile walls of their largest fortifications. Trapped by experience and training in a world which was about to change suddenly and fundamentally, Totten and his fellow engineers were for a long time blind to the developments which made their system of seacoast defenses obsolete even before it was completed.

When the engineers developed their plan for the seacoast defense system after the War of 1812, this change had not yet occurred. They naturally based their plans, and the assumptions underlying those plans, on the extant technology. In 1816 the guns available for fortification armament far outweighed the guns of contemporary warships. Shore guns had greater range, in most cases, and certainly greater destructive power than the guns which could be brought against them. A typical line-of-battle ship in the British Royal Navy, for example, mounted thirty-two-pound guns on its lower gun decks and twenty-four-pounders on the main deck. (Both types were named, as were all guns of this period, after the weight of the cast ball they fired.)[1] The guns available for arming the coastal forts included a variety of calibers including not only twenty-four- and thirty-two-pounders, but forty-two-pounders and, after 1811, a fifty-pounder gun invented by George Bomford (later head of the Ordnance Bureau) called the Columbiad. This last appeared as a 100-pounder as well, and both Columbiad types could fire both solid shot and shell.[2] Even though both these types disappeared from the ordnance lists during the 1820s (for reasons unknown), and the War Department did not officially list the thirty-two- and forty-two-pounder types until 1829 and 1831, respectively, the engineers believed that the coastal fortification had a vastly superior armament than any warship.[3] Since, in addition, engineers assumed that any ship's fire would be less accurate than the fire from a shore battery, the superiority of the latter's armament reinforced their belief in the primacy of the casemated masonry fort as the main agent of coastal defense. There was little doubt that the masonry was vulnerable to well-directed artillery fire. But there was equally little doubt that the strength of the masonry was sufficient to withstand the relatively inaccurate and feeble fire of a warship. The initial developments in American artillery during the early nineteenth century further reinforced this belief.

Even though the original Columbiad type disappeared in the 1820s, the value of a gun capable of firing both shot and shell was not long overlooked. With Bomford now at the head of the Ordnance Bureau, a new gun bearing the same name, although larger, appeared in 1841. This was the eight-inch Columbiad, followed by a ten-inch model in 1844. Both calibers remained a part of seacoast ordnance until 1858 when improved models of both guns appeared.[4] Both the 1841-1844 and 1858 model Columbiads were powerful guns. The eight-inch Columbiad fired a sixty-four-pound shot up to a maximum range (at 27° elevation) of nearly 4,500 yards. The ten-inch model fired a 128-pound shot over 5,600 yards (at 39°15′ elevation). Until the mid-1860s no naval gun could match these guns either in terms of weight of shot or of range. In comparison, the forty-two-pounder naval gun (restricted in its elevation) had a range of just under 2,000 yards.[5]

During the early nineteenth century, however, naval armament was itself in the midst of a revolutionary change. This change centered on the development of the Paixhans shell gun, a gun which would fundamentally alter the mechanics of sea warfare. The French had long sought some means of negating the superiority of the British navy. General Henri-Joseph Paixhans of the French artillery argued, in the 1820s, that the best means of doing this would be to develop guns which fired explosive shells. While ships might resist solid shot, Paixhans contended that "nothing is easier than to produce a kind of artillery which they cannot resist."[6] Basically, Paixhans believed that guns designed to fire shells horizontally (instead of vertically as was the case with the already existing howitzers and mortars) would be far more dangerous to the wooden-hulled warships then in use. He envisioned a system which combined his shell-firing guns with small steamers; such a radical shift in naval armament and propulsion would, he believed, make the Royal Navy obsolete.

Recognizing the revolutionary nature of his scheme Paixhans urged as a first step the modification of existing guns. He went on, however, to design a gun specifically suited to his theories. This gun became known as the Paixhans gun, and in size and shape it was remarkably similar to the American 1811 Columbiad designed by George Bomford.[7] The gun fired a hollow sixty-pound shell filled with four pounds of gunpowder.[8]

In trials the gun proved tremendously effective against wooden ship targets. By 1837 the French were mounting these guns in their ships. Since the Paixhans gun did not have the range of the more traditional shot-firing guns, a part of the armament, by necessity, continued to be the more traditional guns. The British, aware of the system and of the threat it posed, quickly followed suit. By the 1840s both navies included shell guns as a part of their ships' armament, and the U.S. Navy also had a few.[9]

American engineers did not feel that the Paixhans shell gun invalidated their masonry fortifications. Indeed, they argued that the gun made such defenses stronger. "The only practicable way yet discovered of demolishing a fortification," the Board of Engineers stated in 1840, is "by dint of solid shot and heavy charges, fired unremittingly, during a long succession of hours upon the same part of the wall" so that eventually the weight of the wall forced it to collapse into the holes smashed by shot. This type of breaching required "perfect accuracy" and "great power of penetration by the missile." Neither, stated the board, was possible for ships using the Paixhans shell gun, or any other for that matter:

> The requisite precision of firing for this effect is wholly unattainable in vessels, whether the shot be solid or hollow; and if it were attainable, hollow shot would be entirely useless for the purpose, *because everyone of them would break to pieces against the wall,* even when fired with a charge much less than the common service charge.[10]

To test these arguments the engineers undertook some experiments. They constructed a target wall with its length divided into thirds. One-third was of granite, one-third of bricks, and the last of "free stone." Two guns, one a Paixhans type and the other a standard thirty-two-pounder, were then fired at this target. In every case the solid shot penetrated further and did more damage, while the hollow shells broke up against the target. Any ship, concluded the board, "contemplating the description of batteries, [which] should change any of her long 24 or 32-pounder guns for Paixhans guns, would certainly weaken her armament."[11] While shell guns firing against ships was an entirely different situation, the board effectively denied that the Paixhans gun altered the superiority of masonry fortification.

In the short run this conclusion was undoubtedly correct. Nevertheless in the long run the Paixhans shell gun did fundamentally alter the traditional shore battery versus ship equation. Paixhans himself pointed out that the only sure defense against the shell gun was armor plate, although he mistakenly asserted as well that no major ship could carry the weight of the seven to eight inches of armor he believed necessary.[12] While in the United States the Stevenses, John and Robert, were the main early proponents of armor-clad warships, they had support both here and abroad. By the 1850s French experiments indicated that solid iron plates of ten and fourteen cm. thickness could withstand a heavy battering from thirty-pound shot fired at close range. In one test a ten-cm. plate gave way only after being hit fourteen times within one square meter. In other tests a ten-cm. iron plate withstood nine shots, and a fourteen-cm. iron plate thirteen shots, before splitting into fragments still attached to a wooden backing by bolts. These experiments, and similar tests conducted in England, led to the construction of armored floating batteries used in the siege of Sebastopol during the Crimean War. Based on the success of these batteries, in 1856 the French decided to end the construction of wooden-hulled warships. And, as the construction on other similar vessels went forward, the French launched the first armored warship, the *Gloire,* in November of 1859.[13]

The ironclad or armored warship posed a new and difficult problem for coastal defense planners. Since an ironclad warship was far less vulnerable to fire than its wooden-hulled predecessors, potentially it could duel with a shore battery with far more hope of success. Once stronger than the typical warship's hull, the masonry walls of seacoast forts were now relatively weaker. For American engineers and ordnance officers the way out of this dilemma lay in the development of new and more powerful guns which could overcome the protection of the warship's armor.

In the United States ordnance research in the mid-nineteenth century centered on finding a solution for a persistent problem with heavy seacoast guns—a tendency to burst due to flaws in the metal. Unlike field guns, which were often made of brass or bronze, large American ordnance was made from cast iron. The eight- and ten-inch Columbiads, for example, were cast-iron guns, and it was impossible to predict how many shots could be fired from such guns before internal stresses led to fracturing and bursting. A painful illustration of the problem occurred in 1844 when a twelve-inch wrought-iron gun constructed by Navy Captain Robert F. Stockton exploded aboard the U.S.S. *Princeton,* killing Secretary of State Abel P.Upshur and Secretary of the Navy Thomas W. Gilmer, as well as several navy officers and seamen. This accident in particular spurred both army and navy ordnance specialists to find a means of manufacturing large ordnance capable of firing without bursting.

The army's investigator was Captain Thomas Jefferson Rodman of the Ordnance Department, who began his study of the problem at the Fort Pitt Foundry in 1845. Very quickly Rodman concluded that in order to cast a gun strong enough to withstand the stresses of the internal powder explosion over a number of firings, "the metal needed to be thrown upon a strain, the exterior portions being under a strain of extension and the interior under one of compression."[14] The traditional method of casting a gun was to cast it solid in a mold, and then drill out the bore once it had cooled. Rodman observed that this procedure caused the cast iron to develop internal strains during the cooling period exactly the opposite of those he considered necessary. The solution, he decided, was to develop a means of cooling the cast iron from the interior by pumping water through a core pipe around which the gun was cast. Doing this, he predicted, would create within the cast iron the internal stress he wanted and allow the metal to develop its greatest strength.[15]

Rodman's superiors, George Talcott and George Bomford, were highly skeptical and the Ordnance Bureau denied Rodman any financial support for a trial system. Rodman then patented his theory and undertook to test it by private means. Trials of Rodman's process finally began in 1849 and continued during 1851, 1852, and 1856. Matched pairs of guns, each cast from the same metal but one cast and cooled in the traditional way and the other cast and cooled by Rodman's method, underwent test firings until they burst. Although in every case the Rodman-cooled gun exceeded the performance of the gun cooled by the traditional method, the Ordnance Bureau refused to consider the results as proving Rodman's case. In 1857 the bureau carried out a larger experiment, casting three guns, one by the traditional method at the West Point Foundry and a matched pair (as in previous trials) at the Fort Pitt Foundry. The results overwhelmingly favored the Rodman process. The West Point gun burst at the 169th fire, the traditionally cooled Fort Pitt gun at the 399th fire, and the Rodman-cooled gun at Fort Pitt endured 1,600 fires without bursting.[16] The superiority of the Rodman method was clear, and in November of 1859 Secretary of War John B. Floyd directed that all future heavy ordnance be cast by using this cooling method.[17]

Another, and very different, solution to the problem of bursting guns was that developed by naval researcher John A. Dahlgren. Already at work at the Washington Navy Yard, Dahlgren was nearly killed when an experimental thirty-two-pounder exploded in 1849. He immediately set out to improve the quality of heavy ships' ordnance.[18] Through a series of experiments, Dahlgren discovered that the pressure within the gun when fired was far greater at the breech. His solution, presented in the form of a design for a nine-inch gun, was to shift metal from the muzzle end of the gun and concentrate it around the breech. Such a gun would thus weigh no more than a gun of smaller caliber cast in the old way, but would be far stronger in the critical area and thus less likely to burst or explode. Because of the smooth swelling of the gun toward the breech, Dahlgren guns soon acquired the nickname "soda-bottles." Like Rodman, Dahlgren had to overcome internal opposition to his ideas, but during the late 1850s the navy began to arm its ships with the new guns which included an eleven-inch model as well as the original nine-inch design.[19]

Although the term "Rodman gun" really only described a gun manufactured by a new casting procedure, the Dahlgren gun was a new piece of ordnance which did not physically resemble the naval guns it replaced. The experiments of both Rodman and Dahlgren were alike, however, in making possible cannons far more powerful than those in use a scant ten years before. Like the Paixhans gun the Dahlgren was primarily a shell gun. The nine-inch fired a seventy-pound shell while the eleven-inch fired a massive 127-pound shell. Both models could fire solid shot as well, however, the nine-inch model firing a ninety-pound shot and the eleven-inch a huge 170-pound shot. The masonry walls of the engineers' coastal fortifications were not designed to withstand the blows of missiles this powerful.[20]

While the investigations of Rodman and Dahlgren led directly to major changes in American ordnance, they were not the only Americans attempting to solve the problems involved in constructing large-caliber cannon. In the United States two important investigators were Daniel Treadwell and Robert Parrott, whose research went in different directions but who both contributed a great deal to ordnance development. Beginning in 1845 Treadwell, a Harvard professor, argued that due to the pressure of the exploding gunpowder within a cast-iron cannon, the inner surface would

be strained beyond its elastic capacity while the strain on the outside portion was only one-ninth the load it could actually bear.
Furthermore, if a gun were constructed of a number of concentric
rings, the comparative resistance of the rings to the force of the
gunpowder explosion was the inverse of the square of the rings'
diameters. Hence, concluded Treadwell, it was impossible "to increase the strength of cast-iron cannon, in any useful degree, by an
increase of their thickness beyond that now given to them."[21] In
1855 Treadwell patented a gun with a thin cast-iron barrel sur-
rounded by wrought iron or steel hoops shrunk in layers. The process sought the same end result as that induced by Rodman's cooling method, and ultimately Treadwell's proposals became the basis
for a series of large cannon produced by the Armstrong firm in
England. But the U.S. War Department showed little interest, and
his ideas had little impact in the United States until after the Civil
War.[22]

The works of Robert P. Parrott, however, had great impact.
Both Rodman's and Dahlgren's guns were still smoothbores.
Parrott, on the other hand, was interested in rifled cannon. He
employed Rodman's casting method and developed a method of
shrinking a heated cast-iron band over the breech of the barrel,
thus strengthening that critical portion of the gun without adding a
prohibitive amount to the weight of the gun. He produced a ten-
pounder, his first model, in 1860. By the following year larger
twenty- and thirty-pounder calibers were available. By the summer
of 1862 Parrott guns existed in calibers up to a 300-pounder. This
last had a ten-inch bore and fired a projectile weighing 250 pounds.
The more common 200-pounder had an eight-inch bore and fired a
shell actually weighing 150 pounds, with a maximum range of
approximately 8,000 yards.[23]

The advent of the Parrott rifled gun marked a watershed in the
history of American ordnance development. The construction of a
fifteen-inch smoothbore Columbiad, cast using the Rodman cooling method (and thus often termed the Rodman gun) in 1861, and
the later experimental construction of a monster twenty-incher,
pushed smoothbore cast-iron ordnance to the limits of its potential.
The somewhat crudely constructed Parrott guns not only had
greater range than the smoothbore Rodman Columbiads but were
more accurate because of their rifling.[24] This gave the Parrott's

lighter shells as much effective power as the heavier shells and shot of the Columbiads and Dahlgrens, particularly at longer ranges.

Designed in accordance with the much less powerful ordnance of the early nineteenth century, the masonry casemated seacoast fortification was simply incapable of resisting for very long the impact of the huge shells fired by the new Rodman, Dahlgren, and Parrott guns. There was, in addition, no indication that the rapid change in size and power of ordnance would soon cease and every indication that such change would continue. Once ships were armed with powerful long-range rifled guns, the casemated fortification with its high, exposed masonry walls—even when it had the massive Rodman-type guns for its armament—was too vulnerable to remain the key element in the American system of coastal defense.

American engineers did not recognize this situation at first. Major John G. Barnard argued in 1861 that the principles underlying rifled artillery could not, in all likelihood, be applied to guns of large caliber. Rifled artillery was not, said Barnard, "a formidable projectile against iron-clad ships." In order to seriously damage a vessel, the "smashing" effect of a large projectile was necessary. "Range and accuracy," said Barnard, "are . . . of little value, unless the projectile possesses the necessary destructive qualities." Rifled guns, in his opinion, would "not prove to be the most effective for destroying masonry walls, nor do they possess any decided superiority over the solid-shot gun of but eight-inch caliber, when used against iron-plated vessels."[25]

Barnard recognized the importance of iron clad warships and pointed out that "hereafter it is not with ordinary fleets of wooden ships that sea-coast batteries will be called upon to contend."[26] But Barnard disagreed with those who believed that the coming of the ironclad doomed the masonry fortification. "Do the best you can to make your floating structure shot-proof," he rhetorically replied to such critics, "and they [still] cannot endure the protracted battering which they *must* endure if they would 'engage at breeching distance' a *properly-built* and properly-armed stone or earthern fort." In the contest for invulnerability between the fort and the ship, Barnard believed all the advantage lay with the former:

> Admitting, for the sake of argument . . . that there is any reason for believing that well-built masonry batteries may be

breached by guns in iron-clad vessels, [Barnard pointed out that] it is easy to turn the balance the other way by resorting to the same means for procuring invulnerability [that the iron-clad vessel employs], viz, *iron plates.*[27]

Even the newly designed British ironclad employing sloped armor plate and primitive turrets would not be able to stand the fire of the new American fifteen-inch Rodman gun. "The 15-inch shell," said Barnard, "would probably be effectual against the inclined-sided battery, and would be likely to convert Captain Coles' cupolas [the turrets] into *shooting-caps* indeed." The results of a joint British and French naval cannonade against the Russian fortress of Sebastopol during the Crimean War did nothing to alter Barnard's conviction, shared by the other American engineers, that the day of the casemated fortification was not yet over. Wrote Barnard, "*no single case* in which fleets have contended with masonry works have the results of their cannonade upon masonry walls been such as to indicate that the latter were not capable of sufficient endurance— that they were . . . so little damaged as to be, to all intents and purposes, intact."[28]

Even though the far-reaching developments in ordnance technology and the growing use of ironclad warships had not altered the engineers' view on the proper means and devices for coastal defense, only the widespread use of these new weapons in the Civil War would ultimately force the engineers to reevaluate their theories of coastal defense. As the Union forces sought to close or capture Confederate ports, and tighten the grip of the blockade, both the army and the navy had to grapple with the problems posed by those major fortifications seized by the Confederacy as well as the additional or repaired works established to protect Southern harbors and anchorages. In the light of the practical field experience gained in this effort, American seacoast defense planners, particularly the Corps of Engineers, drew a number of conclusions regarding the efficiency of the existing fortification system as well as the validity of the theories which underlay its design.

One important assumption very soon tested was the ability of a coastal fortification to interdict a ship channel simply by the fire of its guns. The lack of response to the argument advanced by General Edmund P. Gaines, in both 1829 and 1840, that steam-powered ships could easily pass through the fire of the forts on the Mississippi below New Orleans, suggests that few engineers took this possibility seriously before the Civil War. Events soon proved Gaines's prediction an accurate one. During the early morning of April 24, 1862, Union Commodore David G. Farragut took his fleet of seventeen ships up the river and past the Confederate Forts St. Philip and Jackson below New Orleans with little loss. Confederate gunboats sank one small vessel well above the forts and three vessels failed to make it past the forts before daylight. By noon on April 25 Farragut's ships were off the city of New Orleans. Cut off and threatened by attack from a land force, Fort Jackson's garrison mutinied. With the loyalty of Fort St. Philip's garrison now open to question, the Confederate commanders surrendered both forts on April 28.[29]

Confederate engineers had made an attempt to obstruct passage up the river by constructing a barrier of chained hulks. But this was at best only a hastily contrived defense, and the Federal navy had little trouble breaching it in the days before Farragut's attack. Some analysts might then suggest that the Union flotilla was able to pass the forts so easily because they were poorly armed. Certainly neither Fort Jackson nor Fort St. Philip contained anywhere near their theoretical armament. Fort St. Philip, in fact, had only thirteen guns and a few mortars. Yet, in comparison to the armaments available for American coastal forts in 1861, both forts were relatively well armed. Fort Jackson contained a total of sixty-seven guns, including three ten-inch Columbiads, five eight-inch Columbiads, a rifled seven-inch gun, and six forty-two-pounders. Fort St. Philip's thirteen guns consisted of six eight-inch Columbiads, six forty-two-pounders, and a rifled seven-inch gun. Farragut's flotilla escaped material damage not because the defending forts were poorly armed but because his ships were fast enough to steam past the forts before the defending gunners could load and fire more than a few times. That Farragut ran past the forts during the night was simply a sound tactical decision which could be expected of any commander attempting to get past a coastal battery.[30]

Farragut provided a further demonstration that a coastal fort would not interdict a channel when his fleet ran past the forts guarding Mobile, Alabama, on 5 August, 1864. In contrast to the

attack at New Orleans, at Mobile Farragut's fleet began its movement at dawn. Also Farragut now had four monitor-type ironclads
reinforcing his wooden-hulled steamers. The forts opened fire just
after seven o'clock and the leading Union ship, the *Hartford,*
passed Fort Morgan an hour later. Despite a heroic resistance by a
Confederate flotilla led by the ironclad *Tennessee,* the Union fleet
succeeded in taking command of Mobile Bay by mid-morning.[31]
Again, despite the volume of fire from the defending forts (primarily Fort Morgan, the nearer of the two) the Union fleet suffered
little damage. The only vessel lost was the monitor *Tecumseh* which
struck a torpedo and sank. Otherwise damage was restricted to
"rigging, and also several guns and gun-carriages . . . cut and
damaged by fragments of shell."[32] Although the Confederates
made an attempt to obstruct the channel with submarine torpedoes,
in order to facilitate the passage of blockade runners they left a
gap of some 500 yards in the line of obstructions. In any case, the
array of torpedoes was hastily emplaced and, aside from the sinking of the *Tecumseh,* failed to slow the Union fleet. As at New
Orleans, the naval guns did not silence the forts. But, those same
forts became essentially useless once the Union flotilla got past.
Quite clearly, the guns of a coastal fortification, even when the
channel was partially obstructed and it had the support of floating
defenses, could not prevent a strong fleet from getting by.

Two episodes early in the war further eroded the theoretical
foundation of the coast defense system by casting doubt on the
previously universally shared assumption that the shore battery was
superior to the ship, a belief shared by most naval officers and a
fundamental premise of all coastal defense theories. The first of
these episodes came in August 1862 when a five-vessel Union
flotilla attacked two small forts, Fort Clark and Fort Hatteras,
defending the entrance to Hatteras Inlet. Originally planned as a
joint army-navy venture, the army landing went awry, but the Confederates had abandoned Fort Clark anyway before the soldiers got
ashore. The following day the ships bombarded Fort Hatteras from
extreme range. With two guns dismounted and the magazine
threatened, the fort surrendered. The second episode was an attack
in November 1862 on Forts Beauregard and Walker which protected the entrance to Port Royal Sound. Like the attack on the
Hatteras forts this was nominally a joint army-navy venture. How-

ever, the army contingent lost its landing boats and its artillery in the wreck of a quartermaster ship. Reluctantly the naval commander, Captain Samuel F. DuPont, undertook to reduce the forts by naval fire alone. To reduce the effectiveness of the forts' return fire, the Union vessels, ten ships and five gunboats, steamed in a circular pattern. The ships began the attack at 8:30 A.M. and to DuPont's surprise Fort Walker surrendered at 11:30. Unable to fire more than three guns in reply, the garrison had fled to the mainland. The garrison of Fort Beauregard kept up a brief desultory fire, but because of the range involved the Union flotilla simply ignored this. Unable to prevent ships from passing into the sound, the garrison abandoned the post during the late afternoon. Although all the forts captured in both expeditions were small, badly built, and weakly armed, the successful outcome in both cases persuaded many observers that naval bombardment could, in fact, reduce shore batteries.[33]

Despite his success in Port Royal Sound, DuPont did not share this belief and only under great pressure did he make an attempt in April 1863 to reduce Fort Sumter by naval bombardment. In this case the engineers's traditional assumptions proved sound; the attack was a disaster. Even though all of the vessels were ironclads (all but two being monitor type) and kept moving in an attempt to throw off Confederate aim the U.S.S. *Keokuk* (not a monitor) sustained fatal damage, sinking the next morning. The U.S.S. *Ironsides* (also not a monitor) was hit ninety-three times. Of the seven monitor-type ironclads in the attack, DuPont later stated that only two were fit to renew the attack the next day. In return the vessels got off only 139 shots, forty of which struck Fort Sumter. Damage done to the fort was apparently minimal.[34]

To Admiral DuPont the experience confirmed his long-held belief that naval bombardment alone, even by ironclads, could not destroy coastal batteries. "The disparity between forts and vessels is well established," he told the Joint Committee on the Conduct of the War. "With the new ordnance, and certification modifications" DuPont remained confident that fortifications would "maintain their supremacy."[35] He did agree with Secretary of the Navy Gideon Welles that no ordinary vessels could have survived the fire brought to bear on the flotilla which attacked Fort Sumter. Indeed, despite the heavy and accurate Confederate fire, none of his ships (except the *Keokuk*) sustained serious damage. But, argued DuPont, mere survivability was not the whole issue. "Endurance," he said "must be accompanied [by] a corresponding power to inflict injury upon the enemy." Armed with the fifteen-inch Dahlgren the monitor-type ironclads had to come in very close to inflict any damage, and thereby exposed themselves to intense counterfire. Furthermore, according to DuPont, not only were the large-caliber guns slow to load, but a single turreted monitor-type vessel carried just two of them. This combination of factors prevented the ships from maintaining a rapid and continuous fire which DuPont considered essential when attacking coastal fortifications.[36]

In contrast to the conclusions drawn by DuPont and the other Federal naval officers, the Confederates responsible for the defense of Charleston recognized very quickly that Fort Sumter was indeed vulnerable to the fire of the ironclads. DuPont believed that only two shots had penetrated the masonry of the fort's wall, but an English observer of the attack, F. H. Thralston, indicated that the wall was struck several additional times. "The most severe blow," wrote Thralston, "was about three or four feet below the crest of the parapet, where two or three balls struck and loosened everything clear through for a space of about six feet in length." Since the Union vessels fired high in an attempt to silence Sumter's barbette-mounted guns, many shots were completely over the fort. But those that did hit the wall did so with great impact. "I think," concluded Thralston, "one thing has been proved—that brick forts can't stand 15-inch shot, etc., for a very long time." There was the clear possibility that the impact of the fifteen-inch shot near the base of the wall might well have reduced the entire scarp. The Confederates soon began removing guns and ammunition from the fort and by mid-August only thirty-eight guns remained.[37]

The failure of the naval attack forced the army to begin a land-based operation against Fort Sumter. Troops under the command of General Quincy A. Gillmore landed at the southern end of Morris Island in July. The failure of a sudden assault on Battery Wagner, located near the northern end of the island, forced Gillmore to begin siege operations against both it and Fort Sumter.

Gillmore had experience at this type of operation, since he had already led an expedition which took Fort Pulaski outside

Savannah, Georgia. There, in April 1862, Gillmore arranged twenty guns and sixteen mortars in eleven siege batteries. Ten of the guns were rifled pieces, five being thirty-pounder Parrott guns and the rest older rebored and rifled cannon. The range to the fort from all the guns was at least 1,600 yards, a range previously unheard of for any breaching attempt. These batteries opened fire just past 8:00 A.M. on April 10, 1862, and by early afternoon the beginning of a breach was already evident. During the next day's firing a breach appeared, opening an entire casemate. Within a few more hours the adjacent casemate was in a similar condition, and Gillmore ordered the batteries to direct their fire at the next embrasure. At 2:00 P.M. the garrison raised a white flag. In less than two days firing, Gillmore's batteries dismounted eleven of the fort's guns and opened a large breach. Return fire hit none of his guns and killed only one man. At the time the feat was without precedence:

> The circumstance reported Gillmore altogether new in the annals of sieges, that a practicable breach was made at that distance [a mean of 1,700 yards], in a wall 7½ feet thick, standing obliquely to the line of fire, and backed by heavy casemate piers and arches, cannot be ignored by a simple reference to the time-honored military maxims that "forts cannot sustain a vigorous land attack."[38]

Gillmore's calculations indicated that in terms of the weight of metal fired, "the breaching of Port Pulaski at 1,700 yards required less than the breaches made in Spain [during the Napoleonic Wars] with smooth-bores exclusively, at 500 yards." Gillmore recognized in particular the power of his rifled guns. "With heavy James or Parrott guns," he told General Totten, "the practicality of breaching the best constructed brick scarp, at 2,300 to 2,500 yards with satisfactory rapidity, admits of very little doubt."[39]

Now, on Morris Island, Gillmore prepared to make an even more dramatic demonstration of the power of the new heavy-rifled guns. During August, as the siege of Battery Wagner went forward, Gillmore built seven batteries directed at Fort Sumter. By the middle of the month he had a total of seventeen guns in position, all being rifled pieces and all but two being Parrott guns. By the standards of the time the ranges from these batteries to Fort Sumter were incredible. The closest breaching battery was over 3,400 yards away, the farthest nearly 4,300 yards, and the average range was nearly 4,000 yards. Undaunted, Gillmore opened fire on August 17. Although snipers in Battery Wagner and a heavy storm interfered with his gunners, they maintained a steady barrage until the evening of the twenty-third. By then, in Gillmore's words, "The fort was reduced to the condition of a mere infantry outpost . . . incapable of annoying our approaches to [Battery] Wagner, or of inflicting injury upon the iron-clads."[40] Rumors that the Confederates were attempting to remount guns in the ruins of the wall breached by Gillmore's batteries led to a resumption of the bombardment in October which completely destroyed the southeast face of the fort.[41] Since Fort Sumter stood on an artificial island in the middle of the harbor, Gillmore could not occupy the ruins, and the Confederates regarrisoned the rubble. Nevertheless, his week-long August shelling literally destroyed Fort Sumter. The message was clear to Gillmore, who reported,

> Our masonry scarps will have to withstand the shocks of the heaviest projectiles from batteries afloat. Can they do this without the protection of iron armor? If not, then the many-storied castle, of which the entire wall is exposed to the concentrated fire of an enemy's fleet, possesses an inherent and fatal element of weakness inasmuch as it accumulates many guns in a small place with inadequate means of protection.[42]

Technological change not only ended reliance on stone or brick fortifications, it also produced other coastal defense devices previously considered either unreliable or unfeasible. Chief among these was the electrically fired torpedo, pioneered by Fulton and Colt. Under the able direction of Matthew Fontaine Maury, an ex-United States navy officer formerly stationed at the Washington Naval Observatory, the Confederacy began experimenting with such devices early in the war. Undeterred by some initial failures, proponents of the new weapon saw their hopes realized in December 1862 when the Union gunboat *Cairo* sank in the Yazoo River after hitting two torpedoes. This first success encouraged the Confederacy to utilize the devices on a larger scale, and various versions soon appeared as a part of the defenses at the South's important ports. Other successes and near successes followed, including the sinking of the Northern ironclad *Tecumseh* during Farragut's attack on Mobile and several near misses on Union vessels at Charleston.[43]

The devices did not always function as planned, of course. English blockade-runner F. H. Thralston mentioned being told by Langdon Cheves (who had charge of the torpedo defenses) that during DuPont's attack on Fort Sumter the Federal vessel *New Ironsides* had been directly over a torpedo. "But," wrote Thralston, "the confounded thing, as is usually with them, would not go off when it was wanted."[44] Even so, the existence of the devices, and the lack of effective countermeasures, at least partially dictated the movements of the Union ships during attacks on the Charleston defenses. Confronted now by a previously scorned but deadly device, naval officers reluctantly admitted that torpedoes were an effective and useful weapon. "The secrecy, rapidity of movement, control of direction, and precise explosion," reported DuPont's successor Admiral John A. Dahlgren, "indicate, I think, the introduction of the torpedo element as a means of certain warfare. It can be ignored no longer."[45]

Likewise, postwar coastal defense planners could not ignore other devices developed by the Confederacy, such as the small, nearly submerged torpedo ram called *David*. Using a spar-torpedo, an explosive device at the end of a long boom or spar which the vessel could attach to the hull of an enemy ship (much like Fulton's proposed harpoon gun arrangement of a half-century before), the prototype *David* attacked the *New Ironsides* outside Charleston in October of 1863. The attack put the *New Ironsides* out of commission for a year.[46] Somewhat similar was the world's first combat submarine, the *C.S.S. Hunley* which sank the Union blockader *Housatonic,* also outside Charleston. Federal naval officers did not at first recognize that the *Hunley* was anything more than another David-type torpedo ram, but they recognized the effectiveness of the type. During the Civil War, Confederate underwater devices damaged fourteen Union navy vessels and sank twenty-nine. This was undisputed proof that such devices worked and their successful development added an entirely new dimension to coastal defense planning.

Thus, by the end of the war the familiar means and methods of coastal defense were demonstrably altered by new types of ordnance, new types of ships, and altogether new types of weapons previously scorned as mere gadgets. All these changes posed problems for postwar coastal defense planners. While it was clear that the masonry casemated fortification could no longer serve as the nation's most important agent of coastal defense, there was little indication of how completely the traditional theories and assumptions of coastal defense might have to be revised. Having invested nearly a half-century in the development of the existing coastal defense system, American military planners and theorists were ill-equipped to institute immediately a fundamental change in that system or to propose a new one. They needed time to adjust and experiment before moving on into a future where past experience might no longer be a sure guide.

NOTES

1. Frederick L. Robertson, *The Evolution of Naval Armament* (London: Constable and Co., Ltd., 1921), p. 48.

2. The origins of the name Columbiad, as well as the gun's development are discussed in Emanuel R. Lewis, "The Ambiguous Columbiads," *Military Affairs,* vol. 28, no. 3 (Fall 1964), pp. 111-122.

3. William E. Birkhimer, *Historical Sketch of the Organization, Administration, Materiel and Tactics of the Artillery, United States Army* (Washington, D.C.: Chapman, 1884), pp. 280-281.

4. Birkhimer, *Historical Sketch,* p. 283; Lewis, "Ambiguous Columbiads," pp. 116-117.

5. John Gibbon, *The Artillerist's Manual* (New York: D. Van Nostrand, 1860), Appendix.

6. Henri-Joseph Paixhans, *Nouvelle Force Maritime* (Paris, 1822), vol. 7, trans. and excerpted in "New Maritime Artillery," *American Quarterly Review,* vol. 4, no. 8 (December 1828), p. 483. Paixhans's ideas are also discussed in James Phinney Baxter, *The Introduction of the Ironclad Warship* (Cambridge: Harvard University Press, 1933), pp. 17-32; and Robertson, *Naval Armament,* pp. 166-176.

7. Paixhans's gun was an eighty-pounder weighing about 8,000 pounds and with a bore diameter of 8.7 inches (22 cm.). Bomford's 1811 Columbiad was a fifty-pounder, weighing around 6,300 pounds and with a bore of 7.25 inches. While the Paixhans gun is larger, the general configuration of the two guns is nearly identical. For a line drawing of the Paixhans gun see Robertson, *Naval Armament,* p. 173; and for a photo-

graph of fifty-pounder Columbiad see Warren Ripley, *Artillery and Ammunition of the Civil War* (New York: Van Nostrand Reinhold Co., 1970), p. 71. At least some American artillerymen believed that Paixhans had gotten his ideas from Bomford's original design. See Lewis, "Ambiguous Columbiads," p. 117.

8. Robertson, *Naval Armament*, p. 172.

9. Ibid., pp. 172-173; Baxter, *Ironclad Warship*, p. 26.

10. Board of Engineers, "Report on the Defence of the Atlantic Frontier, From the Passamaquoddy to the Sabine," April 23, 1840, Senate Document 451, 26th Congress, 1st session, Serial 360, pp. 28-29. As indicated in ch. 1, this report was apparently written largely by Joseph G. Totten.

11. Ibid., p. 29.

12. Baxter, *Ironclad Warship*, p. 24; Robertson, *Naval Armament*, pp. 248-251.

13. Baxter, *Ironclad Warship*, pp. 72-76, 92, 109.

14. Thomas J. Rodman to General J. W. Ripley, April 11, 1862, *A Collection of Ordnance Reports and Other Important Papers Relating to the Ordnance Department,* vol. 3, 1860-1889 (Washington, D.C.: Government Printing Office, 1890), pp. 229-30.

15. Ibid.

16. Ibid., pp. 231-233. Rodman published a compilation of his experiments in 1861. See Captain Thomas J. Rodman, *Reports of Experiments on The Properties of Metals For Cannon and the Qualities of Cannon Powder; With an Account of the Fabrication and Trial of a 15-Inch Gun* (Boston: Charles H. Crosby, 1861). A contemporary account of Rodman's experiments is Major John G. Barnard, "The Fifteen-Inch Gun," *Notes On Sea-Coast Defence* (New York: D. Van Nostrand, 1861), pp. 33-37. Recent secondary accounts which discuss Rodman include Emanuel R. Lewis, *Seacoast Fortifications of the United States* (Washington, D.C.: Smithsonian Institution Press, 1970), pp. 59-61; and Frank E. Camparato, *The Age of Great Guns* (Harrisburg, Pa.: Stackpole, 1965), pp. 181-182.

17. H. K. Craig, Chief of Ordnance, to Secretary of War John B. Floyd, November 25, 1859, *Annual Reports and Other Important Papers Relating to the Ordnance Department,* vol. 2, 1845-1860 (Washington, D.C.: Government Printing Office, 1880), pp. 678-679.

18. Taylor Peck, *Roundshot to Rockets: A History of the Washington Navy Yard and U.S. Naval Gun Factory* (Annapolis: U.S. Naval Institute Press, 1949), p. 106; Camparato, *Age of Great Guns,* pp. 143-144.

19. Peck, *Roundshot to Rockets,* pp. 107-110; Ripley, *Artillery and Ammunition of the Civil War,* pp. 90-93. Ripley suggests that one major

reason for the navy's hesitation in adopting the Dahlgren gun was the gun's great weight. The eleven-inch gun weighed some 15,700 pounds, which some naval officers saw as too heavy for shipboard ordnance.

20. Ripley, *Artillery and Ammunition of the Civil War*, p. 97.

21. Daniel Treadwell, *On the Practicability of Constructing Cannon of Great Caliber Capable of Enduring Long-Continued Use Under Full Charges* (Cambridge, Mass.: Metcalf and Co., 1856), p. 18.

22. Camparato, *Age of Great Guns*, pp. 197-198.

23. Robert P. Parrott, *Ranges of Parrott Guns and Notes For Practice* (New York: D. Van Nostrand, 1863), pp. 3-5, 7; Ripley, *Artillery and Ammunition of the Civil War*, pp. 110, 371; Camparato, *Age of Great Guns*, pp. 144, 182. Eight-thousand yards was, of course, extreme range and could be attained only using a light shell (eighty pounds) at maximum elevation (30°-35°). Using a 100-pound shell, and firing at an elevation of about 25°, the range was in the neighborhood of 6,000-7,000 yards. This was still in sharp contrast to the range of smoothbore guns.

24. Albert Mauncy, *Artillery Through the Ages*, National Park Service Interpretive Services, History no. 3 (Washington, D.C.: Government Printing Office, 1949), p. 161, suggests that at 2,000 yards the "striking velocity of a smoothbore's shot was only a third of its muzzle velocity while the more streamlined rifle projectile lost its velocity more slowly." The initial muzzle velocity of rifled and smoothbore shells was about the same at this time. [John G. Barnard reported an initial velocity of 1,328 FPS for the shell of the fifteen-inch Rodman gun, while Parrott's 100-pounder had a velocity of 1,250 FPS. But, tests during the 1880s indicated that at 1,000 yards a rifled gun converted from a ten-inch smoothbore, hit with twice the power of the original gun. See Rogers Birnie, Jr., *Gun Making in the United States* (Washington, D.C.: Government Printing Office, 1907), pp. 17-18, 33. Birnie's Treatise originally appeared in the *Journal of the Military Service Institution* in 1888.]

25. John G. Barnard, *Notes on Sea-Coast Defence*, pp. 42-45, 57.

26. Ibid., p. 48.

27. Ibid., p. 59n.

28. Ibid., pp. 690-95. The conclusions drawn by American officers who observed the Crimean War were much the same as those expressed by Barnard. See Richard Delafield, *Report on the Art of the War in Europe In 1854, 1855, and 1856* (Washington, D.C.: George W. Bowman, 1861), pp. 25-26, 38, 53.

29. A good, brief history of naval operations in the Civil War is Howard P. Nash, Jr., *A Naval History of the Civil War* (New York: A. S. Barnes and Co., 1972). For the story of Farragut's attack on New Orleans see

pages 126-140. For the earlier views of Gaines on the ability of a steam fleet to pass the forts of the lower Mississippi see *ASP, MA,* vol. 4 (Serial 019), Document 407, p. 105.

30. Nash, *Naval History of the Civil War,* p. 132.

31. Nash, *Naval History of the Civil War,* pp. 247-255; Viktor E. K. R. von Scheliha, *A Treatise on Coast-Defence* (London: E. and F. N. Spon, 1868), reprint edition (Westport, Conn.: Greenwood Press, 1971), pp. 108-114. Although a Prussian, von Scheliha served as the Confederacy's Chief Engineer in the Department of the Gulf. Fort Gaines capitulated on August 6. Fort Morgan held out until August 23, by which time it was a ruin.

32. von Scheliha, *Treatise on Coast-Defence,* p. 122.

33. Rowena Reed, *Combined Operations in the Civil War* (Annapolis: U.S. Naval Institute Press, 1978), pp. 11-15, 23-31.

34. "Letter From the Secretary of the Navy in Answer to Resolutions of the House and Senate in Relation to the Operations of Armored Vessels Employed in the Service of the United States" (Armored Vessels in the Attack on Charleston), *Executive Document 69,* 38th Congress, 1st session, Serial 1193, pp. 53, 55-60 (hereafter cited as "Armored Vessels"); Reed, *Combined Operations,* pp. 293-294.

35. "Report of the Joint Committee on the Conduct of the War: Heavy Ordnance," Senate Committee Report no. 142, 38th Congress, 2d session, Serial 1213, p. 96 (hereafter cited as "Heavy Ordnance").

36. "Heavy Ordnance," pp. 92, 95-96; "Armored Vessels," pp. 76, 80-81, 101-102.

37. "Heavy Ordnance," pp. 94-95; "Armored Vessels," p. 85; Reed, *Combined Operations,* p. 294; Frank Barnes, *Fort Sumter,* National Park Service Historical Handbook Series, no. 12 (Washington, D.C.: Government Printing Office, 1952, revised edition, 1962), p. 27.

38. Quincy A. Gillmore, *Official Report to the United States Engineer Department of the Siege and Reduction of Fort Pulaski, Georgia, February, March, and April, 1862,* Papers on Practical Engineering, no. 8 (New York: D. Van Nostrand, 1862), pp. 24, 32-36, 41.

39. Ibid., pp. 49, 51.

40. Quincy A. Gillmore, *Engineer and Artillery Operations Against the Defences of Charleston Harbor in 1863,* Professional Papers, The Corps of Engineers, no. 16 (New York: D. Van Nostrand, 1868), pp. 57-63.

41. Ibid., p. 79.

42. Ibid., p. 122.

43. Alex Roland, *Underwater Warfare in the Age of Sail* (Bloomington: University of Indiana Press, 1978), pp. 150-153, 160.

44. "Armored Vessels," p. 85.

45. Admiral John A. Dahlgren to Assistant Secretary of the Navy Gustavus Fox, cited in Roland, *Underwater Warfare,* pp. 162-163.

46. Roland, *Underwater Warfare,* p. 162.

FIVE
A System In Flux

The end of the Civil War also marked the end of the coastal defense system planned, constructed, and defended by the Board of Engineers following the War of 1812. To most men concerned with the problem of coastal defense, the need for a new system taking into account new and more powerful weapons was clear. Yet not having foreseen the sudden demise of the prewar system, coastal defense planners had no alternative system ready to propose. Caught by rapid and continuing technological change, these planners struggled to assess the impact of the new weaponry this change produced and analyze the effect such weapons would have on the traditional theories and means of coastal defense. For coastal defense planners, particularly the Corps of Engineers, the next twenty years would be a period of study and experimentation as they sought to establish a new system of coastal defense.

The single most obvious lesson of the Civil War was that the casemated masonry fortification was no longer a suitable form for a seacoast fortification. This was clear even before the war ended. A board of engineers appointed in January of 1864 recommended the replacement of masonry parapets by earthen ones, particularly in places where land batteries could be employed against them.[1] Since this board did not have time to prepare any detailed plans for this change before its members returned to field duty, Secretary of War Edwin M. Stanton authorized the formation of another board in September 1866. Almost immediately this board, which included a number of distinguished engineer officers, echoed its predecessor by stating that the Totten-designed casemates and embrasures of the prewar era could not resist modern artillery. Arguing the necessity of further testing in order to develop a new casemate design, the board recommended that there should be "no further construction" of the former types.[2]

Other analysts reinforced this conclusion. One of these was Viktor E. K. R. von Scheliha, a Prussian who served the Confederacy as Chief Engineer in the Department of the Gulf and published a treatise on coastal defense in 1868. "Exposed masonry," he stated bluntly, "is incapable of withstanding the fire of modern artillery." In his view the rapid destruction of Forts Pulaski and Sumter, as well as the subjugation of Forts Jackson, St. Philip, and Morgan established this point beyond dispute. "The progress made in naval architecture and in artillery since 1861," argued von Scheliha, "has necessitated a thorough change of the principles . . . and methods employed heretofore in coast defense."[3]

Admiral David D. Porter shared these views. Although a sailor and not an engineer, Porter believed his experience in attacking Confederate coastal positions gave him the qualifications to discuss the subject. And if he had ever believed in the principles of shore defense as expounded by the engineers before the war, he no longer did. It was a common maxim, remembered Porter, "that one gun on shore [is] equal to ten on board ship." Yet, he argued, while this "may be true so far as regards ten guns in a vessel and one gun in a fort . . . the rule gives way when a very large number of guns are brought to bear on the fort." In Porter's opinion, "we have no forts on our part of the continent which can stand the concentrated fire of heavy ships, Monitors and Ironsides combined."[4]

Naturally, some engineers were reluctant to admit that the old system of defenses was obsolete. Brevet Lieutenant-Colonel William P. Craighill (a future Chief of Engineers) argued in 1868 that, in fact, the events of the Civil War proved that "guns afloat cannot contend successfully with guns ashore, even if the former are carried by ships thickly clad with iron, and the latter, not of the heaviest caliber known to our service, are mounted in the casemates of what we are accustomed to hear called an old-fashioned masonry fort." Craighill examined in detail the unsuccessful Union attack on Fort Sumter launched by Admiral DuPont in 1863. In this attack, he argued, monitor-type ironclads (the best type of vessel for an assault upon a coastal battery) absorbed extensive damage while inflicting little injury on the fort. Discounting Confederate obstructions in the channel (which Craighill believed, in contrast to many other analysts, had not hindered the movements of the Union flotilla), the encounter became "strictly a contest between *guns,* afloat and ashore." Under these conditions, said Craighill, results of the engagement proved that if ironclad vessels were kept

> under *a very heavy fire at close range for a short time,* . . . [or] if we can so line the channel with batteries of the heaviest guns, *that the iron-clads will be under fire a sufficient time to be ruined,* . . . *that time need not be long.* If they stop to fight they are lost. If they move on . . . being still exposed to a constant fire they are equally lost.

Craighill was primarily interested in asserting the continued supremacy of the shore gun over the shipboard gun (a premise disparaged by those who shared the views of Admiral Porter), and he did not insist that the casemated fortification was the only worthwhile type of shore battery. But, said Craighill, it was "erroneous" to believe that such forts were now useless.[5]

To some extent Craighill misdirected his counterargument. Even though numerous analysts and the Board of Engineers now believed that "like wooden navies [the masonry fortifications had] outlived their usefulness," no one suggested that the need for coastal batteries was at an end.[6] Von Scheliha explicitly included fortifications as one of the key factors in successful local defense and Admiral Porter suggested (in words similar to those of Craighill), "The value of fortifications on land is not in the least diminished. . . . Their importance is greater than ever."[7] What both Porter and von Scheliha did emphasize, in contrast to Craighill, was that to be useful fortifications had to be properly designed, and more important, forts could not be relied on as the sole agents of coastal defense. According to von Scheliha, a "perfect" system of coastal defense depended upon "fortifications, that will withstand the fire of modern artillery" working in conjunction with obstructions (such as submarine mines) and active operations by both the army and the navy.[8] In a similar fashion

Porter stated that forts "could be built that cannot only resist, but can destroy" attacking ships. But, without "obstructions in the channel," no fort could prevent a fleet from passing by and escaping from the fire of the battery.[9] "The sinking of a vessel by artillery-fire alone," argued von Scheliha, "is a more difficult thing than is commonly supposed . . . and is usually the result of a fortunate chance, which has directed the shot to some vital spot." He calculated that the heavy-guns shore battery could be loaded, aimed, and fired in four minutes. Additional calculations indicated that a steam warship could run the gauntlet of effective fire in just twelve minutes. Thus, said von Scheliha, a shore battery needed 100 guns to hit each vessel of a twenty-ship flotilla twenty times. Yet, this was the punishment absorbed by Farragut's flagship at Mobile and neither it nor any other vessel sustained serious damage. Clearly, "artillery fire alone will never again prevent a steam-fleet from forcing a passage, the channel of which has not been obstructed."[10] For analysts of the changes in the means of coastal defense necessitated by the advent of new weaponry, the key issues involved both the development of a new design for coastal fortifications and the simultaneous development of auxiliary systems, particularly obstructions but also submarine torpedoes, floating batteries, torpedo boats (like the Confederate "Davids"), and searchlights.

The analysts who argued that the masonry casemated fort was now obsolete also suggested potential alternatives. In concurrence with the recommendations of the engineers' 1864 report, most argued in favor of well-constructed earthen batteries since, as the engineers said in 1868, "earth is the cheapest and best of all materials to stop shot."[11] On the other hand, most batteries built with earth or sand protection contained guns mounted *en barbette*, and such batteries offered little protection to the gun crews. Any rapid and concentrated fire from attacking ships (as analysts noted it did during the war) would drive the crews from the guns and silence the fort. It was, stated von Scheliha, "not only necessary to avoid, in the construction of [a] battery, all material not able to withstand the effect of heavy artillery fire . . . it is also absolutely necessary to give the guns and gun-detachments a more efficient protection than is afforded them by mounting the guns en barbette." To do this, von Scheliha suggested the use of iron-plated casemates or revolving turrets, protected by a sand or earth parapet. The armor on either casemate or the turret, he said, had to be at least twenty inches thick and angled or sloped so that enemy shot would ricochet rather than strike a flat surface.[12] Instead of masonry fortifications, Admiral Porter urged the use of monitor-type turrets, believing that "this is the only method to build a fort that will resist successfully ships and assaults."[13]

The idea of using armor plate to protect coastal defenses was not new. General Totten suggested the possibility during the 1850s, and in Europe engineers were already beginning to employ armor in their fortifications. A leader in this movement was the Belgian engineer, General Henri Brialmont, who mounted the guns of his forts in rotating cupolas or turrets (even though the forts themselves were typically akin to conventional bastion works). French engineers also followed this pattern. The masonry walls of their forts had the protection of eighteen feet of earth (or more) and by the end of the century the only visible features of French forts were the partially submerged domes of the turrets.[14]

In the United States, one of the primary functions of the engineer board appointed by Stanton in 1866 was the investigation of the viability of using iron plate in the construction of permanent fortifications. In contrast to the direction taken by the Europeans, this 1866 board very quickly concluded that the use of iron turrets (including one proposed by a man named Ryan designed to mount eight of the fifteen-inch Rodman guns) was the least economical means of constructing adequate coastal batteries.[15] Furthermore, said the board, it was unlikely that attempting to protect the entire scarp of a masonry fort by iron plate would be effective. In test firings the iron plate examined by the American engineers broke quickly under the impact of heavy shells. In addition, the use of iron armor in this fashion would be very expensive and since the then available iron-plate armor might (and probably would) become outdated very quickly, any forts shielded by it would soon be "unfit to resist the means of attack of a future year." The board concluded, "It has been hitherto assumed rather than demonstrated that iron is the true substitute for masonry. A resort to it may be compulsory in some cases, but it will not do to embark upon extensive construction in that material upon [an] assumption."[16] Instead of recommending the use of armor plate, the board went on in 1869 to outline an entirely new system of coastal defenses, one which broke in numerous ways with past practice and established the basis for an entirely new line of development in American coastal defense design.

In fortification construction the board recommended the use of inexpensive ("cheaply constructed") barbette batteries with wooden gun platforms. Recognizing the flaws in the barbette design, the board proposed the substitution of a depression or dis-appearing gun carriage for the standard barbette carriage. Such a carriage would bring the gun down below the level of the parapet for leading and thus provide protection for the gun crew. But the board did not stop with this. In addition, it recommended the use of mortars as a part of seacoast armament. It was, admitted the board, difficult to hit a moving target with the high-angle fire of mortars but it argued that such weapons could prove very valuable (particularly when used in large numbers) in defending anchorages. The board was very much aware that the decks of an ironclad were less armored than the hull sides and thus more vulnerable. Going beyond this, the board echoed the conclusions drawn by von Scheliha and Porter, and emphasized the need for a comprehensive system of channel obstructions, a system of "defense by tor-pedoes," and broke even more with tradition by calling for the con-struction of specially designed floating batteries and harbor defense vessels.[17]

Many of these recommendations ran counter to the statements and conclusions expressed by nearly all of the prewar engineer reports on the system of coastal defenses, a fact which the board report of 1869 acknowledged. However, as the board's report argued in regard to the use of floating batteries, the situation was now different. The long-ignored torpedoes had proved a potent weapon during the Civil War and the 1869 board report viewed them as less expensive than any other means of harbor defense, while simultaneously being perhaps "as formidable an opponent to a hostile fleet as even [a] battery itself." Similarly the board willingly admitted that past reports on the efficiency of harbor defense vessels had typically found them useful only in rare cases. But "all now admit," said the board, "that a well devised armored 'floating battery,' combining the powers of the battery and the 'ram' may be a very valuable accessory," particularly useful in combating those enemy vessels which successfully ran past the fire of a coastal battery. Since the board clearly agreed with von Scheliha that "no fleet can force a passage if kept under the fire of heavy guns" if kept there by "properly constructed obstructions," the coastal battery remained the cornerstone of this new system of defenses. Now, however, these batteries would no longer look like the familiar enclosed fortifications of the antebellum years. These batteries would also theoretically operate in concert with numerous ancillary and auxiliary devices slighted or ignored in the past. Not only did Chief Engineer A. A. Humphreys find these recommendations "sound and prudent," but they also garnered the approval of both General William T. Sherman and Secretary of War William Belknap. The country had the beginnings of an entirely new coastal defense system.[18]

Yet, as important a step as the system proposed in 1869 was, in many respects it was ahead of its time. Many of the devices included as a part of the system either did not exist or were only in the testing stage of development. There was, for example, no disappearing gun carriage in service, even though designs for them existed. Any batteries built would require modifications once the engineers found a suitable carriage, modifications which carried an inestimable price tag. Furthermore, no systems of either torpedo defense or obstructions existed. Both areas needed further study and experimentation before any such devices would see actual service. By implication, then, the study represented little more than a stopgap until future developments allowed the creation of a complete system. "The inadequacy of methods of construction hitherto used is fully proved," said the board. Yet, it immediately and candidly admitted that no substitute for those methods was clearly indicated.[19] Amid a welter of continuing, and sometimes conflicting, changes in ordnance it was difficult to suggest a system which would still be adequate when more powerful guns appeared. As things stood, the engineers could not actually implement the system they proposed.

In these circumstances it is not surprising that Congress gave this proposed system only a lukewarm reception. Congressmen of the late 1860s and early 1870s were as unlikely as those of preceding decades to enthusiastically appropriate money for coastal fortifications and other defensive devices, especially when the possibility existed that those devices could become obsolete overnight. In the House of Representatives during the late 1860s, opponents of the coastal fortifications managed either to defeat or to reduce the appropriations. At one point this was done by an amendment to the appropriation bill which prevented the Corps of Engineers from spending more than half the appropriation.[20] This kind of Congressional hesitancy continued into the 1870s. Opponents of the fortification appropriation contended that the expenditure of money on them was "wasteful" and such fortifications would prove useless during any future war. In 1871 John F. Farnsworth of Illinois declared in regard to fortifications, "These defenses are no defense."[21] Supporters of the fortifications, like William Niblack of Indiana, suggested that it was "true economy to expend a little more money so as to adapt our present fortifications" to the kind of ordnance becoming available. Niblack also pointed out that in 1870 and 1871 the Appropriations Committee simply and automatically cut the estimates submitted by the Chief of Engineers in half. Niblack, however, had little support. Regardless of party or region, a majority of Congressmen apparently were unwilling to expend large sums for coastal defenses. Even those who saw a need for fortifications (and other defensive devices, such as torpedoes, which the fortification appropriation included) sought the smallest possible sum that would suffice.[22] To a great extent this was because even supporters of the fortification system were well aware that continued change in ordnance and ironclad design tended to justify critics' charges that the system was likely to prove useless in the future. Although usually willing to advance money for military projects the House Committee on Military Affairs concluded in 1874 that to complete and arm the nation's fortifications "would cost a very large amount, much greater than the Government is now ready to expend." Rapid change in weapons technology had "unsettled the problem of sea-coast defense, and induced the belief that heavy expenditures at present, while the construction of guns, ironclads, and works of defense are in a transition state, are not advisable."[23] Initially that year, the engineers requested $3,601,000. Confronted with the parsimonious mood of Congress the corps reduced this to $1,407,000 and the Appropriations Committee cut this reduced estimate even further, to $994,000, or about 2 percent of the military budget.[24] The boom fell all the way in 1876. Reasoning that improvements in guns and projectiles made continued spending on construction "wasteful," and suggesting that reliance ought to be on torpedoes and ironclad defense vessels, the House Appropriations Committee slashed the engineers' request for $3,500,000 to the comparatively paltry sum of $315,000, of which only $100,000 was earmarked for fortification "repair" and the rest for experiments in torpedoes and ordnance. The total amount was less than 1 percent of military spending and, as an indication of the degree of support this action had in Congress, the bill passed the House with no debate.[25] Significantly, in the Forty-fourth Congress the Democrats controlled the House of Representatives for the first time since 1859. Not only was the Democratic Party the traditional foe of large military budgets (at least rhetorically), but the use of the army in the South during the election of 1876 angered House Democrats who now had even more reason to reduce military expenditures and thereby strike back at the army. Congress did not single out fortifications; spending cuts were across the board. With the Democrats in control of the House for the rest of the decade it is not surprising that Congress continued to provide only token amounts for coastal defenses. Construction, already nearly at a standstill, stopped completely for lack of funds, and the system of defenses proposed in 1869 remained largely on paper.[26]

At the same time, however, Congressional concern over the possibility that the batteries of any new coastal defense system might soon be rendered obsolete by continued advance in weaponry was well founded. Improvements in the design and performance of both ordnance and armor plate continued at a rapid pace throughout the last thirty-five years of the nineteenth century (and indeed beyond). For a long time, however, these changes did not alter the composition of American coastal armament. In 1865 the most powerful gun available for use in coastal batteries was the fifteen-inch Rodman smoothbore (see Fig. 3), designed just before the beginning of the Civil War. Although already surpassed in range and power, the engineers defended the continued use of the fifteen-inch gun on the basis that its shot did more damage to ships' armor than did the shells of rifled artillery. In contrast to the rifled projectiles, which "punched" a hole in armor, the heavy shot of the big smoothbore gun "racked" a ship's armor, causing joints to split and bolts to break. As engineer John G. Barnard stated in

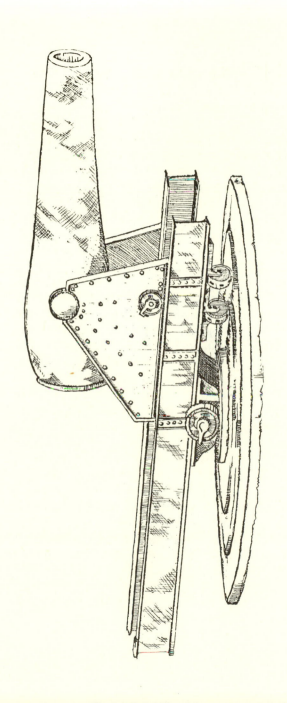

1861, advocates of the racking approach sought "to stave in the whole side" of a ship. Doing this required shot "of large diameter moving at moderate velocity," a combination of factors provided by the fifteen-inch Rodman.[27] As long as the shot of this gun could damage a ship's armor, "racking" was feasible. During British tests at Shoeburyness in the late 1860s, a fifteen-inch gun charged with 100 pounds of powder drove its 450-pound shot clear through a target consisting of eight inches of armor plate backed by eighteen inches of teak as well as the target backing and four sets of timber frame, actually pushing nearly a ton of wood and metal along the ground. However, the accepted powder charge for the gun was actually only sixty pounds, and while with such charges the gun might penetrate armor at 100 yards it would not do so at longer ranges. The British reported that when firing steel shot, the gun could penetrate the armor of the Royal Navy's newest ships at seventy yards and that of its earliest class of ironclad ships at 700 or 800 yards. Using American cast-iron shot, however, the gun could not (using the standard sixty-pound powder charge) penetrate the armor of the newest ships at any range.[28] Quite clearly, effective racking fire could only be carried out at a relatively short range, especially since the relatively weak and crude armor of the early 1860s was already viewed as outmoded and a search under way for newer and stronger armor.[29] In addition, the greater range of rifled guns suggested that a fleet armed with them could bombard American defenses while remaining outside the range of the defending guns.[30] For these reasons, in 1867 American ordnance officers recommended the purchase of equal numbers of rifled guns and smoothbores, a step which ended at least theoretically both the total dominance of the big smoothbore gun as a coastal defense armament and the racking approach associated with that gun.[31]

In practice, however, the fifteen-inch smoothbore gun continued as the predominant type in service because there was simply no satisfactory rifled gun available to supplement or supplant it. The chief problem was a difficulty in finding a suitable gun metal for heavy-rifled artillery. Cast iron was the metal generally used for American heavy ordnance, and the Civil War Parrott guns were of this metal. Although the Parrott guns performed adequately during the war, they also burst with disconcerting frequency. Twenty-four burst during Gillmore's siege of Fort Sumter, and as early as

February 1865, the Canadian-born inventor and ordnance designer Norman Wiard blamed the inability of the Union forces to capture Charleston on the "disastrous failure" of the Parrott guns.[32] Even though Parrott defended his guns by suggesting that they burst from premature detonation of the shell caused either by friction against the bore within the gun or from sand in the muzzles, tests conducted by the Ordnance Department suggested that the fault lay in the cast iron used in their construction. The Chief of Ordnance concluded in 1871, "We must try some other material for heavy guns."[33]

European ordnance manufacturers were already ahead of the Americans in the struggle to find a metal suitable for heavy-rifled guns. Instead of cast iron, both Britain and France used the "built-up" method developed during the 1850s by William Armstrong. This construction method involved shrinking steel or iron hoops around the central core, or around a basic cast-iron barrel, a procedure similar to that suggested by the American professor, Daniel Treadwell. Some French guns were breechloaders, but the British during the 1870s armed their ships with powerful, long-range rifled muzzle-loading guns in calibers up to twelve and sixteen inches.[34]

This built-up process of gun construction was expensive. In the 1860s, in an effort to prolong the life of older guns and simultaneously save money, British Army Captain William Palliser proposed that old smoothbores be rebored and wrought-iron tube be inserted converting the older gun into a rifled one. Since the United States had a large number of sound, but not outdated, smoothbore guns available, American ordnance officers eagerly embraced this conversion method, rather than the more expensive "built-up" process. By the insertion of wrought-iron (later steel) tubes, ten-inch Rodman smoothbores became eight-inch rifled guns. Trials indicated that the muzzle first-insertion of the Palliser system did not result in as sound a gun as did a breech insertion of the tube, although in either case the guns remained muzzle loading. Even though this gun had twice the power and three times the accuracy of the ten-inch smoothbore at a 1,000-yard range, using specially hardened shot, it could only penetrate eight inches of armor at that range. While a reliable rifled gun, by the 1880s it in no way matched the power of European guns of similar caliber.[35]

American ordnance officers were well aware that, as the Chief of

Ordnance stated in 1874, "steel is the best material for guns."[36] Well into the 1880s, however, no American steel producer had the facilities for forging the high-quality steel parts needed for ordnance.[37] Furthermore, by the 1870s American ordnance officers also recognized the potential of the breechloader. In an effort to overcome these problems, the Ordnance Department first attempted to graft a Krupp breechloading mechanism onto the converted eight-inch rifles. Although both the breech system and the conversion system operated successfully while tested separately, the combination of the two was a failure in 1881. "The overstrained system broke down completely," wrote artillery Lieutenant William Birkhimer in 1884. "The pieces bursting one after the other as they were subjected to trial."[38] Confronted by this failure, the department made another attempt with cast iron, testing a twelve-inch breechloading cast-iron rifle in 1886. During tests the bore of the gun began to noticeably erode before the forty-first test round. By the 637th test round the board concluded that it would not be safe to continue firing. Cast iron was simply not durable enough to be the gun metal for a high-powered rifled gun. In addition, Captain Rogers Birnie, Jr. pointed out that the gun took eight months to cast (plus eighteen months to finish) and was the only successfully cast gun in five attempts. The results of the tests, said Birnie, suggested that under the high internal pressures generated by modern powders, the endurance of such a gun "would be an uncertain factor."[39] The Ordnance Department agreed. "It is the firm conviction of the Bureau," reported Ordnance Chief S. V. Benet in 1888, "that the true policy now to pursue is in the manufacture of all steel guns." Both the Ordnance and Navy Departments now placed their faith in the built-up, forged steel gun, even though as late as 1886 many of the forgings still had to be purchased abroad.[40]

While American ordnance development stagnated, American engineers made substantial progress in the development of a system of defense by submarine torpedoes, by the 1870s increasingly referred to by the modern term *submersible mine.* The engineer battalion stationed at Willett's Point, New York, had responsibility for the creation of this system. By the middle of the 1870s the Willett's Point Engineer School of Application possessed 300 mines, the necessary apparatus for twenty shore stations, and had developed plans for implementing a system of defensive mine fields at several important harbors.[41] Impressed by the possibility of utilizing mines instead of fortifications for coastal defense, during the late 1870s Congress earmarked a hefty portion of the small fortification appropriations for research and development of such a system, but did not provide enough money for the construction of the galleries and bombproof casemates the system (developed by the engineers) required.[42] Simultaneous cuts in the authorized strength of the army forced a reduction in the engineer battalion's strength down to 150 men. This was far too few, protested the engineers, to properly lay the mine fields should an emergency arise. So, while there was a plan for a system of defensive mine fields, that system existed only on paper through the early 1880s.

Thus, by the early 1880s, although the United States did not have the effective modern ordnance which could equal that mounted in European warships, it had a system of mine-field defense but it was not yet in place. Yet, even if the mine-field system was ready and in position, the engineers suggested, in opposition to the views of a number of Congressmen, that the lack of powerful coastal guns would mean that the coast was still defenseless. "However efficient in itself," said Chief Engineer Humphreys in 1878, "[torpedo defense] cannot stand alone."[43] Shore batteries and mine fields operated in harmony. Without the obstacle presented by a mine field, enemy vessels would soon escape the fire of the shore battery; without the existence of the shore battery, "the enemy could stop and remove the . . . [mine field] at his leisure and then pass on."[44] Since the country had no modern ordnance, the only guns available were the now obsolete fifteen-inch Rodman guns and the relatively weak converted eight-inch rifled gun. There were not enough of these available, however, to arm even the existing coastal batteries. In 1885 only 308 fifteen-inch guns and 160 of the converted guns were in service.[45] In these circumstances the engineers argued that the coast was "virtually defenseless."[46] An effective system of coastal defenses simply did not, and without increased Congressional support could not, exist. Alarmed by the "stringent economies" of Congress during the late 1870s, the engineers stressed with increasing urgency the need to rebuild the country's coastal defense system; and, the arguments they used differed little, if at all, from those developed by their predecessors before the Civil

War. Despite the massive technological change in weaponry during the mid-nineteenth century, the principles and premises of coastal defense remained unchanged.

The engineers recognized that the United States was isolated from Europe by the Atlantic barrier. But while the country "might, at first view, be regarded as too remote physically, and . . . politically too insulated, to be endangered by the convulsions which, from time to time, disturb the nations of the earth," neither geographical isolation nor the "pacific" tendency of the United States could ensure continued peace. Disputes between nations, as past experience demonstrated, were inevitable. "The certainty of the return of periods of embarrassment and strife with foreign nations," suggested Chief of Engineers H. G. Wright in 1880, ". . . affords a sufficient reason of itself for securing ourselves in the best manner against the more serious evils of these unavoidable collisions."[47] Furthermore, the Atlantic was less a barrier than it seemed. "Our country," argued his predecessor, A. A. Humphreys, in 1876, "is contiguous throughout its northern boundary with the most powerful maritime power of the earth [Great Britain] and close upon our southern shores is another, whose strength is not to be despised [Spain]."[48] Based upon Halifax, Nova Scotia or Bermuda, the Royal Navy, suggested Wright, could easily dominate the waters of the East coast. An enemy squadron assembled at one or the other (or both) of these locations would threaten every important point from the Penobscot River in Maine to New Orleans. Fast, powerfully armed ships could arrive off our coasts or at our port cities "in a few days or even hours of the declaration of war." It would be unavailing for regular troops or militia to assemble at an unprotected city threatened by even one of these modern vessels. All that such troops could do would be to build crude and temporary earthworks mounting obsolete guns. Lying outside the range of these guns, the enemy vessel or vessels would "pierce such temporary parapets through and through, dismount the guns, and explode any magazines." Clearly, under present conditions, the first months of a conflict with a strong enemy would be a series of disasters.[49]

Those concerned with keeping down the cost of seacoast defenses failed, said the engineers, to recognize that in the long run such defenses were a positive economy rather than an expensive luxury.

"There is nothing so costly to a nation as a lack of preparation for war," said Chief Engineer Humphreys. This statement echoed the sentiments of a paper presented in 1871 to the Essayons Club of the Corps of Engineers by then Captain William R. King. The question, argued King, was "simply one of insurance, or, how much can we afford to pay for insuring a given amount of property against an event of a given probability of occurance?" The cost of seacoast defenses was far outweighed by the potential loss should a seaboard city fall into enemy hands. Using a similar line of reasoning, Humphreys argued that American coastal cities "would suffer ten times more than the cost of all the forts necessary to secure them."[50]

Although the economic argument might win over businessmen and commercially minded Congressmen, the engineers also suggested that the requirements of national honor demanded the existence of suitable defenses. Under present conditions, said Wright, "injuries to our citizens abroad and insults to our flag [cannot] be resented with that vigor and promptitude demanded by the dignity and honor of the nation."[51] The honor of the United States was involved, said Humphreys, when the nation had to appeal to the sword; however, "that appeal should be accompanied by the consciousness that the weapon appealed to would not be inferior to that held by the adversary." The lack of seacoast defenses meant that the United States would suffer from just such an inferiority even in a dispute with a "comparatively weaker power." Adequate seacoast defenses would provide the United States "with a justly founded self-confidence" in its dealings with foreign countries.[52]

While the foregoing arguments provided the justification for seacoast defenses, the function of those defenses remained essentially the same as in the antebellum period. As defined by the engineers the function of coastal defenses was sixfold. The first objective was to close the important harbors, securing them for "our military and commercial marine." Second, they would deprive an enemy of easy access to positions where he could establish a base for expeditions up and down the seaboard. Third, the defenses covered the great cities from attack, and protected them from the threat of either seizure or raids for tribute. Fourth, the defenses would prevent the blockade of the "avenues of interior navigation." Fifth, coastal defenses would cover the coasting trade and provide places of refuge for merchant shipping. Finally, defenses were necessary to protect naval yards, giving the navy secure bases from which to operate.[53]

All six functions were identical to those outlined by the Bernard Board of 1821. Unlike their predecessors, the engineers of the 1870s and 1880s did not suggest that the defenses were meant to forestall an invasion of the country. They suggested that occupation of sea-coast cities was a possibility, but argued that the danger "of an attempt by an enemy to land and march any distance into a populous district" was not great.[54] This was in accord not only with the views of most civilian leaders but most military men as well. "Of course no foreign power would undertake an invasion of the United States with a view to carrying on military operations within our borders," wrote infantry Lieutenant Arthur L. Wagner in his prize-winning 1884 essay for the *Journal of the Military Service Institution*.[55] Similarly, General William Tecumseh Sherman suggested that there was "no remote apprehension" of an invasion by any other nation.[56] The engineers agreed with such assessment. "It is of no part of the task assumed by the system of fortifications," said Wright, " . . . to guard against the invasion and protracted occupation of a well-peopled district, or of a point around which the forces of that country could soon be rallied." Wright suggested that critics of the system of defenses were incorrect in assuming that this was the function of the system. Instead, the coastal defenses were intended "to cover the really important and dangerous points . . . [necessitating] a *distant* landing and a march towards the object through the people."[57]

Although the engineers of the 1880s did not suggest that invasion was likely, like their predecessors they pointed out that the importance of protecting the seacoast was recognized by major nations of Europe with whom the United States was likely to have disputes. "Other maritime nations," noted Wright in 1881, "are building . . . defenses for the protection of their own coasts." A year earlier he pointed out that "Great Britain did not hesitate to appropriate $40,000,000 for the defense of its most important harbors" following the great changes in weaponry during the mid-nineteenth century. "We may well profit," Wright suggested, "by her example."[58]

Great Britain was a good example for the engineers, since it was so clearly the dominant naval power of the world. Pointing out that the British continued to build coastal defenses not only suggested that this was a sound policy but also provided the engineers with the opportunity to renew their attack on critics who contended that the navy could defend the coast. Using a line of reasoning lifted directly from the reports made by General Totten before the Civil War, postwar engineers argued that naval defense of the coast required a force equal to an attacking flotilla at every point which the enemy might threaten. Assuming, said Chief Engineer Wright, that the country had one one harbor, a defensive fleet could "be certain of meeting the enemy should he assail it." If the defending fleet was inferior in strength, "there would be no reason to look for a successful defense." If the defending and attacking fleets were equal in strength, "the defense might be complete," but chance might decide the outcome and the consequences of defeat would be the loss of both the defending fleet and the port. A superior defending fleet would, admitted Wright, also make the defense complete, but in that case an enemy would "employ himself cutting up our commerce on the ocean," ignoring the defended port altogether. On the other hand, if a defending fleet of superior strength awaited the enemy outside the harbor, it might be damaged by storms and rendered temporarily inferior—or it could attempt to blockade the enemy's fleet in its own harbor. If the enemy had strong batteries, his fleet could sally out without hesitation. A victory would mean that he could proceed without further hindrance to the capture of our now undefended port; defeated, the enemy "could retire under the shelter of his defense." In any case, Wright also contended, complete blockade of an enemy port was impossible. Successful naval defense, then, required superiority of strength and also required the defending fleet to remain in position in the harbor, yielding the ocean to the enemy without a struggle. The situation became more complex when each country had numerous harbors, as was the case with the United States. But the basic principle remained the same. Indeed, the more points the enemy could choose to attack, "the greater the chances that he will meet no opposition whatever."[59]

Hence, despite the popularity of the idea, the engineers (and most other military men as well) continued to regard a reliance on the navy for coastal defense an unsound and dangerous approach. "A system of naval defence alone for our coast," declared Arthur L. Wagner, "would be expensive and dangerously insufficient." Quincy A. Gillmore pointed out that "the idea that a navy . . . can furnish a sure defense . . . finds no practical application among naval powers." Instead, as Wagner argued, "to protect its harbors and leave its navy free to act on the offensive, the United States must defend its coast with fortifications."[60] Permanent defenses were a sure defense, a fact recognized by all the major powers and proven by history. As General Wright argued in 1880, in words taken almost verbatim from the prewar reports of the Board of Engineers, "There has been but one practice among nations as to the defense of ports and harbors and that has been a resort to fortifications and obstructions by torpedoes or otherwise." War, said Wright, "can only be excluded from our territory by fortifications."[61] The navy was not a defensive force, but an offensive one.

Fortifications and mine fields were not only the surest means of coastal defense, they were the cheapest. The cost of modern ironclad warships, the engineers calculated, came to more than $600,000 per gun. Repair costs for British ironclads ran from $20,000 to $50,000 per year for each vessel. In contrast, the cost of permanent fortifications was, on a per gun basis, unlikely to be a tenth as great, while repair costs were "comparatively trifling." The works proposed by the Board of Engineers in 1869, earth and sand barbette batteries, were "the cheapest works that can be devised."[62]

In addition to their low cost and their surety as a means of defense, permanent works had the added virtue of being a continuously visible deterrent to enemy attack. A defense by fortifications and mine fields, said Gillmore, is "designed quite as much to prevent attack as to defeat it." Confronted by strong batteries and mine fields an enemy would have to decide to run over the mines, risking destruction by them, or stop while under fire to remove them. In such circumstances, an enemy would "prudently elect to do neither." Thus, coastal defenses were, in Gillmore's words, "a most powerful conservator of the national peace and safety. Their true office is to avert war." To those who saw them instead as symbols of militarism or unnecessary monuments to the egocentric ideas of the engineers, Gillmore replied, "They are the guardians if not the champions of the public good . . . costing but a trifle for maintenance and repairs . . . and incapable of exerting any influence dangerous to the liberties of the people."[63] It was, believed the engineers, imperative that Congress recognize the need and value of permanent coastal defenses, and begin to appropriate the necessary money to strengthen them.

In the past these arguments came before Congress in the form of annual or special reports or, more rarely, in a memorial submitted by an individual officer. Now, in the 1880s, such views found a new forum. Articles devoted to convincing skeptical or uninformed civilians appeared in popular magazines, stressing the present weaknesses of the country's defenses and arguing the necessity of stronger ones. Often military officers wrote these articles, clearly attempting to focus public attention on the problem as an indirect way of bringing pressure to bear upon Congress. Retired Major General William B. Franklin, for example, suggested in an 1883 *North American Review* article that while essentially no money was being spent on defenses, Congress alone was not to blame for this: "Had the people felt the interest in the subject which it deserves," he argued, "the power [of Congress to appropriate money for defenses] would have been exercised." When the country was attacked, and its defenses found wanting, Franklin suggested that the people of the country "must bear the blame themselves." He urged the American people to "awake" to the necessity of defending the coasts. "Every year," he wrote, "the chiefs of the engineers and ordnance of the army and the heads of bureaus of the Navy Department . . . have given warnings of the dangers we incur by our inaction." It was no exaggeration, said Franklin, "to say there is no sea-board city . . . that could not at this time be laid under contribution by a single iron-clad ship, which [could] . . . quietly steam [back] out to sea without danger of damage from anything which any fort or ship of the United States can do."[64] Similarly, in an article the following year, retired artillery officer Henry A. Smalley contended that the "diffuseness" and "dry elaboration" of official reports deterred "the general public from a careful examination of them." As a result, the warnings "of the ablest and most experienced officers of our army and navy . . . remain practically unheeded." The harbor defenses of the country, said

Smalley, "have been shamefully neglected." Smalley quoted at length from numerous official reports to present the engineers' case. Unlike Franklin, however, Smalley blamed Congress for failing to provide the necessary money for the coastal defenses. Since, he hypothesized, Congress was "deafened by the constant reiteration of the evidence and conclusions presented by the engineers and other military leaders, an appeal to the country at large seems necessary."[65] Henry P. Wells concluded a detailed analysis of American mines (torpedoes) and worldwide ordnance in an 1886 *Harpers Magazine* article, by contending that a million men "armed with a profusion of every appliance of a modern first-class army and intrenched about New York City could not protect it from capture and destruction or contribution by even a second-rate European naval power." Wells suggested that public apathy to blame for this state of affairs. He argued that "upon our national legislature rests responsibility. It, and it alone, must determine whether we make timely preparation for our future defense, or continue an apathy which must, if persisted in, ultimately over-whelm us in national humiliation and disaster."[66] Both the engineers in their official reports and the authors of articles like these hoped to persuade Congress to increase the annual appro-priations for fortifications construction and ordnance develop-ment. During the early 1880s, nevertheless, Congress remained largely unmoved. In 1882 an effort by New York Congressman Anson McCook to increase the fortification appropriation to $500,000 failed. McCook raised the spectre of the Chilean navy lay-ing waste the California coast, but opponents argued that the country could not make modern guns so that building forts was "in vain," or that Congress would vote necessary funds if the coast was actually threatened. Instead of $500,000 Congress provided a total of $375,000 of which only $175,000 was for fortifications, the remainder being allocated for torpedo (submersible mine) develop-ment and experimentation with heavy ordnance.[67]

In 1884 supporters of the engineers' position gained a bare majority on the House Appropriations Committee and that com-mittee reported a bill appropriating $1,000,000 for new fortifi-cations at "deep-water harbors." Republican Congressman Roswell Horr of Michigan argued strenuously in support of this measure. "You might as well try to stop a mad rhinoceros by firing green peas out of an old-fashioned pop-gun,'' he contended, ''as try to stop a modern warship from sailing into any harbor in the United States'' with the forts and guns then on hand. Yet, while Horr got ''great applause'' for his remarks, the House eventually voted to substitute a minority report presented by William Holman of Indiana. Holman echoed pre-Civil War rhetoric by asserting that ''real fortifications'' could be improvised if needed, and the minority recommended only $175,000 for construction of new works.[68]

In contrast to the situation during earlier periods, the 1884 debate and vote on the substitution of the minority followed party lines. The House Appropriations Committee consisted of nine Democrats and six Republicans. Two of the Democrats, E. John Ellis of Louisiana and John Hancock of Texas, sided with the Republicans giving them a narrow eight to seven majority. In the House as a whole, however, the Democrats outnumbered the Republicans 197 to 118. Although a few Democrats crossed over, not enough did so to alter the outcome.[69]

Nothing was materially different by 1885. In that year the Appropriations Committee recommended a total of $955,000, which, while larger than previous appropriations overall, only provided $100,000 for the repair and preservation of existing defensive works. This was actually less than the amount appropriated for the same purpose during the three previous years. Furthermore, the total amount offered by Congress was in sharp contrast to both the $7,303,000 sought by the engineers and the $4,935,000 favored by a Roswell Horr, now leading a minority of the committee.[70]

This continuing fiscal stringency meant that there could be little or no construction of new seacoast batteries. Yet, by this time it is also evident that concern was growing within Congress over the weakness of the country's coastal defenses. Beginning in 1881 Congress substantially increased appropriations for the development and manufacture of improved ordnance. In addition, the naval appropriations bill of 1883 included authorization for a board of army and navy officers to recommend potential locations for a national gun foundry, as well as suggest suitable manufacturing methods.[71] It was within this climate of increasing concern that in 1885 Congress included a far-reaching clause in the fortification appropriation bill, requiring President Grover Cleveland to appoint a board headed by the Secretary of War, whose duty would be to "examine and report at what ports fortifications or other defences are most urgently required, the character and kind of defences best adapted for each," and the "armament . . . torpedoes, mines, or other defensive appliances" necessary to defend the coasts.[72]

This board—soon known as the Endicott Board after its head, Secretary of War William C. Endicott—represented the first significant attempt to analyze American coastal defense policy and practice since the Civil War. Because of its importance, a number of analysts have tackled the question of why Congress authorized the board, while simultaneously appropriations for defenses remained at the low levels reached in the 1870s. One suggestion is that the arguments of the engineers were now taking effect. Other historians suggest that concern over the state of the coastal defenses was fostered by the closing of the land frontier and the end of the Indian Wars coupled with strains in the friendly relations between the United States and Great Britain. Furthermore, by the mid-1880s the United States seemed on the verge of successfully developing the kind of new, high-powered, breech-loading guns which would make coastal defenses effective once again.[73]

All of these reasons were undoubtedly factors in the creation of the Endicott Board, yet they do not fully explain what was clearly a complex situation. Had the arguments of the engineers and their supporters finally convinced Congress to do something about the decayed and all but useless coastal defenses, appropriations for new construction ought to have climbed in the ensuing years. Instead, appropriations remained at their established levels. Furthermore, as the strains in the Anglo-American relationship eased, it became clear that the Ordnance Department's search for a suitable heavy gun was not yet over. It would be "premature," Ordnance Chief Stephen V. Benet said in 1885, to pronounce the twelve-inch cast-iron rifle then being tested a success. As already indicated, the Ordnance Department eventually reported that this gun would not meet the country's needs and continued to urge the development of all steel guns.[74]

To a large extent, the Endicott Board represents a step away from the traditional practice of allowing the engineers to define the nation's coastal defense system, both in terms of the actual defenses needed and the basic purpose of such a system. Congress mandated that the Endicott Board include two civilians in addition to the Secretary of War, two line (rather than staff) naval officers, two ordnance officers, and only two members of the Corps of Engineers. Although the military men on the board outnumbered the civilian membership, the make-up of the board suggests that Congress hoped to create an advisory panel whose members would have a range of opinions and which would be independent of the existing military bureaucracy.

Since debate on the fortifications bill of 1885 centered on the issue of developing modern, heavy ordnance (with almost no discussion of the Endicott Board itself), any conclusions regarding the reasons for the board's creation and composition must be conjectural. But whatever the exact reasons for its creation, the Endicott Board was a watershed in the history of American coastal defense policy. Its recommendations would define and shape that policy for the rest of the nineteenth century and beyond.

NOTES

1. Annual Report of the Secretary of War (1864), House Exec. Document no. 83, 38th Congress, 2d session, Serial 1230, p. 32.

2. Proceedings of the Board of Engineers, Proceedings and Reports, 1866-1882, Records of the Board of Engineers, 1866-1920, Entry 461, RG 77, NA, vol. 1, p. 6.

3. Viktor Ernest Karl Rudolf von Scheliha, *A Treatise on Coast-Defence* (London: E. and F. N. Spon, 1868), reprint edition (Westport, Conn.: Greenwood Press, 1971), p. 7.

4. David B. Porter to Gideon Welles, Feb. 1, 1865, in von Scheliha, *Coast-Defence*, pp. 158-173, and quoted on p. 159. "I know of no instance," said Porter, emphasizing the need to combine land and naval forces in an attack on a coastal position, "where troops and ships, properly combined, have attacked a land-work when the land-work was not taken.", p. 160. It should be noted that Porter incorrectly believed that an intense mortar bombardment would reduce Forts Jackson and St. Philip in 1862.

5. William P. Craighill, "Guns Ashore and Guns Afloat." Paper read before the Essayons Club of the Corps of Engineers, Oct. 12, 1868, no. 6, Printed Papers (Willett's Point, N.Y.: Battalion Press, 1868). Underlining is in the original.

6. "Report on Experimental Firings," Reports of the Board of Engineers, Proceedings and Reports, 1866-1882, Records of the Board of Engineers, 1866-1920, Entry 461, RG 77, NA, vol. 1, p. 185.

7. Porter to Welles, in von Scheliha, *Coast-Defence,* p. 172.

8. Von Scheliha, *Coast-Defence,* p. 4.

9. Porter, in von Scheliha, *Coast-Defence,* p. 159.

10. Von Scheliha, *Coast-Defence,* pp. 47-48.

11. Reports of the Board of Engineers, 1866-1882, Records of the Board of Engineers, 1866-1920, Entry 461, RG 77, NA, vol. 3, p. 54.

12. Von Scheliha, *Coast-Defence,* pp. 44-45.

13. Porter, in von Scheliha, *Coast-Defence,* p. 172.

14. William M. Black, *Pamphlet on the Evolution of Fortification,* Occasional Paper no. 58, Engineer School, U.S. Army (Washington, D.C.: Government Printing Office, 1919), pp. 95-98; Quentin Hughes, *Military Architecture* (London: Hugh Evelyn, 1974), pp. 225-230; Ian Hogg, *Fortress: A History of Military Defence* (London: MacDonald and Jane's, 1975), pp. 103-108.

15. Proceedings and Reports, 1866-1882, Records of the Board of Engineers, 1866-1920, Entry 461, RG 77, NA, vol. 1, p. 50. The members of the Board of Engineers in 1866 were Col. Henry Brewerton, Col. John G. Barnard, Lt.-Col. Horatio G. Wright, Major Quincy L. Gillmore, Major Henry L. Abbot, and Captain C. B. Reese (the secretary of the board).

16. Ibid., p. 191. This may also be found as "Report of the Board of Engineers Upon Their Experiments in Connection With an Efficient System of Sea-Coast Defences for the United States," House Exec. Document no. 271, 41st Congress, 2d session, Serial 1426, p. 5. This report is also excerpted in the Annual Report of the Chief Engineer (1870).

17. "Report of the Board of Engineers on Experiments in Connection with an Efficient System of Sea-Coast Defences," pp. 7-11; Proceedings and Reports, 1866-1882, Records of the Board of Engineers, 1866-1920, Entry 461, RG 77, NA, vol. 1, pp. 91-92.

18. "The Board of Engineers on Experiments in Connection With an Efficient System of Sea-Coast Defences," pp. 11-12. In 1869 the members of the Board of Engineers were John G. Barnard, George W. Cullum, Z. B. Tower, and Horatio G. Wright.

19. Ibid., p. 5.

20. *Congressional Globe,* 39th Congress, 2d session (vol. 40, pt. 3), pp. 1583-1584, 1763, 1774, 1942.

21. *Congressional Globe,* 41st Congress, 3d session (vol. 43, pt. 2), p. 1536.

22. Ibid., pp. 1536-1537; *Congressional Globe,* 42d Congress, 1st Congress, 1st session (vol. 44, pt. 4), pp. 3298-3299.

23. House Report 384, 43d Congress, 1st session, Serial 1624.

24. *Congressional Record,* 43d Congress, 1st session (vol. 2, pt. 2), p. 1403. The debate on the fortification bill during this session of the 43d Congress produced a long and interesting discussion of the coastal defense system, its rationale, and its cost.

25. *Congressional Record,* 44th Congress, 1st session (vol. 4, pt. 2), pp. 1093-1094; *Statutes At Large,* vol. 19, p. 59. Figures for annual War Department expenditures may be found in United States Bureau of the Census, *Historical Statistics of the United States: Colonial Times to 1957* (Washington, D.C.: Government Printing Office, 1960), pp. 718-719.

26. For a brief analysis of the antagonism toward the army during the mid-to-late 1870s see Robert Utley, *Frontier Regulars* (New York: Macmillan, 1973), pp. 62-63.

27. John G. Barnard, *Notes on Sea-Coast Defence* (New York: D. Van Nostrand, 1861), pp. 59-60.

28. Charles B. Norton and W. J. Valentine, *Report on the Munitions of War* (Paris Universal Exposition: Reports of the United States Commissioners) (Washington, D.C.: Government Printing Office, 1868), pp. 102-103; Ian Hogg and John Batchelor, *Naval Gun* (Poole, Dorset: Blandford Press, 1978), p. 65.

29. Norton and Valentine, *Munitions of War,* pp. 162-177; William H. Jaques, *Modern Armor For National Defence,* Questions of the Day, no. 32 (New York: G. P. Putnam's Sons, 1896), pp. 24-25; Hogg and Batchelor, *Naval Gun,* p. 41.

30. Henry R. Lemly, *Changes Wrought in Artillery in the Nineteenth Century, and Their Effect Upon the Attack of Fortified Places,* Department of Military Art, United States Artillery School Essay (Fort Monroe, Va.: U.S. Artillery School, 1886), p. 6.

31. William E. Birkhimer, *Historical Sketch of the Organization, Administration, Materiel and Tactics of the Artillery, United States Army* (Washington, D.C.: Charman, 1884), pp. 288-290.

32. Norman Wiard, *Memorial Addressed to the Joint Committee on the Conduct of the War,* February 27, 1865, Pamphlet Collection, Library of the State Historical Society of Wisconsin, p. 3. For a secondary account of Wiard's complaints and the problems with American guns during the Civil War see Frank E. Comparato, *The Age of Great Guns* (Harrisburg, Pa.: Stackpole, 1965), pp. 193-202.

33. Robert P. Parrott, Nov. 15, 1864, "Statement of R. P. Parrott," Appendix F in Quincy A. Gillmore, *Engineer and Artillery Operations Against the Defences of Charleston Harbor in 1863,* Professional Papers, The Corps of Engineers no. 16 (New York: D. Van Nostrand, 1868), pp. 310-314; Annual Report of the Chief of Ordnance, 1871, *Exec. Document 1,* pt. 2, 42nd Congress, 2nd session, Serial 1503, p. 225; Birkhimer,

Historical Sketch, p. 267. (Birkhimer mistakenly dates the remark of A. B. Dyer, Chief of Ordnance, as 1870 rather than 1871.) For a summary of the attitude within the Ordnance Bureau toward the Parrott guns see Rogers Birnie, Jr., *Gun-Making in the United States* (Washington, D.C.: Government Printing Office, 1907), pp. 18-19. This brief history of gun-making was originally published in the *Journal of the Military Service Institution* in 1888. At that time Birnie was a Captain in the Ordnance Department.

34. Lemly, "Changes Wrought in Ordnance," pp. 6-7; Hogg and Batchelor, *Naval Gun,* p. 71; Norton and Valentine, *Munitions of War,* pp. 92-100, 104-121. The 16-inch "Woolwich" gun used by the Italian and Royal Navies fired a 1,700-pound shell. The Royal Navy began shifting to equally powerful breech-loading guns during the 1880s.

35. Birnie, *Gun-Making in the U.S.,* pp. 22-26; Birkhimer, *Historical Sketch,* p. 292. The steel tube for this conversion was introduced in 1883. In comparison with the then current guns in European service, some of which fired shells weighing over 1,000 pounds, this gun fired only a 180-pound shell. The Army's Chief of Ordnance, A. B. Dyer, called these converted guns makeshifts "permissible in time of war, but unpardonable waste in peace" in a paper read at the Naval Academy in 1874. See J. W. King (Chief Engineer, U.S. Navy), *Heavy Rifled Guns: Modern European Artillery* (Pittsburgh: H. F. Mann, 1879), p. 8.

36. Comparato, *Age of Great Guns,* p. 209.

37. William H. Jaques, *Heavy Ordnance for National Defence* (New York: G. P. Putnam's Sons, 1885), pp. 19-20. At this time Jaques was a Lieutenant in the U.S. Navy.

38. Birkhimer, *Historical Sketch,* p. 273.

39. Birnie, *Gunmaking in the U.S.,* p. 56.

40. S. V. Benet to William C. Endicott, March 20, 1888. *A Collection of Ordnance Reports and Other Important Papers Relating to the Ordnance Department* (Washington, D.C.: Government Printing Office, 1890, vol. 3), p. 364; Birnie, *Gunmaking in the U.S.,* pp. 87-88.

41. Annual Report of the Chief of Engineers, 1874, *Exec. Document 1,* pt. 2, 43rd Congress, 2nd session, Serial 1636, p. 25; Annual Report of the Chief of Engineers, 1875, *Exec. Document 1,* pt. 2, 44th Congress, 1st session, Serial 1675, pp. 29-32.

42. Annual Report of the Chief of Engineers, 1881, Report of the Board of Engineers, *Exec. Document 1,* vol. 3, pt. 2, Serial 2011, pp. 57-58.

43. Annual Report of the Chief of Engineers, 1878, *Exec. Document 1,* pt. 2, 45th Congress, 3rd session, Serial 1844, p. 4. For an example of the contrary view, apparently popular in Congress, see the remarks of Rep. William S. Holman of Indiana in 1890: "Whatever we shall need . . . for coast defense in coming years . . . will be found entirely available in our torpedo system." *Congressional Record,* 51st Congress, 1st session, vol. 21, pt. 3, p. 2887.

44. Quincy A. Gillmore, "Letter to Chief Engineer H. G. Wright, Respecting the Present Condition of Our Sea-Coast Defenses, and the Importance of Strengthening Them," Appendix No. 2, Annual Report of the Chief of Engineers, 1881, *Exec. Document 1*, no. 1, pt. 2; vol. 2, pt. 1, 47th Congress, 1st session, Serial 2011, p. 407.

45. Report of the Board on Fortifications or Other Defenses (Endicott Board Report), Exec. Document no. 49, 49th Congress, 1st session, Serial 2395, p. 20.

46. Annual Report of the Chief of Engineers, 1883, *Exec. Document 1*, pt. 2, 48th Congress, 1st session, Serial 2183, p. 52.

47. Annual Report of the Chief of Engineers, 1880, Houses Exec. Document no. 1, pt. 2, 46th Congress, 3d session, Serial 1953, pp. 4-5.

48. House Report 354, 44th Congress, 1st session, Serial 1709, pp. 180-181.

49. Annual Report of the Chief of Engineers, 1880, p. 6. As in the past, the engineers tended to cite and recite what they saw as particularly useful statements. Sometimes they actually quoted previous reports; sometimes the material was included without any reference to the original report it came from. In this case Wright paraphrased statements made by A. A. Humphreys in 1876. See House Report 354, 44th Congress, 1st session, Serial 1709, pp. 179-180. As much as anything else this habit demonstrates the consistency of engineer attitudes in regard to coastal defense policy.

50. William R. King, "Economy of Sea Coast Defenses," Paper read before the Essayons Club of the Corps of Engineers, May 15, 1871, Printed Papers, no. 29 (Willett's Point, N.Y.: Battalion Press, 1871); Annual Report of the Chief of Engineers, 1878, Exec. Document no. 1, pt. 2, 45th Congress, 3rd Session, Serial 1844, pp. 4-5. The analogy between coastal defenses and insurance was very popular with those who pressed for more expenditure on defenses. It was repeated in various ways down through the end of the century and survives in a different form today.

51. Annual Report of the Chief of Engineers, 1880, p. 5.

52. Annual Report of the Chief of Engineers, 1878, p. 5. The annual report for 1879 consists largely of lengthy quotes from that of 1878.

53. Annual Report of the Chief of Engineers, 1880, p. 14.

54. Ibid., p. 13.

55. Arthur L. Wagner, "The Military Necessities of the United States, and the Best Provision for Meeting Them," *Journal of the Military Service Institution of the United States,* vol. 5, no. 29 (September 1884), pp. 237-271.

56. William T. Sherman, in testimony before the House Armed Services Committee, *Congressional Record,* 43rd Congress, 1st session, vol. 2, pt. 2, p. 1409.

57. Annual Report of the Chief of Engineers, 1880, p. 13.

58. Pointing out that European countries continued to invest in coastal

defenses was a consistent theme in the engineers' reports. See, for example, the Annual Report of the Chief of Engineers, 1880, p. 5, and the Annual Report of the Chief of Engineers, 1881, p. 5.

59. Annual Report of the Chief of Engineers, 1880, pp. 10-12; House Report 354, 44th Congress, 1st session, Serial 1709, p. 180; Quincy A. Gillmore, "Letter to Chief Engineer H. G. Wright," pp. 403-405.

60. Gillmore, "Letter to Chief Engineer H. G. Wright," p. 403; Arthur L. Wagner, "Military Necessities of the United States," p. 246.

61. Annual Report of the Chief of Engineers, 1880, p. 8.

62. Ibid., p. 15; House Report 354, 44th Congress, 1st session, Serial 1709, p. 180.

63. Gillmore, "Letter to Chief Engineer H. G. Wright," p. 409.

64. William B. Franklin, "National Defense," *North American Review* vol. 137, no. 324 (November 1883), pp. 594-604.

65. Henry A. Smalley, "A Defenseless Sea-Board," *North American Review,* vol. 138, no. 328 (March 1884), pp. 233-245.

66. Henry P. Wells, "The Defense of Our Sea-Ports," *Harpers Magazine,* vol. 71, no. 426 (November 1885), pp. 927-937.

67. *Congressional Record,* 47th Congress, 1st session, vol. 13, pt. 1, pp. 596-601; *Statutes At Large,* vol. 22, p. 93.

68. *Congressional Record,* 48th Congress, 1st session, vol. 15, pt. 6, pp. 5804-5820, 5869-5870.

69. Ibid., pp. 5869-5870. In addition to Ellis and Hancock, the Democratic members of the Appropriations Committee in 1884 were Samuel Randall of Pennsylvania, William H. Forney of Alabama, William Holman of Indiana, Richard W. Townshend of Illinois, Waldo Hutchins of New York, John F. Follett of Ohio, and James N. Burnes of Missouri. In addition to Horr, the Republicans on the Committee were J. Warren Keifer of Ohio, Joseph G. Cannon of Illinois, Thomas Ryan of Kansas, William H. Calkins of Indiana, and William D. Washburn of Minnesota. Hutchins and Keifer did not vote on the substitution. Ellis, Horr, and Washburn voted against the final bill, apparently believing it provided far too little money.

70. *Congressional Record,* 48th Congress, 2nd session, vol. 16, pt. 3, p. 2306; *Statutes At Large,* vol. 23, p. 434.

71. Edward Ranson, "The Endicott Board of 1885-86 and the Coast Defenses," *Military Affairs,* vol. 31, no. 2 (Summer 1967), pp. 74-75; *Statutes At Large,* vol. 21, pp. 109, 468; *Statutes At Large,* vol. 22, pp. 93, 471; *Statutes At Large,* vol. 23, p. 158.

72. *Statutes At Large,* vol. 23, p. 434; *Legislative History of the General Staff of the Army of the United States,* compiled by Chief Clark R. P. Thian under the direction of Adjutant General H. C. Corbin (Washington, D.C.: Government Printing Office, 1901), p. 520.

73. The best summaries regarding the formation of the Endicott Board are: Rowena Reed, "The Endicott Board—Vision and Reality," *Periodical: The Journal of the Council on Abandoned Military Posts,* vol. 9, no. 2 (Summer 1979), pp. 3-17, and Ranson, "The Endicott Board of 1885-86 and The Coast Defenses."

74. Annual Report of the Chief of Ordnance, 1885, Exec. Document no. 1, pt. 2, 49th Congress, 1st Session, Serial 2374; S. V. Benet to William C. Endicott, July 17, 1886, and March 20, 1888, in *A Collection of Ordnance Reports and Other Important Papers Relating to the Ordnance Department* (Washington, D.C.: Government Printing Office, 1890), vol. 3, pp. 356-357, 362-364.

SIX
A System Reestablished

The Endicott Board made its report in January 1886, a bare ten months after its creation the previous March. Even so, the board's report was detailed and far-ranging. Going beyond an examination of the current status of the country's coastal defenses, it reexamined the rationale for coastal defenses and proposed a massive program of construction and development designed to reestablish a sound system of defenses commensurate with the country's needs. In doing this, the Endicott Board not only fulfilled its function of describing the kinds of defenses required at the nation's ports, it also established the parameters for all future discussion of American coastal defense well beyond the turn of the century. The report of the Endicott Board, in short, marked an end to two decades of confusion and stopgap planning in American coastal defense policy.

The Endicott Board began its report with a brief summary of the recent history of American coastal defenses. In 1860, it argued, the nation's system of coastal defenses was unsurpassed in efficiency and "entirely competent to resist [the] vessels of war of that period." The rapid development of modern artillery and armored, steam-powered warships, however, meant that by the 1880s these defenses were obsolete and unable to prevent attacking warships from entering the ports they supposedly protected. During the twenty-odd years following the conclusion of the Civil War, argued the board, the country had grown wealthier than ever before. Yet the rich and growing cities of the seaboard were "defenceless" and in this condition simply invited a naval attack. The country seemed oblivious to the fact, said the board, that "plunder of one of our sea-ports might abundantly reimburse an enemy for the expenses of a war conducted against us."[1] Such a conclusion was so apparent to the members of the board that they found it "impossible to understand the supineness which has kept the nation quiet—allowing its floating and shore defenses to become obsolete and effete—without making an effort to keep progress with the age, while other nations . . . have not considered themselves secure without large expenditures for fortifications."[2]

If any Congressmen had supported the creation of the Endicott Board in the belief that the inclusion of naval officers and civilians would modify the rationale for coastal defenses so consistently propounded by the engineers, they were quickly disappointed. Both the Endicott Board's brief historical analysis and its enumeration of the functions of a coastal defense system echoed the arguments and reasoning of the engineers throughout the preceding seventy years. According to the Endicott Board, the primary purpose of a coastal defense system was to protect the nation's important commercial ports from attack or bombardment, particularly in those cases where the port city doubled as the site of a navy yard or anchorage. A second purpose of coastal defenses was the protection of merchant shipping when it reached the coast. Protecting American commerce on the ocean was the navy's responsibility, said the board, but merchant ships also needed secure ports of refuge to which they would come to escape enemy commerce raiders. Associated with this was the third purpose of coastal defenses: protection of the vessels employed in the vital coastal trade along the seaboard. These ships, too, required places where they could seek refuge, otherwise enemy vessels could disrupt the American economy with little trouble.[3]

All of the purposes which the Endicott Board suggested coastal defenses served were similar, and in most respects identical, to those indicated by the various Boards of Engineers in the past. The Endicott Board placed less emphasis on the need to protect naval yards and rendezvous points; but aside from this, it continued the tradition of linking the need for coastal defenses to the need to protect economic and commercial interests. As the Endicott Board pointed out, only a handful of Confederate commerce raiders had nearly wrecked United States commerce during the war. A war with a European enemy, one with a far stronger navy than the Confederacy ever possessed, would mean an even greater threat to trade, as well as the possibility of raids on coastal cities. A system of coastal defenses would, contended the board, reduce the level of such depredations while simultaneously allowing the navy the freedom to carry the war "to the enemy's commerce." Quite clearly the Endicott Board saw any future war as having a large economic dimension, and by arguing that coastal defenses would reduce the economic damage done by an enemy was subtly implying that such defenses were a form of insurance. Not only was this a familiar line of reasoning, used by the engineers throughout the nineteenth century, but, taken in its entirety, it also dovetailed neatly with the navy's strategic emphasis on commerce raiding.[4]

The Endicott Board made no overt mention of invasion, but it did suggest that the "capture" of a coastal port was a possibility. Since the board went on to argue that by taking a major American coastal city, an enemy could "derange . . . the transportation of troops/and materiel of war . . . at critical junctures during military operations," there was the veiled implication that an enemy could, and would, land troops in substantial numbers on the coast.[5] No small-scale raiding party could hope to seize a port and disrupt railway communications for very long; only a fully equipped force of substantial size could do so without facing complete destruction. Without actually saying so, the board thus raised the spectre of invasion just as the engineer boards of the past had done. At the same time, though, the emphasis was clearly and unequivocally on the threat an enemy would pose toward American commerce and trade rather than on the threat of a military invasion.

The system of coastal defenses proposed by the Endicott Board shared more than its basic premises with the systems proposed in the past. Like the Board of Engineers in 1869, the Endicott Board emphasized that while fixed shore batteries were the key element of their system, these batteries alone were insufficient. Echoing the views of previous reports, the Endicott Board pointed out that guns alone could not "bar the progress of an armored fleet." Shore guns needed the support of floating auxiliaries and a system of submarine mines to be fully effective. "Submarine mines," the board stressed, "are not accessories of the defense, but are essential features, whenever they can be applied." To protect these vital mine fields, the board recommended the temporary use of the existing smoothbore and converted rifled guns until these could be replaced by small-caliber all-steel rifled guns. In addition, the board urged the mounting of searchlights which would illuminate the mine fields and prevent enemy attempts to remove the mines at night.[6]

Although the Endicott Board accepted the new prevailing view that coastal fortifications needed to be supplemented by mine fields, searchlights, and various forms of floating defenses, it also recognized the necessity of providing modern high-powered guns for the coastal batteries. It was, of course, possible to buy such modern guns from European manufacturers; yet the board pointed out that since European arms manufacturers were already producing weapons at capacity simply to meet the demands of their own governments, there would be long delays before arms bought abroad could be delivered. Additionally, foreign purchase would mean money going overseas rather than into the American economy, and this would certainly fail to "encourage home industries" or "promote the national wealth." More importantly, the coming of war could put an end to the import of foreign arms and would mean the United States could be cut off from further supplies as well as replacement parts. It was hardly sound strategy to be dependent upon foreign sources for weapons. For these reasons, the board categorically rejected the alternative of foreign purchase.

Nevertheless, it remained true that "the necessary facilities for the production of . . . masses of steel, and the machines for fashioning this metal into guns and armor" could not "now be found in this country." And, the board noted, it was unlikely that "even the richest and most flourishing of our steel works" would voluntarily make the huge capital investment in such machinery without some kind of long-term national commitment to purchase the arms produced. Businessmen needed to be assured that Congress would maintain its interest, and the board suggested that whatever appropriation Congress granted needed to be permanent. To get things started, the board proposed an immediate appropriation of $8,000,000 (an amount equaling 20 percent of the War Department's expenditures in 1885), contending that this large amount was necessary to induce domestic steel manufacturers to begin tooling for the production of heavy guns. As a further measure, the board endorsed the already proposed idea of creating two national gun factories—one for the army and one for the navy—where large-caliber all-steel guns could be fabricated under the direct control of the respective services' ordnance departments.[7]

In most respects the recommendations of the Endicott Board simply echoed and reinforced the proposals and conclusions presented by past boards. This board, however, went much further than past boards in its proposed utilization of various types of floating defenses. As already seen, the engineers traditionally viewed such devices with some scorn and had long argued that the navy should not be seen as the major agent of direct coastal defense. While the engineers acknowledged that at times floating defenses might prove useful as auxiliaries, they consistently contended that this form of defense was prone to unforeseen accident and could not exceed in strength the similar types of vessels an enemy would use to attack a port city. On the other hand, by the 1880s naval officers were taking a much more active interest in the problem of coastal defense. This increasing naval interest undoubtedly reflected to a large degree the consistent reiteration by many Congressmen that the navy was the "front line" of the coastal defenses. The American navy was by tradition and by deliberate arrangement a defensive force. Even Congressional supporters of the naval building programs of the 1880s, a period which supposedly marked the beginning of the "modern" all-steel navy, accepted the view that the proper function of the navy was limited to breaking up enemy blockades and driving off foreign vessels, activities "essential to the maintenance of the safety of our coast line."[8]

The 1880s were also a time of increasing naval professionalism. The establishment of the Office of Naval Intelligence (whose original purpose was to report on foreign naval developments such as ship design and strategic thinking) in 1882 and the founding of the Naval War College in 1884 indicate the increasing importance placed on education and professional information within the navy. In terms of naval policy, much of the information read and written by increasingly professional officers reinforced the traditional role of the navy by, for the first time, suggesting detailed ways the navy could carry out its obligation to defend the coast. For example, an 1884 study of worldwide naval tactics and strategic thought undertaken by Commander William Bainbridge-Hoff (and published as a pamphlet by the infant Office of Naval Intelligence) contained a substantial section presenting various views on the proper means of naval coastal defense. In analyzing American needs, Bainbridge-Hoff pointed out that modern vessels could bombard American seacoast cities from ranges of 10,000 to 12,500 yards "without . . . running any serious risks from the coast batteries, or other shore or submarine defenses." Thus, he argued, the only way effectively to oppose such a fleet was with "a fleet designed for coastwide defense." The vessels which would make up such a fleet could be either small torpedo boats—fast, inexpensive, and designed to launch self-propelled "modern" torpedoes—or larger gun-armed, armored warships. To be fully effective the latter required powerful guns, shallow draft, good speed, and enough armor or watertight compartments to make them "nearly unsinkable."[9]

Captain (later Admiral) William T. Sampson echoed these ideas in a long detailed proposed system of naval coastal defense presented before the U.S. Naval Institute in 1889. Sampson admitted that "a considerable difference of opinion" existed between the army and the navy on the issue of coastal defense. Doubtless hoping to defuse some army criticism of his proposed scheme, Sampson agreed with the army that if the navy was employed as the sole agent of coastal defense, "it would require a navy enormously greater than would be necessary" given the existence of properly constructed fortifications. "It is understood," said Sampson, "that no such naval establishment is contemplated." Land defenses, if placed far enough in advance of the cities they protected, were "a sufficient and complete protection." But if the city to be defended was close enough to deep water that an enemy fleet could bombard it without forcing a passage by the defending forts, or if the channel was too broad to be covered by gunfire, or the current was too swift and the water too deep to allow the extensive use of mine fields (as was the case at the mouth of the Mississippi River), then Sampson disagreed with his army counterparts and argued that "the defense must be made, in whole or in part, by floating structure."[10] Such floating defenses should not, further contended Sampson, simply be ordinary naval vessels assigned to coastal defense duty. "A naval force that is adapted to the wide range of its duties at sea," he argued, "is not well adapted to the work of defending a coast.'' Instead Sampson urged the construction of powerfully armed, shallow draft vessels capable of maneuvering in water too shallow for enemy warships. In addition, he proposed that other specially designed vessels be built for coastal duties, including torpedo boats, gunboats, and rams. Sampson supplied his views on the proper displacement, speed, and armament of each type, and went on to estimate the numbers of each type required to defend specified locales. The complete naval defense of Massachusetts Bay, for example, required two first-class vessels (see Fig. 4) armed with two fourteen-inch and two ten-inch guns each, two rams, and ten torpedo boats. Only by the provision of such defenses could, in Sampson's view, the stranglehold of an enemy blockade at a major port be broken.[11]

Naval Lieutenant Richard Wainwright took a slightly different approach in a *United Service* article the same year. All analysis of coastal defense, he complained, assigned the navy an offensive role and no part of the defense. This, he argued, ''not only injures the navy, but also the country at large.'' Naval officers alone, believed Wainwright, knew and understood the kinds of vessels an enemy might use in an attack on the United States. A naval officer was to him clearly the best source of information on how an enemy would carry out an attack, and how to defeat him. Fortifications, he admitted, had the advantages of unlimited weight of guns and a steady platform, but as the Civil War had demonstrated, permanent batteries could not keep out a fleet, even when mine fields were present. ''The more we overhaul our experience of the past,'' said Wainwright, '' . . . the more evident becomes the necessity of a navy to defend our coast.''[12]

Given such an apparently widespread attitude among naval officers during the 1880s, and particularly given the fact that Sampson was one of the naval members of the Endicott Board, it is not surprising that the board placed more than usual emphasis on the role of the navy in coastal defense. In the report of Committee Number 5, the naval subcommittee of the Endicott Board, Sampson set forth most of the arguments he would later repeat in his 1889 scheme for naval defense of the coast. Floating defenses, he stated, had three component elements: floating batteries, gunboats, and torpedo boats. In comparison to regular sea-going naval vessels, the former sacrificed speed and endurance in return for heavier

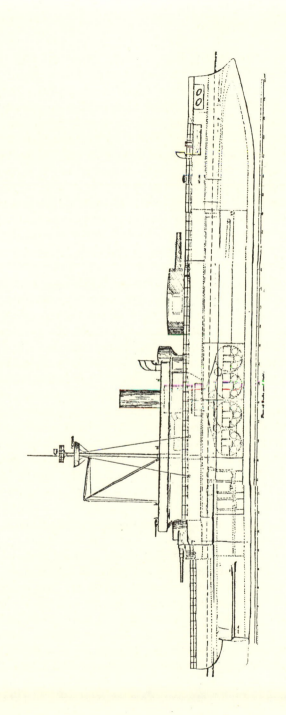

gunpower and armor. Hence, floating batteries had "advantage" over all types of regular sea-going ships. Furthermore, while floating batteries were important agents of defense, their mobility, coupled with the threat posed by defending torpedo boats, meant an attacking enemy had to be circumspect in his blockading attempt. Faced by the possibility of counterattack, the blockader would have to withdraw some distance from the coast, especially at night, and would have to exercise caution in his approach toward the coast during daylight hours.[13]

Sampson admitted that the efficiency of a gun ashore was, within its effective range, greater than that of one on board a ship. Nevertheless, when enemy ships could approach close to shore, the approaches to a port were too broad to be covered solely by land-battery gunfire. When the nature of the ground made construction of fortification impractical, floating defenses were necessary. Since each locale demanded certain types of defending vessels, the naval officers on the Endicott Board proposed the basic designs for four types of "floating batteries." Even the largest of these displaced only 7,000 tons, but carried the heavy armament of two sixteen-inch guns and one ten-inch gun (mounted on naval barbette carriages), protected by eighteen inches of armor backed by six inches of wood and two inches of steel. "Only three vessels afloat," said Sampson, "are armed with guns of similar power," while "no vessel afloat . . . is as well protected by armor."[14] When summarized in the text of the main Endicott Board report, Sampson's views were accepted without revision. While batteries designed to the recommended specifications would be costly, the Endicott Board's report left no doubt that they were an important part of the system of defenses.[15]

Like the landmark Board of Engineers report of 1869, the system of coastal defenses proposed by the Endicott Board was far more sophisticated and complex than any previous system. Because of its complexity and because of the numerous auxiliaries to fortifications now considered necessary, the cost of the system was immense. The Endicott Board estimated that completing the necessary defenses for twenty-seven ports would cost well over $126,000,000. Construction of permanent batteries and fabrication of their armament would cost $93,000,000, while the rest of the total sum included estimates of nearly $19,000,000 for floating batteries, nearly $10,000,000 for torpedo boats, and over $4,000,000 for submarine mines. Recognizing that such vast amounts would never clear Congress as a lump appropriation, the board recommended a first-year appropriation of $21,500,000, an amount equal to over 50 percent of the War Department's total expenditures in 1885. This initial sum would then be supplemented by annual appropriations of $9,000,000 until completion of the work.[16]

Considering that the 1885 appropriation for all aspects of the coastal defense system totaled only $655,000 (with $450,000 ear-marked for gun experiments and construction), the huge amount now recommended, representing a request to essentially double the military budget, boggled Congressional minds. In contrast to the amount proposed by the Endicott Board in July 1886, the House Appropriations Committee suggested the comparatively insignifi-cant amount of $670,000, or roughly the same amount allocated the previous year. In making the committee's case, Representative William Forney of Alabama pointed out that the country was then at peace with the entire world. He pointed out, in addition, that the board reported a total of over 2,000 guns then available. Ignoring the fact that these guns were at best obsolescent (many were still smoothbore guns of Civil War vintage), Forney gave voice to the majority view that since "we have those guns, as our country is at peace . . . and as we have the fortifications which the Board testify were so efficient in former years . . . it is not necessary for us to enter at this time upon the immense work which the Board recom-mend." Within the House, proponents of increased spending for coastal defenses responded by calling the Appropriation Com-mittee's report "hardly a decent apology" for an adequate appro-priation. Representative Byron M. Cutcheon of Michigan argued that it was only a matter of time before the country was again at war. Both he and Representative William McAdoo of New Jersey recognized that at least some of the opposition to fort construction was based on the traditional fears about large standing armies. McAdoo, in particular, countered this belief by arguing that forts were "no menace to the people," and might very well "prevent war by not inviting attack,"[17] as he once more advanced the by now familiar contention that seacoast defenses were a deterrent. Such arguments were in vain. Although the Senate recommended a more generous appropriation of $6,010,000 the House refused to budge. Neither side compromised during the ensuing conference and ultimately no appropriation cleared Congress in 1886.[18]

From the engineers' point of view, the situation improved only marginally during the next few years. Congress again appropriated no money for new construction in 1887 and 1888; and in October of the latter year Chief of Engineers James C. Duane complained that due to the lack of funds "everything connected with our permament defenses" was "going to rack and ruin." Although Duane estimated that a sum of nearly $5,000,000 was necessary, Congress provided only the now traditional amount of $100,000 for "protection, preservation, and repair" of the existing works. This was not enough, reported Duane, for at the various sites the "slopes [were] overgrown with grass and weeds and gullied by the rain; walks and roads [were] ragged and untrimmed and full of holes and breaks; ditches and drains filled up or fallen in and pools of stagnant water [were] on the parades and in the casemates." The entire picture Duane painted with his words was one of "total abandonment and decay."[19]

As in the years prior to the appearance of the Endicott Board report, supporters of the effort to strengthen American coastal defenses took their case to the public media. An engineer officer, Eugene Griffin, for example, summarized the Endicott Board's recommendations in an 1888 *North American Review* article in which he argued, "Our wealthy seacoast cities lie at the mercy of any hostile fleet." Opposition to increased spending on coastal defenses was, said Griffin, based on either one of four commonly used arguments: political expediency, the belief that the United States was secure from attack, the belief that necessary defenses could be improvised in an emergency, or the belief that there was no need for immediate action since guns and armor were constantly improving. All, in Griffin's opinion, were specious; there was no sound reason "that Congress should still neglect to make provision for our defenseless coasts."[20]

Based on the complaints of the Chief Engineer and the angry criticism of Congress expressed by Griffin, the most obvious conclusion is that, through a misguided sense of fiscal responsibility, a shortsighted Congress was failing in its clear obligation to provide adequate coastal defenses. This is the most often arrived at view, but it deserves some further investigation. Certainly some Congressmen opposed military spending for petty or spurious reasons; yet it is also true that most were well aware that, as late as 1889, the country did not possess a proven design for a modern steel gun or the facilities to produce such a weapon in large quantity. Congress allowed the navy to establish a gun factory at the Washington Arsenal in Troy, New York, during the following year.[21] The fortification appropriation for 1888 indicated Congressional concern over the problem of designing and manufacturing suitable artillery. Although Congress earmarked only $100,000 for battery repair and preservation, it provided $500,000 for construction of and experimentation with gun carriages, $1,500,000 for the purchase of steel for guns, $2,500,000 for the construction of twelve-inch breech-loading cast-iron mortars, and another $500,000 to cover the costs of purchasing and testing guns, carriages, and armor.[22]

Aided by such support, by the end of the 1880s American ordnance development began to escape from the doldrums. The first steel gun manufactured in the United States entered the testing phase of development in 1891, and the Ordnance Department predicted in the fall of 1892 that fifteen eight-inch, eight ten-inch, and three twelve-inch guns would be available by December—exclusive of guns being built under contract by the Bethlehem Iron Company.[23] From this point on gun production increased steadily. By 1895 the army's gun factory at Watervliet had produced thirty eight-inch, thirty-three ten-inch, fourteen twelve-inch guns, and eight twelve-inch mortars, while the Bethlehem Iron Company had delivered ten eight-inch guns and was finishing ten ten-inch pieces. Furthermore, after nearly fifteen years of study and trial, the Ordnance Department finally determined on a suitable disappearing carriage in 1894. This was the Buffington-Crozier model 1894, the carriage originally developed in the late 1870s by then Major A. R. Buffington and modified by Captain William Crozier.[24]

The development of American heavy guns and the adoption of a disappearing carriage solved two major problems in the establishment of the Endicott Board's recommendations. Like the engineers' board of 1869, the Endicott Board suggested the possibility of using armored turrets or fixed armored casemates for shore batteries. But partly because of test results and partly on the grounds of cost, the engineers continued to lean in the direction of soundly designed barbette batteries or heavily bunkered batteries for disappearing guns. Such positions could only be accurately designed and built when the kind of gun and carriage to be used in them was known. For Congress, apparently, the key issue was the development of American all-steel high-powered guns, for as these became available, funds for construction of batteries and emplacements did as well. Specifying that the money was for batteries at Boston, New York, and San Francisco, Congress provided $1,221,000 in August of 1890, and there was surprisingly little debate on the bill. The major issue, in fact, was not the appropriation but involved a controversy of several years standing over which committee, appropriations or military, has jurisdiction over the ordnance appropriation.[25] Congress followed up the 1890 appropriation with a further $1,250,000 over the next two years. While the estimates coming from the Engineer Department continued to be higher than this, these amounts were clearly as much as that department could effectively spend, for by the end of 1892 the department still had some $9,000 in unspend funds.[26]

It appears significant, too, that in the Fifty-first Congress the Republicans once again controlled both House and Senate. At least in the Senate, votes on coastal defense measures followed party lines. In June 1890, for example, the Senate voted thirty-two to fifteen to increase the appropriation for the fabrication of seacoast mortars from $250,000 to $400,000. Four Democrats joined twenty-eight Republicans in forming the majority; all fifteen members in opposition were Democrats.[27] Equally indicative of this party split on the issue of coastal defense is the fact that when the Democrats gained control again in the Fifty-second Congress, appropriations for coastal defenses fell off. This situation continued until the Fifty-fourth Congress when the Republicans regained control and appropriations once again rose sharply. In 1895, for example, the total appropriation for coastal fortifications—excluding the amounts for submersible mines—was only $500,000, or about 1 percent of military expenditures. In 1896 the appropriation jumped dramatically to $3,050,000, or 6 percent of military spending. Spending remained at this level, averaging about 4 percent of all military expenditures, for the next two years.[28]

Despite the relative increase in appropriations, the engineers continued to complain that Congress was not providing enough money. Nevertheless, work on the construction of batteries and emplacements went steadily, if slowly, forward. In 1897 the Chief of Engineers, John M. Wilson, reported that fourteen twelve-inch, eighteen ten-inch, and five eight-inch guns were in place, supported by seventy-three twelve-inch mortars and two five-inch and four six-pounder rapid-fire guns. In addition, Wilson stated that by July 1, 1898, a further ten twelve-inch, sixty-four ten-inch, and twenty-eight eight-inch guns would be in position along with another 159 twelve-inch mortars and ten five-inch rapid-fire guns. This was an impressive total, particularly in comparison to the state of the coastal defenses only a decade earlier.[29] The coming of war with Spain in 1898 further spurred construction of coastal defenses, as suddenly East and Gulf coast ports, afraid of Spanish cruisers marauding along the seaboard, demanded protection. By June of 1900 fifty-seven twelve-inch, 105 ten-inch, and seventy-five eight-inch guns were actually emplaced together with fifty-three rapid-fire guns of various calibers and 242 twelve-inch mortars.[30]

Such totals suggest that, by any comparative standard, the United States had a fairly impressive coastal defense system. Since these guns and mortars were distributed over only thirty locales, an average port city was thus protected by approximately two twelve-inch, three ten-inch, and two or three eight-inch guns—along with two rapid-fire guns and eight twelve-inch mortars. Many ports exceeded this average. By June of 1900 Boston, for example, had twenty-four twelve-inch mortars in place along with ten ten-inch guns, three twelve-inch guns on disappearing mounts, and seven rapid-fire guns of various calibers. Despite such figures, the engineers suggested that, in fact, the defenses were only 50 percent complete, and only twenty-five port cities had sufficient guns mounted to permit an effective defense against a naval attack.[31]

Unquestioning acceptance of the engineers' claims led at least one historian of the army to conclude that by the turn of the century, American coastal defenses were in a "depressing state" due to a "lackadaisical" Congress whose failure to provide enough money meant that the country possessed only a "partial harbor defense."[32] Since by 1900 Congressional appropriations for fortifications and defenses (including allotments from a general national defense appropriation in March 1898) totaled over $22,000,000, this assertion deserves further examination. One aspect of the problem, important in assessing the importance of engineer statements regarding the percentage of work completed, is the size and extent of the coastal defense system as proposed by the Endicott Board and revised during later years. As of 1896 planners saw a need for a total of 661 guns and over 1,000 mortars assigned in varying numbers to different sites.[33]

The planned defenses of New York, as an example, included twenty-one twelve-inch guns, fifteen ten-inch guns, and nine eight-inch guns along with 176 twelve-inch mortars, submarine mines, and the already discussed floating defenses. At the same time the planned defenses of Boston included twelve twelve-inch guns, fifteen ten-inch guns, five eight-inch guns, and 128 mortars plus mines and floating defenses, while those of San Francisco included eighteen twelve-inch guns, twenty-three ten-inch guns, thirteen eight-inch guns (all on various types of disappearing carriages) plus fifteen twelve-inch, five ten-inch, and six eight-inch guns on barbette carriages and 144 mortars.[34] All of these numbers indicate that planners wanted an awesome number of heavy guns in and around the ports to be protected. As Donald Abenheim has pointed out in an examination of San Francisco's defenses, the totals suggest that coastal defense planners were still locked conceptually into the past when fortifications mounted several hundred guns. While planners recognized the power of modern rifled artillery, in their proposals they still tended to see such guns as simply replacements for outmoded types, without seeing that fewer of the modern guns fulfilled the function of several dozen of the older types.[35] Obviously, this argument can only go so far, since an antebellum casemated fort might have mounted up to 300 guns and no Endicott battery was planned for anything near that total. At the same time the number of guns considered necessary by the Endicott Board, particularly in conjunction with the limited number of sites to be fortified, does indicate that the board "overplanned"; and a failure to provide the complete total of originally recommended guns is not necessarily an indication that the coastal defenses were thereby weak.

In addition, there are other factors which suggest that blaming a "lackadaisical" Congress (and especially penny-pinching Democrats) for the incomplete status of American coastal defenses obscures the true situation. As Chief of Engineers Thomas L. Casey noted in 1893, construction of a coastal battery was a large-scale project. Building one five-gun disappearing battery entailed the excavation of 26,000 cubic yards of earth and the pouring of over 25,000 cubic yards of cement alone, with the additional move-ment of some 12,000 cubic yards of dirt for the embankment. As Casey said, "the element of time cannot be disregarded" when this amount of work is planned on a national scale.[36] Had Congress granted more money, more laborers might have been hired but the limitations on army, and particularly the Corps of Engineers' strength meant that only a limited number of supervisory officers would be available. The fact that the Corp of Engineers also had responsibility for supervising a vast number of river and harbor improvement projects further reduced the number of officers available to supervise fortification construction. Given these cir-cumstances, the engineers constructed emplacements about as quickly as they could and any extra money would in all likelihood simply accumulate unspent.[37]

At the same time, the engineers were building defenses at a rate which approximated the numbers of guns being made available by the Ordnance Department. By 1900 the Ordnance Department had either supplied or contracted for all the guns and mortars necessary for each of the emplacements the engineers had ready or under con-struction.[38] This was a far cry from the situation of the antebellum period when finished fortifications often went unarmed for years.

The kinds of batteries constructed were also very different from those of a half-century before. European countries were in-creasingly utilizing armor in fortification construction, either facing the scarp wall directly with armor plate or using armored cupolas and revolving turrets. Initially, like the other boards formed after the Civil War, the Endicott Board recommended the use of armored turrets and fixed, armored casemates as well as bar-bette emplacements. In practice, however, United States shore bat-teries were almost universally of the barbette type, modified to allow for the use of disappearing carriages or, in two cases, arranged so that the entire gun platform could move up and down. Furthermore, unlike the casemated fortifications of the Third System which concentrated all the defending guns within a small area, late nineteenth century American shore batteries consisted of a number of detached positions connected by telephone communications and trenches. It continued to be critical that the field of fire of these batteries cover the water approaches completely, leaving no "dead" angles in which enemy ships could escape the concentrated fire of the defenders. Nevertheless, while the Third-System defenses were highly visible and built as close as possible to the water's edge, Endicott period batteries were dispersed and concealed. Engineer General Henry L. Abbot pointed out in a series of lectures in 1888 that ships' gunners could use visible landmarks around a battery position as aiming points. "Hence," said Abbot, "those sites are most advantageous which do not favor such methods." Forest behind a battery position, for example, made determining the horizon difficult, while wooded or brush-covered front slopes helped hide the fall of shot. "We must sacrifice neat crests and beautiful slopes," argued Abbot, "trees and bushes must be planted on the parapets and behind the batteries to prevent a clear definition of the guns; the latter themselves must be colored to harmonize with their surroundings in summer and winter." In contrast to the past, when concentration and material strength were key aspects of fortification design, "dispersion and concealment" were now important.[39]

This kind of dispersion meant that coastal fortifications took on an entirely new configuration which required far more ground area than earlier fortifications. This fact posed some problems for coastal defense planners as the needed ground space was not always available. In addition, the increased power and range of modern guns meant that the actual line of defenses needed to be much further forward of the protected port or harbor than in the past. "Where one mile was once more than ample" distance from the fort back to the "object of defense," by the 1890s the engineers believed "eight to ten miles" were necessary. In some situations, it was, of course, not possible to construct defenses this far in front of a port. At Charleston, South Carolina, for example, there was simply no ground on which to build any further out than that already occupied by older fortifications. In such cases, the older works were simply utilized as sites for modern guns. In other cases, particularly at Chesapeake Bay, gun positions moved steadily closer to the mouth of the bay, further away from cities and harbors like Baltimore, Annapolis, and Hampton Roads. For close-in defense, these places relied on reworked and modified older defenses. In most cases, however, as the naval officers of the Endicott Board had pointed out, by the time these older defenses could be effective, an enemy fleet would already be within bombardment range of the city or harbor.[40] In such a situation, where advanced battery sites could not be constructed, the policy was "to sweep all practicable bombardment areas with a heavy fire, and to trust to the cooperation of naval torpedo boats acting offensively."[41] This was clearly a less than ideal arrangement, and the engineers thought it fortunate that it was a necessary one at only a few important port cities.

One gun which became increasingly important during the 1890s was the small-caliber rapid-fire gun. Typically these guns were five-inch or six-pounder pieces, emplaced on "balanced pillar" mountings. Their primary function was to cover the mine fields, but they had the important secondary function of reinforcing the larger guns at short range.[42] By the late 1890s the engineers were beginning to suggest reductions in the numbers of heavy guns and mortars at some sites, and the replacement of these weapons by more of the smaller, faster-firing pieces. "To meet the increased volume of fire," the board suggested it would "be prudent to follow the naval precedent."[43] Although the original Endicott Board recommended a total of only 355 of the rapid-fire guns, 516 were actually in place by 1905, and they accounted for some 43 percent of the defensive gun strength by that time.[44]

In addition to the increasingly popular rapid-fire guns and the newly developed large-caliber pieces, coastal defense armament also included numerous mortars. Recommended originally by the board of 1869 as useful for protecting anchorages or other sites from enemy vessels, mortars were an accepted part of coastal defense armament by the mid-1880s. The Endicott Board included them as a part of the recommended armament without any comment. Apparently, no additional justification was necessary by this time.

The most important virtue of coastal defense mortars was that the deck armor of warships was not built to withstand heavy-caliber projectiles. Since ships' guns fired horizontally rather than lobbing their projectiles to fall vertically, most of the massive armor on capital ships was on the hull sides, and American engineers believed that a slowly moving or stationary bombarding vessel could be attacked at its most vulnerable point. To overcome the inherent inaccuracy of mortar fire, the engineers proposed concentrating the mortars in groups of four, with four such batteries (or sixteen mortars) constituting a battery commanded by a Captain of Artillery. With this type of concentration, mortar fire would "be far more effective than is generally believed."[45] European tests, argued the engineers, demonstrated the validity of this claim. In Germany, eleven-inch mortars, fired at a range of nearly five miles, had a mean lateral dispersion of 105 feet. In a Russian test, the lateral dispersion was nineteen feet, six inches, and the longitudinal dispersion eighty-five feet. Based on these tests the engineers calculated that a British battleship of the *Inflexible* class (making a target 800 feet long and 300 feet wide) would be hit anywhere from two to nineteen times in an hour's firing by sixteen mortars. Since the rifled twelve-inch mortar being developed for American service fired a projectile weighing 625 pounds, they would hit a ship's deck armor or planking with a force of forty-five to fifty foot-tons per inch. Less than a third of this was ample to penetrate a three-inch wrought-iron deck, and thus any ship struck would suffer grievous damage.[46]

American engineers took a good deal of pride in their development of seacoast mortar batteries. Henry L. Abbot suggested before an international audience in 1894 that in regard to this aspect of coastal defense, "American ideas are in advance of any existing European constructions, although . . . the subject is now attracting attention abroad."[47] A part of that attention was doubtless due to the fact that mortars were far less expensive than equal-caliber guns, a factor happily pointed out by American engineers.[48] By 1900, 240 mortars were already emplaced and the Ordnance Department had made provision for supplying a further 132.[49]

One problem with American mortar batteries was the inevitable confusion as four mortar crews struggled to reload their weapons in the confined space of the battery. Eventually, experiments indicated that the rate of fire went up with no loss in effectiveness when only two of the mortars were utilized. These results led to a reduction in the number of mortars per battery from four to two during the years after the turn of the century.[50]

Another problem, however, was the inherent difficulty of hitting a moving target with vertical fire. The Engineer enthusiasm for the use of mortars was, in fact, consistently predicated on the assumption that a bombarding vessel would remain stationary while firing.[51] By the turn of the century the Board of Engineers was suggesting that this assumption was no longer valid, and it recommended a reduction in the number of mortars. Improvements in range-finding techniques and the development of more powerful mortars ensured the continued existence of such batteries as a part of American coastal defense well into the twentieth century.[52]

Developments such as the inclusion of mortar batteries and rapid-fire guns, along with searchlights and modern range finders, suggest that by the end of the nineteenth century American coastal defense was both theoretically and practically more complex than ever before. While the fundamental purpose of such defenses remained essentially unchanged, American engineers and defense planners had to cope with far more elements in the design of defenses and in the tactics of their use.

At least to some extent, training at West Point reflected the altered nature of coastal fortification design. In 1884 a new textbook by J. B. Wheeler replaced the now fifty-year-old text of Dennis Hart Mahan. Although Wheeler's text covered much the same ground as Mahan's, particularly in its lengthy discussion of the evolution of the bastion system, it went much further in its coverage of the particular problems in designing a coastal defense system. Wheeler included a substantial section on this subject in which he accepted the end of the masonry casemated fortification and emphasized the need for channel obstructions. Instead, Wheeler proposed as an example a defensive system including armored turrets mounted on casemated towers, strong enclosed batteries, and various forms of obstructions (including submarine mines along with sunken hulks, booms, pilings, and rope obstructions for fouling ships' propellers).[53]

Since Wheeler's text appeared in 1884, it naturally reflected the then widespread belief that some sort of armored battery would eventually become the dominant design form for American coastal fortifications. As already indicated, this did not occur. Even though the Endicott Board also suggested the eventual use of armored turrets and armored casemates, the barbette battery utilizing some form of disappearing carriage actually became the design form used for American defenses. Not only were such batteries less expensive, but their massive earthen protection was actually superior in most respects to that provided by armor plate. In this regard Wheeler's text was soon outdated. Nevertheless, as the Military Academy's standard text past the end of the century, it provided cadets with a sound introduction to the complex problems of coastal defense.

By the end of the nineteenth century, the system of coastal defenses outlined by the Endicott Board was beginning to take substantial shape. Although during the late 1890s critics of Congressional laxity continued to suggest that the American coasts were open to attack, perhaps even invasion, the strength of the coastal defenses was continuing to grow.[54] The fundamental premises which underlay that system remained unaltered from those developed by the Board of Engineers in 1816, despite the increasing complexity of the practical mechanics of coastal defense. While that complexity would continue to increase, those fundamental premises would continue to remain unchanged as the country moved into the twentieth century.

NOTES

1. House Executive Document 49, 49th Congress, 1st session, Serial 2395, pp. 5-6. This document, which fills an entire volume in the serial set, contains the full text and tables of the Endicott Board Report and the reports of its component subcommittees. In addition to William C. Endicott, the Secretary of War, the Board of Fortifications or Other Defenses included General Stephen V. Benet (Chief of Ordnance) and Captain Charles S. Smith of the Ordnance Department, General John Newton (Chief of Engineers) and Lt.-Col. Henry L. Abbot of the Engineers, Commander William T. Sampson and Commander Caspar F. Goodrich of the Navy, and two civilians—Joseph Morgan, Jr. from Pennsylvania and Erastus Corning from New York.

2. Ibid., p. 2.

3. Ibid., p. 9.

4. Ibid. For an analysis of the navy's strategic thinking see Harold and Margaret Sprout, *The Rise of American Naval Power* (Princeton: Princeton University Press, 1939). Firmly Mahanian in outlook the Sprouts argue that both the navy and the country's civilian leaders ignored the

lessons of history by continuing to opt for this strategy of "commerce raid-ing" and that, as a result, the period from 1865 to 1890 was one of stagna-tion in American naval thought. This view is challenged by more recent students of the era. One good modern, and revisionist, study is Lance C. Buhl, "Maintaining An 'American Navy' 1865-1889," in Kenneth Hagan, ed., *In Peace and War* (Westport, Conn.: Greenwood Press, 1978), pp. 145-173. Buhl suggests that the navy's strategic thought in this period was fully in accord with national needs and national attitudes and condemna-tion of it represents a failure to deal with the issue in its proper context.

5. House Executive Document 49, 49th Congress, 1st session, p. 7.

6. Ibid., pp. 9-10.

7. Ibid., pp. 27-29. The $8,000,000 figure equaled not only 20 percent of the War Department expenditures in 1885, but nearly 25 percent of those actually made in 1886. It equaled roughly 3 percent of all federal expenditures during this period. Here and throughout, figures for annual War Department and federal expenditures are from United States Bureau of the Census, *Historical Statistics of the United States: Colonial Times to 1957* (Washington, D.C.: Government Printing Office, 1960), pp. 718-719.

8. Representative Charles A. Boutelle, *The Congressional Record,* 51st Congress, 1st session, pp. 3161-3163, as cited in Lance C. Buhl, "Main-taining 'An American Navy,' "in Kenneth Hagan, ed., *In Peace and War* (Westport, Conn.: Greenwood Press, 1978), p. 159.

9. William Bainbridge-Hoff, "Examples, Conclusions, and Maxims of Modern Naval Tactics," *Office of Naval Intelligence, Bureau of Naviga-tion, General Information Series No. III* (Washington, D.C.: Government Printing Office, 1884), pp. 133, 139-141.

10. William T. Sampson, "Outline of a Scheme for the Naval Defense of the Coast," *Proceedings of the United States Naval Institute,* vol. 15, no. 2 (April 1889), pp. 182-183.

11. Ibid., pp. 195, 201.

12. Richard Wainwright, "Our Coast Defenses From A Naval Stand-Point," *The United Service* (New Series), vol. 2, no. 1 (July 1889), pp. 46-47.

13. Endicott Board Report, pp. 305-307.

14. Ibid., p. 310.

15. Ibid., p. 9.

16. Ibid., pp. 28-29. Ninety-three million dollars was an amount equal to nearly 40 percent of annual federal expenditures in the mid-1880s. Annual federal expenditures for these years may be found in United States Bureau of the Census, *Historical Statistics of the United States,* pp. 718-719.

17. *Congressional Record,* vol. 17, pt. 7, 49th Congress, 1st session (July 1886), pp. 7097-7113.

18. Ibid., p. 7629.

19. Annual Report of the Chief of Engineers, 1888, Exec. Document no. 1, pt. 2, 50th Congress, 2d session, Serial 2629.

20. Eugene Griffin, "Our Sea-Coast Defenses," *North American Review,* vol. 147 (1888), pp. 64-75.

21. Annual Report of the Chief of Ordnance (1886), Exec. Document 1, pt. 2, 49th Congress, 2d Session, Serial 2465; Annual Report of the Chief of Ordnance, 1888, Exec. Document 1, pt. 2, 50th Congress, 2d session, Serial 2633.

22. *Statutes At Large,* vol. 25, pp. 489-491.

23. Annual Report of the Chief of Ordnance, 1891, Exec. Document 1, pt. 2, 52d Congress, 1st session, Serial 2928; Annual Report of the Chief of Ordnance, 1892, Exec. Document 1, pt. 2, 52nd Congress, 2nd session, Serial 3083.

24. Annual Report of the Chief of Ordnance, 1895, House Document 2, 54th Congress, 1st session, Serial 3378.

25. *Statutes At Large,* vol. 26, p. 315; *Congressional Record,* 51st Congress, 1st session, pp. 2883-2887.

26. *Statutes At Large,* vol. 26, p. 767; *Statutes At Large,* vol. 27, p. 258; Annual Report of the Chief Engineer (1892), House Exec. Document 1, pt. 2, 52d Congress, 2nd session, Serial 3078.

27. *Congressional Record*, 51st Congress, 1st session, vol. 21, pt. 6, p. 5587.

28. *Statutes At Large,* vol. 28, pp. 704-705; *Statutes At Large,* vol. 29, pp. 256-261. The cited figures for fortifications appropriations do not include appropriations for submersible mines and their associated equipment, or appropriations for ordnance development and manufacture.

29. Annual Report of the Chief of Engineers, 1897, House Document 2, 55th Congress, 2d session, Serial 3631.

30. Annual Report of the Chief of Engineers, 1900, House Document 2, 56th Congress, 2d session, Serial 4089.

31. Ibid.

32. William A. Ganoe, *The History of the United States Army* (New York: D. Appleton, 1924), p. 428.

33. Annual Report of the Chief of Engineers, 1896, House Document 2, 54th Congress, 2d session, Serial 3479.

34. Annual Report of the Chief of Engineers, 1893, House Document 1, pt. 2, 53rd Congress, 2d session, Serial 3199, pp. 4-10.

35. Donald Abenheim, "Never A Shot in Anger," *Military Collector and Historian: The Journal of the Company of Military Historians,* vol. 28, no. 3 (Fall, 1976), p. 104.

36. Annual Report of the Chief of Engineers, 1893.

37. In 1898 the Corps of Engineers consisted of 123 officers. Thirteen

were then employed on river and harbor projects, nine were at the School of Application, and fifty-three were doing double-duty—working on river and harbor improvements and on fortifications. Thirty-five engineers were serving with armies in the field. The remaining thirteen were serving in administrative positions. See the Annual Report of the Chief of Engineers, 1898, House Document 2, 55th Congress, 3rd session, Serial 3746, pp. 3-4.

38. Annual Report of the Chief of Engineers, 1900.

39. Henry L. Abbot, *A Course of Lectures Upon the Defence of the Sea-Coast of the United States* (New York: D. Van Nostrand, 1888), pp. 154, 158.

40. Annual Report of the Chief of Engineers, 1889, Exec. Document 1, pt. 2, 51st Congress, 1st session, Serial 2716, p. 6; Annual Report of the Chief of Engineers, 1890, House Exec. Document 1, pt. 2, 51st Congress 2nd session, Serial 2832. For a brief discussion of this change in range and its effect on battery position see Emanuel R. Lewis, *Seacoast Fortifications of the United States* (Washington, D.C.: Smithsonian Institution Press, 1970), p. 89.

41. Henry L. Abbot, "Coast Defense, Including Submarine Mines," *Proceedings of the International Congress of Engineers, Division of Military Engineering, Chicago, 1893* (Washington, D.C.: Government Printing Office, 1894), p. 21.

42. Ibid., p. 25.

43. Letters Received "Safe File," Fortifications and Defenses, 1810-1920, Box 2, Folder E. D. 31841, Entry 225, Record Group 77, NA.

44. Rowena A. Reed, "The Endicott Board—Vision and Reality," *Periodical: The Journal of the Council on Abandoned Military Posts,* vol. 9, no. 2 (Summer 1979), p. 12. See also the report of the Endicott Board, previously cited, and the report of the National Coast Defense Board, Senate Document 248, 59th Congress, 1st session, Serial 4913.

45. Board of Engineers, U.S. Army, *Typical Mortar Battery to Favor Precision of Vertical Fire in Sea Coast Defence* (Willett's Point, N.Y.: Engineer School Battalion Press, 1888), p. 1.

46. Ibid., pp. 2-4. Also see Henry L. Abbot, *A Course of Lectures Upon the Defence of the Sea-Coast of the United States,* p. 108.

47. Henry L. Abbot, "Coast Defense, Including Submarine Mines," p. 25.

48. Henry L. Abbot was explicit on this point in an 1869 paper read before the Essayons Club of the Corps of Engineers. See Henry L. Abbot, "Notes on Mortars in Harbor Defence," Printed Papers of the Essayons Club, no. 11 (Willett's Point, N.Y.: Battalion Press, 1869). Also see Henry L. Abbot, *A Course of Lectures Upon the Defence of the Sea-Coast of the United States,* pp. 123-124.

49. Annual Report of the Chief of Engineers, 1900.

50. Emanuel R. Lewis, *Seacoast Fortifications,* pp. 84, 94; Rowena Reed, "Endicott Board—Vision and Reality," p. 12.

51. Henry L. Abbot, "Notes on Mortars in Harbor Defence," p. 10; Board of Engineers, U.S. Army, *Typical Mortar Battery To Favor Precision of Vertical Fire,* p. 1.

52. Eben E. Winslow, *Notes on Seacoast Fortification,* Occasional Papers, no. 61, Engineer School, U.S. Army (Washington, D.C.: Government Printing Office, 1920), p. 37.

53. J. B. Wheeler, *A Textbook of Military Engineering,* 2 vols. (New York: John Wiley and Sons, 1884), vol. 2, pp. 171-172, 175-176.

54. For an example of this type of criticism see Representative George N. Southwick, "Our Defenceless Coasts," *North American Review,* vol. 162, no. 372 (March 1876), pp. 317-327. The fact that fear of actual invasion continued to lurk in the minds of at least some military men is indicated by the solution to the Naval War College problem of 1899. That problem postulated a thinly disguised Anglo-German alliance and an attack upon the United States. The "solution" suggested that not only was such an alliance "not beyond the realm of possibility" but that the combined attackers would be able to take and hold Boston and most of New England for at least a year. Fortifications and Defenses, 1810-1920, Box 5, Folder E. D. 16637, Entry 225, RG 77, NA.

EPILOGUE
A System Reaffirmed

Concern over the state of the country's coastal defenses faded in the victorious afterglow of the Spanish-American War. After all, the navy had dominated the Spanish in every encounter, and despite the fears of many coast-inhabiting citizens, no Spanish cruisers appeared off any American port cities. Nevertheless, during the years after 1900, construction of coastal defenses continued at a slow but steady rate. It was increasingly apparent, however, that continued advances in military technology made the Endicott Board fortifications obsolescent, if not obsolete. Accordingly, at the end of January 1905 President Theodore Roosevelt created a new board under the leadership of Secretary of War William Howard Taft to review the recommendations of the Endicott Board and suggest that additional means or modifications would place American coastal defenses back among the best in the world. Officially known as the National Coast Defense Board, and informally known as the Taft Board, this group made its report to the President at the end of February 1906.[1]

The Taft Board made no revisions to the principles of coastal defense as reported by the Endicott Board and fully accepted the earlier board's arguments on the necessity of such defenses. Rather than reexamining American coastal defense policy, the Taft Board limited itself from the start to reconfirming that policy, confining its analysis to an examination to the details of the Endicott Board's proposals, modifying them to match technological developments, and simultaneously updating the original cost estimates.[2] Some sites selected by the Endicott Board were now deemphasized while others, most notably the entrances of Chesapeake Bay and Puget Sound, were given increased importance. In addition, the Taft Board recommended the construction of defenses for the country's new colonial possessions and the Panama Canal, sites which the Endicott Board had no need to consider. However, while the Taft Board lengthened the list of locations needing defenses, it suggested little substantial change in the "defensive appliances" which would make up those defenses.

In looking at smaller details, the Taft Board came down firmly in favor of the disappearing gun carriage, effectively ending any debate over the use of armored casemates or turrets. The board also urged the continued use of mortars and submarine mines as well as the use of devices only suggested by the Endicott Board, such as searchlights. The only alteration to these systems urged by the Taft Board was the addition of a range-finding system. Advances in range finding would make the fire of both guns and mortars more effective and allow a relatively small number of large-caliber guns to equal the power and effectiveness of the larger number of small-caliber guns recommended by the Endicott Board. This was not really a change, however, since it represented only a modification made because of a technological advance, not a change in the basic approach.[3]

Only in one area did the Taft Board differ substantially from the Endicott Board, and even here the Taft Board did no more than return to the arguments of even earlier boards. As already seen, the Endicott Board had enthusiastically recommended the adoption of "floating defenses," particularly for the defense of the "outer ring" (the entrances to Long Island Sound and Chesapeake Bay). The Taft Board, though, swung back to the old argument of the engineers that such defenses were inefficient and undependable, a shift which reflected a change in the attitude of naval officers and strategists.

During the 1880s and early 1890s naval officers eagerly sought some role in coastal defense, at least partly in the hope that linking the navy to such a traditional and defensive policy would mean an increase in the importance and perhaps the size of the navy. The naval officers on the Endicott Board certainly favored the building of coastal defense vessels. In addition, the Endicott Board's emphasis on the necessity of floating defenses was also due in part to the relative weakness of American ordnance in the mid-1880s and in part to the fact that many Congressmen continued to see floating defenses as a viable alternative to the engineers' extensive land fortifications, as they had throughout the century.

In reviewing the Endicott Board's recommendations, however, the Taft Board concluded that floating defenses were, in fact, more expensive than fortifications, an argument long used by the engineers in countering proposals for such vessels. The five major floating batteries proposed by the Endicott Board, along with the recommended 150 torpedo boats, carried an estimated price tag of over $28,000,000. Although never committing itself fully to the proposed program, Congress had nevertheless authorized the construction of several monitor-type harbor defense vessels, ten of which were a part of the naval list in 1905 and 1906. Five of these were essentially Civil War vessels, constructed over a twenty-year period and built with iron hulls rather than steel. Designed with low freeboard and shallow draft, these ships were wet at sea and poorly ventilated below decks. Engine room temperatures could exceed 150 °F, with 205 °F recorded by one official inspection party.[4]

During the Spanish-American War these ships formed a part of the American fleet blockading Cuba, and two actually sailed as far as the Philippines. In addition, numerous Civil War ironclad monitors were rebuilt to serve as defense vessels for eastern ports. Convinced of the usefulness of such types, Congress authorized the construction of four new monitors in 1898. Unlike the earlier vessels these 1898 monitors were modern ships, built with efficient boiler systems, electrical auxiliary power, and powerful twelve-inch guns.[5]

None of these 1898 monitors entered service until well after the wartime emergency was over, and by the time they entered service enthusiasm for this type was already waning. Except in extreme cases, monitor vessels were limited to coastal defense duties; none could serve as part of a main battle fleet nor could they be used to extend American naval power beyond coastal waters. By 1905 such limitations were unacceptable to a growing number of naval officers and navy supporters, all of whom shared Captain Alfred Thayer Mahan's conviction that the role of a navy was not passive coastal defense but to contend for "command of the sea." As early as 1901, Lieutenant-Commander James H. Sears argued that while shore defenses might in some cases be strengthened by the presence of specially designed harbor defense vessels, the construction of such vessels absorbed a considerable part of the available money and weakened the "line of battle." It was, declared Sears, "illogical" to believe that the proper function of a navy was to participate "in the defense of the coast as a present actual factor of harbor defenses." Yet, at the same time, Sears argued that coastal fortifications would add little support to American "stature or strength" in any contest with a foreign enemy. "Our peace-loving nation," he wrote, "may be content to rest behind such defenses," but in the end passive defenses such as coastal fortifications would not be enough. Ultimately, suggested Sears, the best defense for the United States coastline was a naval force capable of taking the offensive. Permanent defenses were necessary, since they provided time for relief forces to gather and because they exercised "a deterrent effect"; but in keeping with Mahan's teachings, Sears contended that "the fate of a coast rests in the beginning and in the end, fortified or not fortified, *upon command of the sea.*"[6] Sears, like the majority of naval officers after 1900, was not suggesting that fortifying the coast should cease. Instead, he was pressing the case for a navy capable of taking the fight away from the coast and out on the open ocean. Coastal defense monitors had no place in this kind of navy.

Army officers concerned about the problem of coastal defense concurred. In a 1902 book titled *The Tactics of Coast Defense,* Major John P. Wisser of the Artillery Corps, suggested that the use of the navy as a direct agent of coastal defense violated the basic principles of strategy. Like Sears, Wisser argued that the coastal defenses alone could only avoid defeat; for victory it was necessary for a nation to take the offensive. "Permanent defenses," wrote Wisser, "serve to protect important bases for the navy, exercise a deterrent effect on the enemy . . . and gain time for the navy to repel an invasion or to raise a blockade."[7]

This concurrence between army and navy views on coastal defense brought the arguments surrounding the issue full circle. Proponents of such defenses were by 1906 essentially arguing the same case developed by the original Board of Engineers as early as 1818. Coastal defenses would protect important naval bases, guard centers of trade and commerce, and act to deter any nation from attempting a raid upon a coastal city. Freed from worry about security of its bases the navy would be able to concentrate and seek out the enemy on the high seas. Changes in weaponry and in the associated technology meant that the mechanics of coastal defense were very different in 1906 from what they were in 1816; the fundamental premises of coastal defense were the same.

The first colonists did not express their views on coastal defense in so formal a way. Awareness that the sea was the avenue on which foreign enemies would come prompted them to build the first American coastal defenses. Crude by European standards, these defenses constantly deteriorated until some emergency spurred reconstruction. Consciously or not, the colonists relied upon the Royal Navy as the first line of defense.

Although the Revolutionary War removed the protective bulwark of the Royal Navy, other aspects of the colonial tradition persisted. The federal government was slow to assume total control over the construction of coastal defenses. As in the past, construction of such defenses generally came only during an emergency which excited fears for the unprotected seacoast cities and towns. Even the founding of West Point did not change this practice. Fortifications might be built by American engineers rather than foreigners, but no centralized planning body assumed control over the direction and scope of American defensive measures.

In this regard, the War of 1812 is a watershed. Spurred by vivid memories of the Royal Navy's essentially unchallenged ravages of the American coast, the government created a Board of Engineers in 1816 to act as the central clearing house for coastal defense planning. For the rest of the century, this board, in all its permutations, would dominate the thinking on the subject of defenses. Shaped for nearly fifty years by the presence of Joseph G. Totten, the views of the Board of Engineers would become the nation's most expert opinions on the subject of coastal defense. These opinions and plans did not go unchallenged, but while other views on the best means of coastal defense came and went, the views of the board remained unchanged.

From the beginning the Board of Engineers defined the basic function of coastal defenses as protection of the nation's commercial centers, the country's coastal navigation, and the navy's bases.

The possibility of actual invasion, while alluded to and discussed, never entirely dictated the shape and extent of the system of defenses developed by the board. What was repeatedly emphasized was the fact that coastal defenses would deter foreign aggression by making any potential foe think twice before attacking the coast.

In addition to this, the Board of Engineers did two other things, each of which had far-reaching effects. By acting as the central planning body for coastal defense, the board also acted to institutionalize the planning process and make it a permanent aspect of the American military establishment. At the same time the board advanced the argument that the construction of permanent fortifications would be a one-time expense, while maintaining an army large enough to defend the coastline would be an annual expense.[8] However, by its very nature, this argument led planners to believe that the fortifications, once built, would serve indefinitely thereafter. Technological improvements in weaponry during the middle of the nineteenth century soon invalidated this belief. Despite all the labor and money spent on permanent defenses during the years between 1815 and 1861, the existing coastal defense system was obsolete by 1865. Yet even when the physical means of coastal defense were no longer sufficient, the engineers retained their faith in the need for coastal defenses and in the principles of coastal defense as originally developed by the Board of Engineers after the War of 1812. In the two decades following the Civil War, the engineers continued to argue the urgent need for coastal defense while simultaneously attempting to develop a modern system of such defenses.

The end of this period of confusion and experimentation was marked by the creation and report of the Endicott Board, the first major board to include civilians as well as military men. Given the task of recommending both the means and the extent of the coastal defense system, the Endicott Board proposed an ambitious scheme combining a great number of shore batteries with floating defenses and auxiliaries, such as mine fields and searchlights. The immediate impact of this proposal was slight; Congress did not authorize any additional construction until 1890, and even then appropriations fell far short of the estimates. In the long run, the Endicott Board's proposed system of coastal defenses nevertheless became the basic plan which, despite occasional modification, would guide coastal defense planners well beyond the turn of the century. And the Endicott Board once more reiterated the familiar principles of coastal defense—only the board's endorsement of floating defenses was different from the basic proposals of the Board of Engineers before the Civil War.

Not until after 1900 did the proposed scheme of the Endicott Board come under scrutiny. In 1906 a new board, the Taft Board, reviewed the 1886 program and, despite the intervening improvements in weaponry, made only cosmetic alterations to the Endicott Board's proposals and recommendations. The Taft Board accepted unchallenged and unaltered the principles of coastal defense as argued by the Endicott Board and, before them, every board back to 1816.

During the ninety years from 1816 to 1906, the government spent $143,000,000 on permanent defenses, an amount equal to roughly 4 percent of all War Department expenditures.[9] This percentage varied, of course, during the period. From 1816 to 1860 8 percent of military spending went toward fortifications, a figure which dropped to 1 percent between 1871 and 1889. However, this latter period was one of rapid and continuous change in weaponry. Congress was justifiably reluctant to spend large sums on defenses which would soon become obsolete. Indeed, Congressional concern over the need to develop modern ordnance for American defenses is illustrated by the fact that appropriations for ordnance experimentation and development averaged between two and three times the amounts for fortification construction.[10] When modern all-steel guns became available in the 1890s, appropriations increased dramatically. To some extent this was due to the increasing dominance of the Republican Party—the party traditionally linked to the movement toward a more aggressive foreign policy and greater military strength—but even under the Democrats appropriations for fortifications increased in the 1890s. From 1891 to 1898 an average of 3 percent of military expenditures went into coastal fortifications, a figure which rose to 5 percent in 1896 and 1897.[11]

Such figures testify to the consistent importance of coastal defenses in American military planning. Under the program outlined by the Taft Board, construction continued at a fairly steady pace for the next decade. By that time, however, improvements in warship design, together with the development of ever more powerful long-range guns and better fire control systems, led the Chief of Engineers, Brigadier General Daniel C. Kingman, to once again argue that American defenses were dangerously outmoded. What was necessary was a program of immediate and continuous modernization in order to keep up with the pace of technological change. American entry into World War I postponed any major effort, though, and postwar financial constraints meant that little construction of new permanent coastal positions actually occurred in either the 1920s or 1930s.[12]

Indeed by the end of the 1930s the era of the permanent coastal battery was coming to an end. The emerging threat of aircraft meant that the coastal cities were no longer the only ones threatened by sudden attack, and antiaircraft artillery emerged as an increasingly important component of the traditional coastal artillery organization. Even though the early years of World War II heightened concern over coastal defenses, especially along the West coast and in Hawaii, this concern began to fade as the tide turned and construction of coastal batteries eventually ceased altogether.[13]

By the end of World War II the long age of the coastal defense battery was over. Long-range bombers or missiles, carrying either heavy conventional bomb loads or atomic weapons, shifted the focus of national defense from the shoreline to the sky and made distant interception (or at least early warning) mandatory. A system of permanent coastal defenses was no longer a shield to the nation, no longer a barrier to an attacker.

For nearly a century and a half concern about the need to protect the coast was an integral aspect of American military policy. In his brief and perceptive history of coastal fortifications, Emanuel R. Lewis suggests that this continuing concern about the problem of defending the coast is a reflection of a "defensive tradition" in American military thought.[14] An even more appropriate description would be "deterrent tradition," since the belief that coastal defenses would not only repel attack but might even prevent conflict altogether was fundamental to the development of American coastal defense policy. In its modern context deterrence implies the ability to strike back in overwhelming force, directly at an attacker's homeland. But, at its most basic, deterrence simply means the placing of barriers in an enemy's way, barriers which by their existence prevent an enemy from taking a certain line of action. Within this meaning of the term, American coastal defenses were a deterrent, for their purpose was not only to act as agents of local defense, but simply by their existence forcing any potential enemy to recognize that the cost of any attack would be prohibitive and, perhaps, not attack at all. Thus, American coastal defense policy was intended to provide not only the mechanisms of actual defense, but to demonstrate to all potential enemies that the United States was prepared to defend itself, and by virtue of being prepared, prevent conflict. Colonel Eben E. Winslow expressed this idea clearly in 1920 when he concluded an analysis of American coastal defenses by suggesting that "a seacoast fortification" might have best "performed the function for which it was intended, if it never was called into use at all."[15] Present-day American military policy is based on the same principle; the oft-stated justification for the nuclear deterrent is that by its existence it prevents the very war it would serve. American coastal defense policy was then, at rock bottom, nothing more than the expression of one of the most fundamental premises in American military thought.

NOTES

1. "Coast Defenses of the United States and the Insular Possessions," Senate Document 248, 59th Congress, 1st session, Serial 4913. (The Taft Board Report.)

2. Ibid., p. 10.

3. Ibid., pp. 13-19.

4. John D. Alden, *The American Steel Navy* (Annapolis: U.S. Naval Institute Press, 1972), pp. 93-94. The Monitors in service in 1905 were listed by the Taft Board. See Senate Document 248, 59th Congress, 1st session, Serial 4913, p. 41.

5. Alden, *Steel Navy,* p. 94.

6. Emphasis in the original. James H. Sears, "The Coast in Warfare," *Proceedings of the United States Naval Institute,* vol. 27, no. 3 (September 1901), pp. 477, 505, 492.

7. John P. Wisser, *The Tactics of Coast Defense* (Kansas City, Mo.: Hudson-Kimberly, 1902), pp. 13-14. Major Wisser was well aware of Lt.-Commander Sears's views. He listed Sears in his bibliography and mentioned him on page 14.

8. *American State Papers, Military Affairs,* vol. 2 (Serial 017), Document 206, p. 309. By the twentieth century the engineers were very

much aware of how changes in weaponry could make a fortification system obsolete in a brief time. See Colonel Eben E. Winslow, *Notes on Seacoast Fortification,* Occasional Paper no. 61, Engineer School, U.S. Army (Washington, D.C.: Government Printing Office, 1920), pp. 19-20. The engineers of the 1820s, however, cannot be blamed for believing that the forts they designed and built would last for decades; theirs was a period of little change in weaponry—at least until the 1840s.

9. George A. Zinn, *Index to the Reports of the Chief of Engineering, U.S. Army, 1866-1912,* vol. 2 (Washington, D.C.: Government Printing Office, 1916), p. 1814. Part 1 of this volume contains a summary table showing the total appropriations by states for fortifications in each year going back at least to 1821. Since there is no indication that any of the totals include those amounts appropriated from 1816-1820, I suspect that the figure of $143 million is slightly low. However, the amounts being appropriated during the years just after the War of 1812 were small enough that the total for those four years would not alter the final, summary, total significantly. Figures for annual War Department expenditures, here and throughout, are from United States, Bureau of the Census, *Historical Statistics of the United States: Colonial Times to 1957* (Washington, D.C.: Government Printing Office, 1960).

10. In 1880, for example, while appropriations for fort construction and repair equaled only $100,000, Congress provided $400,000 for armament. From 1876 to 1885, fort appropriations averaged $130,000 ($150,000 after 1879) while appropriations for armament and ordnance experimentation averaged $233,500 ($316,000 after 1879). *Statutes At Large,* vol. 19, pp. 59, 391; vol. 20, pp. 31, 467; vol. 21, pp. 109, 468; vol. 22, pp. 93, 471; vol. 23, pp. 158, 434.

11. Fortification appropriations rose from $540,000 in 1895 to $3,050,000 in 1896 and $1,746,333 in 1897. *Statutes At Large,* vol. 28, pp. 704, 706; vol. 29, pp. 256-261, 641. The figures given do not include amounts for mines and torpedoes.

12. Eben E. Winslow, *Notes on Seacoast Fortification,* Occasional Papers no. 61, Engineer School, U.S. Army (Washington, D.C.: Government Printing Office, 1920), pp. 18-21; Emanuel R. Lewis, *Seacoast Fortifications of the United States: An Introductory History* (Washington, D.C.: Smithsonian Institution Press, 1970), pp. 100-110.

13. Lewis, *Seacoast Fortifications,* pp. 115, 119-125.

14. Ibid., pp. 306.

15. Winslow, *Notes on Seacoast Fortification,* p. 438.

Selected Bibliography

Space limitations prevent the inclusion of all the works, both primary and secondary, examined or consulted in the preparation of this book. Anyone interested in the development of American seacoast defense policy should begin with the various engineer reports and letters and reports of Congressional committees contained in the serial set of printed United States public documents. These are, almost literally, a mine of information. Access to these documents is made easier by a number of excellent indexes, including an extensively annotated index published as a part of the serials set in 1902 and covering the period up to 1893. The records of the Corps of Engineers at the National Archives are a useful supplement to this documentary material. The archival material consulted tended to add only a little new information, and usually simply repeated or confirmed the material available in the printed documents.

Whenever possible, documents will be listed by title, document number, Congressional session, and number and the number of the volume in the serial set in which the document appears. Since only those items of particular importance or significance are listed below, reference to the other items consulted will have to be made through the individual citations in the text, or the indexes listed at the end of this bibliography.

PRIMARY: ARCHIVAL AND MANUSCRIPT SOURCES

Correspondence, Blueprints, and Reports Relating to Defense, 1873-1918. Fortifications and Defences, 1810-1920. Entry 225, Record Group 77, National Archives.

Letters and Reports of Col. Joseph G. Totten, Chief of Engineers, 1803-1864. 10 vols. Papers of Engineer Officers and Others. Entry 146, Record Group 77, National Archives.

Miscellaneous Letters Sent, Records of the Office of the Chief of Engineers. Entry 4, Record Group 77, National Archives.

Reports on Fortifications and Topographical Surveys, July 3, 1812-Oct. 4, 1823. Fortifications and Defenses, 1810-1920. Entry 221, Record Group 77, National Archives.

Reports of Boards of Engineers Relating to Fortifications and Defenses, 1821-1834. Fortifications and Defenses, 1810-1920. Entry 223, Record Group 77, National Archives.

Proceedings and Reports, 1866-1882. Records of the Board of Engineers, Board of Engineers, 1866-1920. Entry 461, Record Group 77, National Archives.

Swift, Joseph Gardner. *The Memoirs of General Joseph Gardner Swift, LL.D., U.S.A., First Graduate of the United States Military Academy, West Point, Chief Engineer U.S.A. From 1812 to 1818,* 1800-1865. Privately printed by Harrison Ellery, 1890.

PRIMARY: UNITED STATES GOVERNMENT PRINTED DOCUMENTS

Bernard, Simon; Totten, Joseph G.; and Elliott, J. D. "Report of Board of Engineers . . . " (Original Bernard Board Report, February 7, 1821). *American State Papers, Military Affairs.* vol. 2 (Serial 017), 16th Congress, 2d Session, Document 206.

Board of Engineers. "Report of The Board of Engineers In Relation to a System of Fortifications." (Revised Report of the Bernard Board, February 1826). *American State Papers, Military Affairs.* vol. 3 (Serial 018), 19th Congress, 1st Session, Document 316.

Board of Engineers. "Report of . . . Upon Experiments in Connection With an Efficient System of Sea-Coast Defenses for the United States. (Report of April 1869). Executive Document 271, 41st Congress, 2d Session, Serial 1426.

Cass, Lewis. "Remarks on a Practical System of Defence." Submitted in conjunction with a report by the Board of Engineers, April 7, 1836. *American State Papers, Military Affairs.* vol. 6 (Serial 021), 24th Congress, 1st Session, Document 671.

"Coast Defenses of the United States and the Insular Possessions." (Report of the Taft Board.) Senate Document no. 248, 59th Congress, 1st Session, Serial 4913, March 5, 1906.

Dearborn, Henry. "Report on Fortifications and Gunboats." *American States."* (Report of April 1869.) Executive Document 271, 41st Congress, 2d Session, Serial 1426.

Gaines, Edmund P. Excerpt from "A Report of a Tour of Inspection of the Military Posts of the Western Department." *American State Papers, Military Affairs.* vol. 4 (Serial 019), 20th Congress, 2d Session, Document 407.

_____. "Memorial of . . . " Re: Systems of National Defense, December 31, 1839, Executive Document 206, 26th Congress, 1st Session, Serial 368.

Gillmore, Quincy A. "Letter to Chief Engineer H. G. Wright, Respecting the Present Condition of Our Sea-Coast Defenses, and the Importance of Strengthening Them." (Appendix no. 2 to the Annual Report of the Chief Engineer, 1881.) Executive Document 1 (no. 1, pt. 2, vol. 2, pt. 1), 47th Congress, 1st Session, Serial 2011.

Gratiot, Charles, Chief Engineer. "Statement of the Fortifications, Their Garrisons, Steam Batteries, etc., Necessary for the Defence of the Coasts of the United States, Their Cost, etc." *American State Papers, Military Affairs.* vol. 6 (Serial 021), 24th Congress, 1st Session, Document 650.

Halleck, Henry W. "Report on National Defence . . . " Senate Document 85, 28th Congress, 2d Session, Serial 451.

Joint Committee on the Conduct of the War. "Report of . . . ; Heavy Ordnance." Senate Committee Report 142, 38th Congress, 2d Session, Serial 1213.

"Letter From the Secretary of the Navy in Answer to Resolutions of the House and Senate in Relation to the Operations of Armored Vessels Employed in the Service of the United States." Executive Document 69, 38th Congress, 1st Session, Serial 1193.

Morton, James St. Clair. "Memoir of American Fortification Submitted to the Honorable John B. Floyd, Secretary of War . . . " Senate Document 2, 36th Congress, 1st Session, Serial 1024.

Poinsett, Joel R. "Letter From the Secretary of War to the House of Representatives . . . Status of Frontier Defences." Executive Document 199, 25th Congress, 2d Session, Serial 327.

_____. "Report on the Military and Naval Defences." (Covering letter for the Board of Engineers Report of April, 1840.) Senate Report 451, 26th Congress, 1st Session, Serial 360.

Totten, Joseph G. "Report of the Chief Engineer on the Subject of National Defences." Executive Document 5, 32d Congress, 1st Session, Serial 637. (Also published independently, Washington, D.C.: A. Boyd Hamilton, 1851.)

_____. "Summary Statement of the General System of Defence . . . " (In conjunction with statement by Secretary of War Lewis Cass.) *American State Papers, Military Affairs.* vol. 6 (Serial 021), 24th Congress, 1st Session, Document 671.

Totten, Joseph G.; Thayer, Sylvanus; Cross, T.; and Tallcott, G. "Report on the Defence of the Atlantic Frontier From Passamaquoddy to the Sabine." (Board of Engineers of 1840.) Senate Document 451, 26th Congress, 1st Session, Serial 360.

United States House of Representatives. "Report of the Board of Fortifications or Other Defenses Appointed by the President Under the Provisions of the Act of Congress Approved March 3, 1885." (Endicott Board Report.) Executive Document 49, 49th Congress, 1st Session, Serial 2395. (Plates in Serial 2396.)

United States War Department. "Fortifications: Instructions and Reports of the Temporary Engineers in the Service of the United States." (1794) *American State Papers, Military Affairs.* vol. 1 (Serial 016), 2d Congress, 2d Session, Document 22.

PRIMARY: MANUALS AND TREATISES

Chase, William H. *Brief Memoir Explanatory of a New Trace of a Front of Fortification in Place of the Bastioned Front.* (Pamphlet published at the office of the *Jeffersonian,* New Orleans, LA, 1846.)

Gibbon, John. *The Artillerist's Manual.* New York: D. Van Nostrand, 1860. Reprint edition, Westport, Conn.: Greenwood Press, 1971.

Halleck, Henry W. *Military Art and Science.* New York: D. Appleton and Co., 1846.

Holden, Edward S. *Notes on the Bastion System of Fortification: Its Defects and Their Remedies.* New York: D. Van Nostrand, 1872.

Lendy, Auguste F. *Elements of Fortification.* London: John W. Parker and Son, 1857.

Maguire, Edward. *The Attack and Defence of Coast Fortifications.* New York: D. Van Nostrand, 1884.

Mahan, Dennis Hart. *An Elementary Course of Military Engineering.* 2 vols. New York: John Wiley and Sons, 1867.

———. *A Treatise on Field Fortification.* New York: John Wiley and Sons, 1848.

Mercur, James. *Attack of Fortified Places.* New York: John Wiley and Sons, 1894.

Muller, John. *A Treatise Containing the Elementary Part of Fortification, Regular and Irregular.* London, 1746. Reprint edition, Ottawa, Ontario: Museum Restoration Service, 1968.

Parrott, Robert P. *Ranges of Parrott Guns and Notes For Practice.* New York: D. Van Nostrand, 1863.

Scheliha, Viktor Ernest Karl Rudolf von. *A Treatise on Coast-Defence.* London: E. and F. N. Spon, 1868. Reprint edition, Westport, Conn.: Greenwood Press, 1971.

Straith, Hector. *Treatise on Fortification and Artillery.* Revised and re-arranged by Thomas Cook and John T. Hyde. London: William H. Allen and Co., 1858. Seventh edition.

Totten, Joseph G. *Report Addressed to The Honorable Jefferson Davis, Secretary of War, On the Effects of Firing Heavy Ordnance From Casemate Embrasures, and Also the Effects of Firing Against the Same Embrasures With Various Kinds of Missiles, In the Years 1852, '53, '54, and '55.* Papers on Practical Engineering no. 6. Washington, D.C.: Government Printing Office, 1857.

United States Engineer Department. *Regulations for the Government of the United States Engineer Department, 1840.* Washington, D.C.: Government Printing Office, 1840.

United States Ordnance Department. *Artillery For the Land Service.* Prepared by Alfred Mordecai. Washington, D.C.: J. and G. S. Gideon, 1849.

United States War Department. *Ordnance Manual, 1862.* Prepared by T.T.S. Laidley. Philadelphia: J. B. Lippincott and Co., 1862.

Vernon, Gay de. *A Treatise on the Science of War and Fortification.* Translated by Captain John M. O'Connor. New York: J. Seymour, 1817.

Wiard, Norman. *Memorial of Norman Wiard Addressed to the Joint Committee on the Conduct of the War, Upon the Subject of Great Guns.* Printed by order of the Committee on Naval Affairs, 1865.

Wheeler, J. B. *The Elements of Field Fortifications.* New York: D. Van Nostrand, 1882.

_____. *A Textbook of Military Engineering.* 2 vols. New York: John Wiley and Sons, 1884.

Wisser, John P. *The Tactics of Coast Defense.* Kansas City, Mo.: Hudson-Kimberly, 1902.

PRIMARY: CONTEMPORARY ACCOUNTS: HISTORIES AND ARTICLES

Abbot, Henry L. "Coast Defense, Including Submarine Mines." *Proceedings of the International Congress of Engineers, Division of Military Engineering, Chicago, 1893.* Washington, D.C.: Printing Office, 1894, pp. 15-28.

_____. *A Course of Lectures Upon the Defence of the Sea-Coast of the United States.* New York: D. Van Nostrand, 1888.

_____. "Notes on Mortars in Harbor Defence." *Printed Papers of the Essayons Club.* Paper no. 9. Willett's Point, N.Y.: Battalion Press, 1869.

Bainbridge-Hoff, William. "Examples, Conclusions, and Maxims of

Modern Naval Tactics." *Office of Naval Intelligence, Bureau of Navigation, General Information Series, Number III.* Washington, D.C.: Government Printing Office, 1884.

Barnard, John G. *Notes on Sea-Coast Defence.* New York: D. Van Nostrand 1861.

Birkhimer, William E. *Historical Sketch of the Organization, Administration, Materiel and Tactics of the Artillery, United States Army.* Washington, D.C.: Chapman, 1884.

Birnie, Jr., Rogers. *Gun-Making in the United States.* Washington, D.C.: Government Printing Office, 1907. Reprint of earlier publication.

Clarke, Sir George Sydenham. (Baron Sydenham.) "Coast Defense." *Proceedings of the International Congress of Engineers, Division of Military Engineers, Chicago, 1893.* Washington, D.C.: Government Printing Office, 1894, pp. 31-44.

———. *Fortification: Its Past Achievements, Recent Development and Future Progress.* New York: E. P. Dutton and Co., 2nd Edition, 1907.

Craighill, W. E.; Shunk, F. R.; and Bergland, E. "Foreign Systems of Torpedoes as Compared With Our Own." *Printed Papers of the Essayons Club, Corps of Engineers.* Paper no. 9. Willett's Point, N.Y.: Battalion Press, 1888.

Craighill, W. P. "Guns Ashore and Guns Afloat." *Printed Papers of the Essayons Club, Corps of Engineers.* Paper no. 6. Willett's Point, N.Y.: Battalion Press, 1868.

Delafield, Richard. *Report on the Art of War in Europe in 1854, 1855, and 1856.* Washington, D.C.: George W. Bowman, 1861.

Ehrenhook, F. von. "History of Submarine Mining and Torpedoes." Translated by Sergeant-Major Frederick Martin, Army Corps of Engineers. *Engineer School of Application, Paper Number I.* Willett's Point, N.Y.: Battalion Press, nd.

Gillmore, Quincy A. *Engineer and Artillery Operations Against the Defences of Charleston Harbor in 1863.* Professional Papers, The Corps of Engineers, Paper no. 16. New York: D. Van Nostrand, 1868.

———. *Official Report to the United States Engineers Department of the Siege and Reduction of Fort Pulaski, Georgia, February, March and April, 1862.* Papers on Practical Engineering, Paper no. 8. New York: D. Van Nostrand, 1862.

Griffin, Eugene. "Our Sea-Coast Defenses." *North American Review.* vol. 147, no. 380 (1888), pp. 64-75.

———. "A View of Our Naval Policy and a Discussion of Its Factors." *Proceedings of the United States Naval Institute.* vol. 12, no. 1 (March 1896), Whole no. 36, pp. 121-139.

Jaques, William H., USN. *Heavy Ordnance For National Defence,* Questions of the Day, vol. 17. New York: G. P. Putnam's Sons, 1885.

_____. *Modern Armor For National Defence.* Questions of the Day, vol. 32. New York: G. P. Putnam's Sons, 1886.

_____. *Torpedoes For National Defence.* Questions of the Day, vol. 34. New York: G. P. Putnam's Sons, 1886.

King, James W. *Heavy Rifled Guns: Modern European Artillery.* Pittsburgh: Stevenson, Foster and Co., 1879.

King, William R. "The Military Necessities of the United States and the Best Provision For Meeting Them." *Journal of the Military Service Institution of The United States,* vol. 5 no. 20 (December 1884), pp. 355-395.

_____. "Economy of Sea Coast Defences." *Printed Papers of the Essayons Club, Corps of Engineers.* Paper no. 19. Willett's Point, N.Y.: Battalion Press, 1871.

Lemly, Henry R. *Changes Wrought in Artillery in the Nineteenth Century, and Their Effect Upon the Attack of Fortified Places.* Department of Military Art, United States Artillery School, Essay. Fort Monroe, Va.: United States Artillery School, 1886.

Lewis, J. F., Royal Engineers. "Fortification For Coast Defense, Including Submarine Mines." *Proceedings of the International Congress of Engineers, Division of Military Engineering, Chicago, 1893.* Washington, D.C.: Government Printing Office, 1894, pp. 47-55.

Lloyd, E. M., Royal Engineers. "The Forts of To-Day." *Ordnance Notes.* vol. 8, Ordnance Note no. 248. Washington, D.C.: Government Printing Office, 1883.

Longridge, James A. "Modern Gun Construction." *Proceedings of the International Congress of Engineers, Division of Military Engineering, Chicago, 1893.* Washington, D.C.: Government Printing Office 1894, pp. 243-273.

Luce, S. B., USN. "Our Future Navy." *Proceedings of the United States Naval Institute.* vol. 15, no. 4 (December 1889), Whole no. 51, pp. 541-559.

Michaelis, Otho E. "The Military Necessities of the United States and the Best Provision For Meeting Them." *Journal of the Military Service Institution of the United States.* vol. 5 no. 19 (September 1884), pp. 272-291.

Miles, Nelson A. "Our Coast Defenses." *The Forum.* vol. 24 (January 1898), pp. 513-519.

Norton, Charles B., and Valentine, W. J. *Report on the Munitions of War.* (Paris Universal Exposition, Reports of the United States Commissioners.) Washington, D.C.: Government Printing Office, 1868.

Sampson, William T. "Outline of a Scheme for the Naval Defense of the Coast." *Proceedings of the United States Naval Institute.* vol. 15, no. 2 (March 1889), Whole no. 49, pp. 169-232.

Sears, James H. "The Coast in Warfare." *Proceedings of the United States Naval Institute.* vol. 27, no. 3 (September 1901), Whole No. 99, pp. 449-527, and vol. 27, no. 4 (December 1901), Whole No. 100, pp. 649-712.

Smalley, H. A. "A Defenseless Sea-Board." *North American Review.* vol. 138, no. 328 (March 1884), pp. 233-245.

Southwick, George N. "Our Defenceless Coasts." *North American Review.* vol. 162, no. 372 (March 1896), pp. 317-327.

Wells, Henry P. "The Defense of Our Sea-Ports." *Harpers Magazine.* vol. 71, no. 426 (November 1885), pp. 927-937.

Van Auken, Wilbur R. *Notes on a Half Century of United States Naval Ordnance, 1880-1930.* Washington, D.C.: George Banta, 1939.

Wagner, Arthur L. "The Military Necessities of the United States and the Best Provision of Meeting Them." *Journal of the Military Service Institution of the United States.* vol. 5, no. 19 (September 1884), pp. 237-271.

Winslow, Eben E. *Notes on Seacoast Fortification.* Occasional Papers no. 61, Engineer School United States Army. Washington, D.C.: Government Printing Office, 1920.

SECONDARY: BOOKS AND THESES

Alden, John D. *The American Steel Navy.* Annapolis: U.S. Naval Institute Press, 1972.

Ambrose, Stephen E. *Duty, Honor, Country: A History of West Point.* Baltimore: Johns Hopkins University Press, 1966.

Arthur, Robert. *History of Fort Monroe.* Fort Monroe, Va.: Coast Artillery School, 1930.

Barnes, Frank. *Fort Sumter National Monument.* National Park Service Historical Handbook no. 12. Washington, D.C.: Government Printing Office, 1952. Revised 1962.

Baxter, James Phinney. *The Introduction of the Ironclad Warship.* Reprint edition. New York: Archon Books, 1968.

Bennett. *The Steam Navy of the United States.* Two vols. Pittsburgh: Warren and Company, 1897.

Black, William M. *Pamphlet on the Evolution of the Art of Fortification.* Occasional Paper no. 58, Engineer School, U.S. Army. Washington, D.C.: Government Printing Office, 1919.

Bright, Samuel R. "Coast Defense and The Southern Coasts Before Fort Sumter." Unpublished M.A. Thesis, Duke University, 1958.

Brown, Wilburt S. *The Amphibious Campaign For West Florida and Louisiana, 1814-1815.* Birmingham: University of Alabama Press, 1969.

Camparato, Frank E. *The Age of Great Guns.* Harrisburg, Pa.: Stackpole, 1965.

Duffy, Christopher. *Fire and Stone: The Science of Fortress Warfare, 1660-1860.* London: David and Charles, 1975.

Fleming, Thomas J. *West Point.* New York: William Morrow, 1969.

Ganoe, William A. *The History of the United States Army.* New York: D. Appleton and Company, 1924.

Hogg, Ian V. *Fortress: A History of Military Defense.* London: MacDonald and Jane's, 1975.

_____. *A History of Artillery.* London: Hamlyn, 1974.

Hogg, Ian V., and Batchelor, John. *Naval Gun.* Poole, Dorset: Blandford Press, 1978.

Hughes, Quentin. *Military Architecture.* London: Hugh Evelyn, 1974.

Kohn, Richard H. *Eagle and Sword: The Federalists and the Creation of the Military Establishment, 1783-1802.* New York: Free Press, 1975.

Lattimore, Ralston B. *Fort Pulaski National Monument.* National Park Service Historical Handbook Series no. 18. Washington, D.C.: Government Printing Office, 1954.

Lessen, Harold I., and MacKenzie, George C. *Fort McHenry National Monument and Historic Shrine.* National Park Service Historical Handbook Series no. 5. Washington, D.C.: Government Printing Office, 1950.

Lewis, Emanuel R. *Seacoast Fortifications of the United States: An Introductory History.* Washington, D.C.: Smithsonian Institution Press, 1970.

Lundeberg, Philip K. *Samuel Colt's Battery: The Secret and the Enigma.* Washington, D.C.: Smithsonian Institution Press, 1974.

Manucy, Albert. *Artillery Through the Ages: A Short Illustrated History of Cannon, Emphasizing the Types Used in America.* National Park Service Interpretive Series, History, no. 3. Washington, D.C.: Government Printing Office, 1949.

Peck, Taylor. *Roundshot to Rockets: A History of the Washington Navy Yard and U.S. Naval Gun Factory.* Annapolis: U.S. Naval Institute Press, 1949.

Peterson, Harold L. *Notes on Ordnance of the American Civil War, 1861-1865.* Washington, D.C.: American Ordnance Association, 1959.

Reed, Rowena. *Combined Operations in the Civil War.* Annapolis: U.S. Naval Institute Press, 1978.

Ripley, Warren. *Artillery and Ammunition of the Civil War.* New York: Van Nostrand Reingold Company, 1970.

Rippy, James F. *Joel R. Poinsett: Versatile American.* Durham, N.C.: Duke University Press, 1935.

Robertson, Frederick L. *The Evolution of Naval Armament.* London: Constable and Company, Limited, 1921.

Robinson, Willard B. *American Forts: Architectural Form and Function.* Champaign: University of Illinois Press, 1977.

Roland, Alex. *Underwater Warfare in the Age of Sail.* Bloomington: University of Indiana Press, 1978.

Silver, James W. *Edmund Pendleton Gaines: Frontier General.* Baton Rouge: Louisiana State University Press, 1949.

Spector, Ronald. *Professors of War: The Naval War College and the Development of the Naval Profession.* Newport, R.I.: Naval War College Press, 1977.

Turnbull, Archibald. *John Stevens: An American Record.* New York: The Century Company, 1928.

Wade, Arthur P. "Artillerists and Engineers: The Beginnings of American Seacoast Fortifications." Unpublished Ph.D. dissertation, Kansas State University, 1977.

Weigley, Russel F. *History of the United States Army.* New York: Macmillan, 1967.

_____. *Towards An American Army: Military Thought From Washington To Marshall.* New York: Columbia University Press, 1962.

SECONDARY: ARTICLES AND ESSAYS

Abenheim, Donald. "Never A Shot In Anger." *Military Collector and Historian: The Journal of the Company of Military Historians,* vol. 28, no. 3 (Fall 1976), pp. 100-107.

Allen, Richard S. "American Coastal Forts: The Golden Years." *Periodical: The Journal of the Council on Abandoned Military Posts,* vol. 5, no. 2 (Summer 1973), pp. 2-7.

Arthur, Robert. "Colonial Coast Forts on the South Atlantic." *Coast Artillery Journal,* vol. 70, no. 1 (January 1929), pp. 41-62.

_____. "Coast Forts of Colonial Massachusetts." *Coast Artillery Journal,* vol. 58, no. 2 (February 1923), pp. 101-122.

_____. "Coast Forts of Colonial New Jersey, Pennsylvania, and Delaware." *Coast Artillery Journal,* vol. 69, no. 1 (July, 1928), pp. 46-59.

_____. "Early Coast Fortification." *The Military Engineer,* vol. 53, no. 354 (July-August 1961), pp. 279-281.

Buhl, Lance C. "Maintaining An 'American Navy,' 1865-1889." *In Peace and War.* Edited by Kenneth Hagan. Westport, Conn.: Greenwood Press, 1978.

Carter, William H. "Bernard." *Journal of the Military Service Institution of the United States,* vol. 51, no. 179 (September-October 1912), pp. 147-155.

Forman, Sidney. "Early American Military Engineering Books." *The Military Engineer,* vol. 46, no. 310 (March-April 1954), pp. 93-95.

_____. "Why the United States Military Academy Was Established in 1802." *Military Affairs,* vol. 29, no. 1 (Spring 1965), pp. 16-28.

Hall, Charles L. "Coastal Warfare—Past and Future." *The Military Engineer,* vol. 3, no. 173 (September-October 1938), pp. 327-329.

Hinds, James R. "Potomac River Defenses: The First Twenty Years." *Periodical: The Journal of the Council on Abandoned Military Posts,* vol. 5, no. 5 (Fall 1973), pp. 2-17.

Hinds, James R., and Fitzgerald, Edmund. "Fortifications in the Field and on the Frontier." *Periodical: The Journal of the Council on Abandoned Military Posts,* vol. 9, no. 1 (Spring 1977), pp. 41-49.

_____. "An Introduction to Fortification of the Musket Period." *Periodical: The Journal of the Council on Abandoned Military Posts,* vol. 8, no. 3 (Fall 1976), pp. 24-28.

_____. "Permanent Fortification in the United States." *Periodical: The Journal of the Council on Abandoned Military Posts,* vol. 9, no. 3 (Fall 1977), pp. 40-53.

Jarman, Sanderford. "Future Coast Defense Artillery." *The Military Engineer,* vol. 12, no. 64 (July-August 1920), pp. 440-441.

Kinney, Sheldon H. "Dry Tortugas." *United States Naval Institute Proceedings,* vol. 76 (April 1950), pp. 425-429.

Kirchner, David P. "American Harbor Defense Forts." *United States Naval Institute Proceedings,* vol. 84 (August 1958), pp. 95-101.

Lewis, Emanuel R. "The Ambiguous Columbiads." *Military Affairs,* vol. 28, no. 3 (Fall 1964), pp. 111-122.

McDonald, Archie P. "West Point and the Engineers." *The U.S. Army Engineers: Fighting Elite.* Edited by Franklin M. David and Thomas M. Jones. New York: Franklin Watts, 1967.

Mullin, John R. "Fortifications in America: Application in the New World." *Periodical: The Journal of the Council on Abandoned Military Posts,* vol. 6, no. 1 (Spring 1974), pp. 10-18.

_____. "Fortifications in America: European Theories and Practice." *Periodical: The Journal of the Council on Abandoned Military Posts,* vol. 5, no. 4 (Winter 1973), pp. 5-13.

_____. "Fortifications in America: Intention and Reality." *Periodical: The Journal of the Council on Abandoned Military Posts,* vol. 6. no. 3 (Fall 1974), pp. 23-26.

Ranson, Edward. "The Endicott Board of 1885-86 and the Coast Defenses." *Military Affairs,* vol. 31, no. 2 (Summer 1967), pp. 74-84.

Reed, Rowena. "The Endicott Board—Vision and Reality." *Periodical: The Journal of the Council on Abandoned Military Posts,* vol. 11, no. 2 (Summer 1979), pp. 3-17.

Riley, Edward M. "Historic Fort Moultrie in Charleston Harbor." *South Carolina Historical and Genealogical Magazine,* vol. 51 (April 1950), pp. 63-74.

Robinson, Willard B. "The Rock on Which the Storm Shall Beat." *Periodical: The Journal of the Council on Abandoned Military Posts,* vol. 9, no. 1 (Spring 1977), pp. 3-16.

Thibaut, Jacqueline. "Deciphering Fort Mifflin." *Military Collector and Historian: The Journal of the Company of Military Historians,* vol. 27, no. 3 (Fall 1975), pp. 100-112.

Watson, Richard L. "Congressional Attitudes Toward Military Preparedness, 1829-1835." *Mississippi Valley Historical Review,* vol. 34 (March 1948), pp. 611-636.

Williams, Ames W. "The Old Forts of New York Harbor." *Periodical: The Journal of the Council on Abandoned Military Posts,* vol. 4, nos. 5-6 (Fall-Winter 1972), pp. 2-14.

————. "Stronghold on the Straits." *Periodical: The Journal of the Council on Abandoned Military Posts,* vol. 6, no. 4 (Winter 1974-75), pp. 2-20.

Young, Rogers W. "The Construction of Fort Pulaski." *Georgia Historical Quarterly,* vol. 20 (March 1936), pp. 41-51.

INDEXES

Checklist of United States Public Documents, 1789-1909. Washington, D.C.: Government Printing Office, 1911.

Cullum, George W. *Biographical Register of the Officers and Graduates of the U.S. Military Academy at West Point, N.Y., From Its Establishment in 1802 to 1890.* 3 vols. Boston: Houghton Mifflin and Company, 1891.

Tables and Annotated Index to the Congressional Series of Public Documents, 1817-1893. Washington, D.C.: Government Printing Office, 1902.

United States Serial Set Index, 1789-1969. 12 vols. Washington, D.C.: Congressional Information Service, 1975-1979.

Zinn, George A. *Index to the Reports of the Chief of Engineering, United States Army, 1866-1912.* vol. 2. Washington, D.C.: Government Printing Office, 1916.

Index

About the Author

ROBERT S. BROWNING III is a Lecturer in the Department of
History at Sam Houston State University. He has published studies
of American military history in *Proceedings of the Colloquium on
Military History* and *America in War and Crises*.